The 52 Weeks

Two Women and Their Quest to Get Unstuck, with Stories and Ideas to Jumpstart Your Year of Discovery

Karen Amster-Young and Pam Godwin

Foreword by Barbara Hannah Grufferman

Skyhorse Publishing

Skyhorse Publishing books may be purchased in bulk at special discounts for sales promotion, corporate gifts, fund-raising, or educational purposes. Special editions can also be created to specifications. For details, contact the Special Sales Department, Skyhorse Publishing, 307 West 36th Street, 11th Floor, New York, NY 10018 or info@skyhorsepublishing.com.

Skyhorse® and Skyhorse Publishing® are registered trademarks of Skyhorse Publishing, Inc.®, a Delaware corporation.

Visit our website at www.skyhorsepublishing.com.

10 9 8 7 6 5 4 3 2 1

Library of Congress Cataloging-in-Publication Data is available on file.
ISBN: 978-1-62087-718-0

Printed in China

"And will you succeed? Yes indeed, yes indeed! Ninety-eight and three-quarters percent guaranteed!"

—Dr. Seuss

Table of Contents

The 52 Weeks Experts & Contributors

Trying Something New
Alex Lickerman, M.D., author of *The Undefeated Mind: On the Science of Constructing an Indestructible Self*
Ellen Leikind, founder, *PokerprimaDivas™*

Wellness
Jennifer H. Mieres, M.D., nuclear cardiologist, author, and leading expert in women's heart health
Lisa Lillien, best selling author and creator of *The Hungry Girl™* brand

Just for Fun
Michele Balan, comedian and finalist of NBC's *Last Comic Standing*
Nadia Stieglitz, founder, *Mice at Play*
Enda Junkins, LCSW, motivational speaker, Laughter Therapy expert

Arts & Culture
Daniella Ohad Smith, Ph.D., design historian, critic on 20th Century art and art advisor
Andrea Blanch, award-winning photographer and founder of *Musée* Magazine

Relationships
Debbie Magids, Ph.D., counseling psychologist, author
Helen Fisher, Ph.D., biological anthropologist, journalist, and author

Facing Fears
Lauren Kantor Gorman, M.D., psychiatrist, faculty member at Mt. Sinai School of Medicine

Giving Back
Joi Gordon, CEO, Dress for Success Worldwide
Marie-Yolaine Eusebe, CEO, Community2Comunity (C2C)
Julie Weiss, Marathon Goddess, 52 Marathons in 52 Weeks

Changing Course
Pamela Weinberg, author, career coach, and co-founder of MYOBMoms, (Mind Your Own Business Moms)
Vivian Steir Rabin, author and co-founder, iRelaunch

Flying Solo, with Jami Kelmenson
Helen Fisher, Ph.D., biological anthropologist, journalist and author
Robin Gorman Newman, founder of Motherhood Later…Than Sooner; author of *How to Meet a Mensch in NY* and *How to Marry a Mensch*
Jennifer Gardner Trulson, author of the award-winning memoir, *Where You Left Me*

For full biographies see page 253

FOR BEN, KEN, ALISON, JULIET, AND ALLIE

THANKS FOR BEING SO PATIENT LONG AFTER THE FIRST 52 WEEKS

Acknowledgments

How crazy is it that we get to write an Acknowledgments page? Where are we supposed to start?

We probably should thank the waitress who served us our three drinks the night the52weeks.com was born. She continued to smile long after we overstayed our welcome!

Thanks to everyone who always saw the potential in our blog and supported us a million weeks ago when the book was just an idea between two friends.

To Shelley Sadler Kenney, an old family friend of Karen's. She saw a book long before we did. A big thanks for her encouragement, her foresight, and for putting us in touch with some great people.

To Karen Lewis, our amazing blog designer who has been with us from the outset and helped us launch the52weeks.com.

To Leigh Goldman, who interviewed us about our blog for Urbanbaby.com. Her inspiring July 2010 article fueled Karen's passion for writing a book and made Pam wonder what she was getting herself into!

To Sue Shapiro, author and generous writing teacher. It was at one of Sue's great events where we first met our future editor.

To Ellen Neuborne, an amazing writer who helped shape our proposal and bring it all together.

Our deepest gratitude to Abigail Gehring of Skyhorse Publishing, who believed in sharing the message of *The 52 Weeks* and was inspired by our idea from the beginning. She has been a calm force and great editor.

To Jessica Papin, our agent from Dystel and Goderich, who was there to help us navigate the world of publishing. She was a cheerleader, voice of reason, and infallible guide throughout the process.

To Ella, graphic designer extraordinaire, an early *52* follower, who generously offered her talent and time.

To Betsy Kent for helping us get our social media sea legs.

To Jami Kelmenson, for her unwavering support of *52* from day one and for bringing her always optimistic, "unstuck," "single and loving it" perspective to the table. She shares her insights in the "Flying Solo" chapter and is a contributing author for our "Giving Back" chapter.

To all of our experts and contributors: your knowledge, advice, and words of wisdom are an invaluable part of the book.

To Piper Hoffman, for her help with editing, formatting and other invaluable "late night" finishing touches on our manuscript.

To Shani R. Friedman, for helping us with all of those lists!

To our doormen for smiling as we went in and out of one another's buildings!

To our blog followers, thank you for your comments, support, and encouragement.

Thanks to our husbands, Ben and Ken, who put up with our questions, mood swings, and each of us talking, shouting, or coordinating *52* while multitasking and promising to get off the phone "in two minutes!"

Finally, to our beautiful daughters who always had input, questions, and criticism to keep us on track. We hope you never stop growing, learning, and trying new things.

Foreword

By Barbara Hannah Grufferman
Author, *The Best of Everything After 50:*
The Experts' Guide to Style, Sex, Health, Money, and More

Here's a little experiment: imagine you're under a spell—or really, a curse. You aren't asleep or even hurt. You aren't imprisoned in a tower or turned into a toad. No, under this spell you are not only alive, but able to live your life exactly the same way you did yesterday. That is the curse. You're going to do exactly the same things every day from now until the end of your life. You're going to eat the same breakfast and the same dinner, wear the same pants with the same shirt, take the same route to work, have the same discussions with the same people about the same topics, and end up with the same results. You're never going to change anything about your life ever again. You can't. Because you're cursed.

It's the Inertia Curse.

Scary, no? I love my little routines (don't we all?), and my comfort zone is very comfortable, but the idea of doing everything just as I've always done it, without anything new ever? Terrifying. Even thinking about it, I feel claustrophobic. Like I'm being buried alive.

And yet, there's something kind of familiar about that feeling. As if maybe I've been there before.

When I was in my twenties, change was constant. I was young, and it seemed like everything was new. New apartments, new jobs, new boyfriends. I was always looking ahead, planning for the future, always confident and excited about what was coming next. In my thirties, I settled into a nice, humming groove, but it was a good kind of settling—like finding my place. I was still planning, still making choices. I got married. I had kids. Still good! But sometime after that . . . It seemed like all the choices had already been made. As if I'd quit planning and had switched to autopilot. I was zipping along and doing and doing and doing, but I wasn't looking ahead anymore or thinking about who I wanted to be. Of course, I had plenty of other things to think about, with a job and a wonderful husband and two fast-growing daughters.

And then, suddenly, I was 50. 50? How did that happen? Whenever I caught a glimpse in a mirror, I didn't even recognize myself. The woman behind the glass didn't look excited and confident. She looked scared and insecure. She didn't know who she was or how she fit into the world anymore. I'd been flying through my life so fast that I'd quit really living it. "Oh, well," I told myself. "It's too late to change." Whatever my life was, I was going to be stuck with it from there on out.

But I didn't want to be stuck with it. Sure, I kept trudging through my routine, but inside, I was feeling more and more frustrated and suffocated, not sure what to do. I was stuck.

Those feelings built for months until one day, it hit me: my age wasn't trapping me. Neither was my family, or my work. I was trapping myself! I was squashing my own confidence and fostering my own fears, and I was hiding inside my comfort zone. I was the reason I was stuck!

That realization opened a floodgate. I stopped fretting about missing out on life and went back to living it. I took charge again: of my health and my happiness and my future. I started looking forward to what was next.

I now say that turning 50 saved my life—because it pushed me out of my complacency and forced me to pay attention again. But the transition would have been easier and more fun if I had gotten help from Karen Amster-Young and Pam Godwin.

Karen and Pam are smart women. They are both happily married with children and lead busy lives. If you met them on the street, you'd think they were "doers"—and you'd be right. But they got stuck anyway, just like I did. Like so many of us.

It turns out they were on autopilot, too. They liked their lives in many ways, but as they passed forty and kept zipping through the same routines, their comfort zones started to feel more like cages.

So one night, over drinks, they came up with a brilliant and simple idea to get back in touch with their lives. They dared themselves to do one new thing every week for a year—and to blog about it. Over the next 52 weeks, they did big and little things, things they'd always been scared of, and things they'd meant to do, but had never quite made time for. They didn't get to a few things and even did a few things they probably wish they hadn't done. At the end of it all, they're still smart and still married (and are still friends!) but they're not quite the same women they were at the beginning. They're unstuck.

During that year of new things, the blog gained an enthusiastic following of people who were feeling trapped in their own lives—and ready to do something about it. So Pam and Karen kept going. Now they've pulled together everything they learned: their struggles, triumphs and insights, as well as some expert advice. The result is this book: a truly inspiring guide to reclaiming your life through the simple power of action.

To me, one of the most treacherous things about the Inertia Curse is how easily we can fall under its spell even when we are basically content. Sometimes contentment is what keeps us stuck! After all, most of us don't want to turn our worlds upside down. And most of us don't need to. But if you're ready to make a few changes, Karen and Pam can help you figure out how.

Life is change, and learning to enjoy change—perhaps even to embrace it—is the first step in learning to love your life.

Well, maybe it's the first 52 steps . . .

Note to the Reader

The 52 Weeks was conceived as a fun idea between two good friends. Our plan was to get going again, get unstuck and just feel better. This book is *our* story, but it is also an inspirational blueprint to help others get moving again.

A "*52* list" is a list of things you want to do, revisit, or conquer. The idea is to try something each week and cross it off! Some weeks you may just want to have fun; other weeks you may want to start tackling a fear; another, you may want to make one small change for better health. No one is grading you. The list can be fluid or set in stone. You can skip a week, or two, or even three. Sometimes, you won't feel like doing any of them. Other times, life may just get in the way. Don't worry; the list will still be there waiting for you.

Everyone's "*52* list" is unique. There are no rules. What matters is that you think about what you want to change, add, or eliminate from your life, make a list, and try to follow through. Each and every thing you do could make you feel better, build confidence, or just laugh. It may also simply confirm that you should never have tried it to begin with! You can go it alone or, like us, you can be accountable to someone—maybe a friend or significant other.

You should anticipate that the things on your list will change throughout the year. You should also expect to encounter both small and big surprises and happy accidents along the way. A cooking class can lead to a business opportunity. A volunteer gig can spark a new career. Dance lessons may bring you together with new, lifelong friends.

Our book features chapters that reflect the areas we explored during our 52-week journey: "Trying Something New"; "Wellness"; "Just for Fun"; "Arts & Culture"; "Relationships"; "Facing Fears"; "Giving Back"; "Reflection"; "Changing Course" (midlife career changes); "Flying Solo" (single, divorced, widowed); and "Your 52."

The stories in this book reflect our *52* to-dos. Our lists won't look like your list. That's the idea. We are all at different places in our lives but still likely feel stuck in one area or many. You can jump around from chapter to chapter in the book. Whatever works for you.

Our anecdotes and stories are intended to inspire you. They were culled from our blog and detail our adventures. There are some amazing guest writers included, too. We think many of you will relate to our triumphs and tribulations. At the very least, we hope they make you smile or think.

The experts and contributors we interviewed share their insights and advice throughout the book. Top doctors, entrepreneurs, TV personalities, CEOs, and others generously offer their tips and stories. At the end of each chapter, are three small sections: "Next Steps" (valuable advice for getting started); "Take Away Advice and Quotes" (aphorisms and quotes intended to amuse and inspire); and "Ideas for the Reader" (things we or our contributors tried). The back of the book features 52 ideas for every chapter. You will also find a few templates or tools at the end of the book, including a "My 52" worksheet. Look for more tools and helpful advice at the52weeks.com to keep you on track.

So get going and get unstuck!

The 52 Weeks

Use this key as you read through the following chapters.

 Karen's 52 Weeks stories and anecdotes

 Pam's 52 Weeks stories and anecdotes

 52 Weeks guest writer stories

 Expert Advice

 Next Steps: advice for getting started, worksheets, and templates

 Takeaway Advice: quick tips, aphorisms, inspirational quotes

 Ideas for the Reader

Introduction

"When you wake up in the morning, Pooh," said Piglet at last, "What's the first thing you say to yourself?"

"What's for breakfast?" said Pooh. "What do you say, Piglet?"

"I say, I wonder what's going to happen exciting today?" said Piglet. Pooh nodded thoughtfully.

"It's the same thing," he said.

—A. A. Milne

• • • • •

Looking back, there was something prophetic about this quote.

This exchange between Pooh and Piglet was featured in one of the first articles that launched our blog, the52weeks.com. At the time, it was just a quote to set the stage for a story about making simple yet seemingly difficult dietary changes at breakfast. For Karen, blueberries represented being "stuck." If she could only start eating these healthy, little, indigo-colored fruit more often, it would symbolize a change, and a small but meaningful step toward reaching her goals.

Later on we realized that eating blueberries every day meant much more than just a breakfast overhaul or "moving away from stuck." There was a bigger message to deliver to others and an important reminder for everyone, including us: Get out there, look around, and shake things up. You never know what's going to happen.

At the time, Karen wrote on the blog, "I did it. This little, stupid change has pushed me out of the starting gate. I hope it will be the fuel I need for the next 51 weeks. I hope that on the 10th week or the 25th week or the 46th week or whatever week, as I set my sights on bigger challenges, I will be inspired by my blueberry project. Regardless, Week 1 is over."

Pam's first *52* outing was a weaving class at a local studio—a "crafty," hands-on excursion—just to have fun. She wasn't confident she would ever actually make it there. She admitted at the time, "I often say I am going to do something and then don't." Pam shared her frustration with her tendency to procrastinate in her first blog entry. She wrote, "A perfect example is launching this blog. Just the thought of trying something new each week for 52 weeks, writing weekly, and having a deadline has got to be one of the craziest ideas I have ever agreed to." In the end, though, she did it. She walked into the weaving class, and she stayed committed to the blog.

Why did we want to share our story and write a book that was inspired by our blog?

Edging into forty-something, we found ourselves in a state of stuck. We had checked off many of our major life goals: career, husband, children, friends—but felt we'd lost momentum.

The 52 Weeks, this book, is a guide to getting "unstuck," getting inspired, and getting going again. Even more importantly, it's about learning to take time for yourself and make space in your life for what's important to you. It's about not giving up and looking within. It's about remembering to have some fun, and about feeling better. It's about all these things and more.

Ultimately, this book turned out to be less of a memoir and more a blueprint for getting out there and creating your own "attainable adventure." With a large helping of how-to advice from experts and contributors, this is our story.

Over drinks one night, as we griped and shared our "woes," we came up with a plan. We would reclaim our forward momentum. We would face our fears, rediscover our interests, try new things, and renew our relationships. We would do it as partners, because no one likes to journey alone. And we would share our experiences in the hopes that women like us would see the possibilities and step out of "stuck" themselves.

It began with our blog. On those virtual pages, we shared our trials, tribulations, and "a-ha!" moments. Together, as a team and with the input of our blog readers, we journeyed through a year of discovery. We laughed and complained and wondered a million times why we'd ever bothered to take on this challenge. When we came through it, we wanted to share what we learned with others who may feel the same way. The blog was just supposed to be a fun project to get us going again. In the beginning, we couldn't have imagined it would take on a life of its own and bring us here.

As we made our way through our respective 52 "to-do" lists—everything from test-driving Maseratis to learning poker to taking dance lessons—we experienced a powerful epiphany: Getting unstuck does not mean you have to run a marathon, climb a mountain, or travel the world. This is not a book about an all-consuming, instant, transformational experience. It's about real life and real experiences. You can create your adventure in the world you live in. You can carve realizations out of the life you have. You can find time, feel better, and move forward. Sometimes you'll make enormous leaps, and sometimes you'll just inch along. Both are okay. This book is intended to inspire, make you think, and remind you not to take it all so seriously. It's about taking stock, facing who you really are, and getting going again.

We sampled different things—some we liked, some we didn't. We discovered things about ourselves and each other—some we liked, some we didn't. But our best realization was that everything we did had value because we did it. Whatever we pursued in any given week, it got us laughing, running, drawing, loving, and moving. It got us out the door; it got us out of "stuck."

From the beginning, we were drawn to simple quotes from Dr. Seuss and others.

Neither of us can say exactly why. Seuss's quotes certainly have universal appeal for kids and adults—that's obvious. But it was more than that: the aphorisms were uncomplicated, manageable life lessons wrapped up in neat little packages; sentences intended to inspire and motivate. Words to keep in mind as we all navigate this confusing, sometimes-exhausting, scary yet wonderful, exciting world. Seuss and other favorites reminded us of what was important. The book features many of these quotes, from Carrie Bradshaw to Jerry Seinfeld, and even Eleanor Roosevelt.

Our greatest realization during the year was that you can't neatly package all of your goals and "to-do's" into 52 weeks. In fact, the "52 mindset" may become a lifelong adventure. The key is to just start with your first 52 and see where it takes you. Yes, it got us going again, but our major realizations came much later, after we had a chance to reflect on what our blog really meant for us individually.

We are excited to share what we learned and inspire others to take those first small steps and have a plan. This is a book about our 52 weeks—and yours.

Chapter One

Trying Something New

"Aim at a high mark and you will hit it. No, not the first time,
nor the second and maybe not the third. But keep on aiming and
keep on shooting for only practice will make you perfect. Finally,
you'll hit the bull's-eye of success."

—Annie Oakley, legendary sharpshooter

Aiming for the Bull's-Eye

Pam

*I expected a big adrenaline rush from the experience. Instead, I left
relaxed, with a sense of calm and a heightened awareness that with
concentration, focus, and keeping your "eye on the prize," you really
can accomplish a hell of a lot.*

*When I went to a shooting range in New York City, I thought it
would just be something different and frivolous to do for my 52. I've always had
a fascination with intrigue, spies, and all that cloak and dagger stuff. To fulfill
this silly fantasy of mine, I've always had an inexplicable urge to try my hand at
shooting a gun. Let me just state for the record that I am the furthest thing you can*

get from a card-carrying member of the NRA. In fact, I am very "anti-gun," but the act of target shooting has always intrigued me. My favorite game at the carnival has always been to blow up the water balloon by shooting water into a clown's mouth with the water pistol. I usually win, too—I just love to concentrate, aim, and . . . squirt!

So my friend Stacy came along and we ventured to Westside Rifle and Pistol Range. It is the only public shooting range in Manhattan and the one place in the borough where a person without a license can shoot a firearm. Since NYC (thankfully) has one of the toughest gun laws in the United States, you must have a handgun permit to fire a pistol. However, with the requisite background check and a mandatory safety course, you are allowed to fire a .22 rifle.

If we hadn't known of our destination, we would have walked right by it. Tucked away amongst shops and the bustle of a busy NYC street, this truly clandestine hideaway emerges after you walk through a small, unmarked street-level door and down a flight of rickety stairs to the basement of the building. I felt like I had entered a time warp. But it didn't end there—the cast of characters was straight out of a B-movie set and true entertainment in itself. There was John, our instructor—a small, squeaky fellow tattooed up to his neck with two holsters tightly strapped to his chest, who talked a lot about going to church; the big teddy bear of a guy with the foreign accent who you knew had lived a thousand lives and had a story to tell behind his charming veneer (but you were afraid to ask what that story was); his "Jack Sprat"-like sidekick; the suburban housewife who came by to pick up the rifle she purchased for her husband's birthday; those two suspect-looking dudes hanging back in the corridor; and the group of law-enforcement types who came in with their instructor and took out the big guns (literally). They were the "real deal."

And then there was Stacy, with long blonde hair, California cute, and polished fingernails—and me. We both wanted to believe we were two-thirds of the "Charlie's Angels" trio—was I Kate Jackson or Jaclyn Smith? Of course, Bosley was nowhere to be found, and maybe we were a little older than the Angels, but one could dream.

After filling out our forms, participating in the safety course, and manually loading 50 rounds of bullets into the magazines, I was handed a .22-caliber Ruger semiautomatic rifle. I definitely felt more like Annie Oakley than Angelina Jolie, but it would do. I put on my protective glasses (finally, the cool glasses!) and headphones (it really is deafening if you don't wear them) and was taken to the "stalls." The bull's-eye and pug-nosed thug targets were hanging for us to aim at just like you see on TV. I used a bull's-eye target and cranked mine in a bit closer than the 50 ft. that's suggested. It was my first time, after all.

It's very quiet in the gallery—bulletproof windows surround you, and headphones drown out the extraneous buzz. I was forced to be still, to slow my breathing, to really focus if I wanted to succeed at this. And succeed I did. The first few shots were pretty pathetic, but once I found my rhythm and kept sight of my target, I even shot a few in the bull's-eye. It had this unbelievable calming effect on me. Of course, just as I really got the hang of it, it was time to go. I rolled up my souvenir bull's-eye targets, cleaned up my shell casings, and quietly headed out.

What began as a guilty pleasure and playful "spy jaunt" turned into a very different experience. I definitely don't advocate the use of guns, but I must admit I thoroughly enjoyed it and learned about myself from this little adventure. I need to concentrate, keep steady and focused, and get out of my comfort zone. Then, when ready, look ahead and aim. The bull's-eye is not as far off in the distance as I think it is.

Dancing with My Star

Karen

"You write better than you dance," my husband joked as we awkwardly tried to do the rumba. The last time we took a dance lesson was the obligatory, pre-wedding class 100 years ago. Let me put it this way: the year I got married, the average price of gas was $1.05 per gallon, Princess Diana and Prince Charles separated, and

3

John Gotti was sentenced to life in prison. The only thing the same today is Hillary Clinton's pantsuits. In 1992, our first dance as Mr. and Mrs. Clueless was to Eric Clapton's "Wonderful Tonight," and I didn't need anything even remotely similar to SPANX Shapewear. And just by coincidence, Scent of a Woman *was released in the theaters and we all watched as actor Al Pacino danced the tango at the Plaza.*

Mr. Sometimes-Still-Clueless is a closet Dancing with the Stars *fan. On the rare occasion when he isn't working and has a few moments before his ridiculously early bedtime, my daughter and I will catch him watching the show. He used to try to hastily switch channels to hide his addiction; he finally relaxed about it when the newest season made its debut last month. I actually find it pretty endearing: a pretty big, football-watching guy glued to an addictive dance show on television to unwind. I am glad he finally "owned" it so I could write about it.*

Coincidentally, I've wanted to take dance lessons . . . again, if you count the one in 1992. Mr. Dancing with the Stars seemed okay with it—actually it was finding the time to take a class together that was difficult. It has been on my "52 list" since the beginning: I wanted to do something as a couple that was new, active, fun, and out of our "couple comfort zone." I also wanted to learn a few moves that would surprise my body and give me a sense of accomplishment. The fact is, like most people, we're "average" dancers—if that. Of course, over the years, mostly in our twenties and thirties, there were some tequila-infused moments when we actually thought we were pretty good; but the salsa? No way. The tango? Yeah, right. I just wanted to know what these dances were all about. Would they feel sexy? Would I feel like a fool? Was I twenty years too late? So I called Fred Astaire Dance Studio in Manhattan. When in doubt, think Fred and Ginger Rogers, I told myself when I booked the lesson.

The location was close to Bloomingdale's—the ultimate New York department store. I was glad it was 9:30 at night and the store was closed. I may have been tempted, just for a minute, to bee-line to the Lancôme counter.

After an elevator ride to the fifth floor, we were greeted at the door by Desi. She was terrific on the phone, so it was no surprise she was the same in person. I looked around at the big dance floor, lights, and huge photo of Fred and Ginger and started to feel a bit hesitant. Thankfully, we soon were greeted by a cheerful, pretty instructor named Gala. She was warm and immediately made me feel comfortable. We chatted for a few moments on the dance floor; then, she casually inquired about our wedding song and before we knew it, it was playing. Okay, this was a bit corny, but it did the trick; we laughed and started following her confident lead, doing the rumba and stepping on each other's toes. I had selected a "sampler" private class, so we went from the rumba to the hustle to the tango and salsa all within 45 minutes. When necessary, Gala danced with each of us and never made us feel uncomfortable or too awkward. I loved it. I loved doing this with my "oh-so-busy" husband, and I loved not being on the treadmill or doing my usual stuff.

By the end of the session, we were moving a little less awkwardly and smiling with a little more spunk in our step despite the fact that it was past a certain someone's bedtime. That is what mattered most—our moods. I really would like to do this again. Certainly with Gala as our teacher and definitely when Bloomingdale's is closed.

The Fighter

Karen

Mark Wahlberg as Micky Ward in the 2010 film The Fighter: *aging quickly. Lives in Lowell, Massachusetts—a tough neighborhood. Endless monotony, potheads, crackheads, gloomy. Supportive girlfriend. Trying to get "out" of his neighborhood, win the title, and rise above his situation.*

Me: aging quickly this winter. Lives in New York City—an especially tough neighborhood this month. Endless snowstorms, potholes, ice, traffic, still eating too much cheese and crackers, gloomy. Supportive family. Trying to get my butt anywhere in this weather that will allow me to continue 52 weeks without losing my mind.

I saw The Fighter *last week. It reminded me that boxing was on my "52 list." I've always wanted to try it, just never have. I also heard it is one of the best workouts if you want results, increasingly popular among women and even hot in Hollywood. So this week, I decided it was the perfect time to put on the gloves and punch something, anything.*

I was angry about all the really important stuff in the world that is unfair and about the "little" things like wanting to sleep more, the garbage piled up in the streets, and just trying to navigate the construction and hurdles in the wintery, frozen New York City streets. I also was mad that, despite some small steps in the right direction, I still haven't made some important, big changes in my life and that I haven't seen the sun in months. I was in the perfect "boxing mood." In fact, an article I recently stumbled upon said boxing is the only fitness exercise during which you can hit without being arrested. That's what I needed this week.

So I called John. John and his wife Stephanie have a fitness studio about ten blocks from my home. Over the years, I have dragged myself to their gym when I feel like I need someone to get me back on track or stay on track or start again or get out of a rut. I wish I could say that I trot happily to my appointments, but I don't.

This week, I was scheduled for a regular training session, but I called John and asked him if I could box instead, since I know he has the equipment and often boxes with clients. John gave me a thumbs up when I walked in the door. I showed up. That was huge for me this week.

After a short warm-up, John helped me put on "inner" gloves that reminded me of my biking gloves (they were actually pink!). The boxing gloves followed. My hands couldn't breathe. I immediately wanted to free them, but I didn't have much time to think about it because he put on training "mitts," held up his hands, and showed me how to jab (one-two) and then cross over and alternate, left-right, left-right.

I was a little uneasy of course, but soon I got the rhythm and did numerous sets. John alternated my boxing with crunches, squats, push-ups, and other exercises, all while wearing gloves. Drinking from my water bottle became a joke but I guzzled some water anyway, spilling it as I clumsily grabbed the bottle between both gloves. My heart was beating fast; yes, I was a bit nervous to be trying something so new, but it was also intense cardio. Once or twice I felt like stopping, but I plowed through it and felt some of my anger at the world dissipate as I boxed with John. Clearing my head was easy since I had to focus on just surviving the session. John was great, reassuring me that I was not the only one who found boxing really difficult, especially the first time. I needed the pep talk. Thanks John.

I didn't love The Fighter, *the movie. I didn't love boxing, either, but I felt great after my session. I may do it again to stay in shape. Not sure. All I know is that I showed up, and that was the biggest knockout of the week.*

Now . . . where are my cheese and crackers?

Poker Face

Pam

A dark, smoky room filled with men, the muffled sound of chips hitting the felt table, and silent tension hanging in the air is what one usually imagines when thinking of poker. A brightly lit classroom filled with women, the sound of squeaky metal folding chairs, and giddy anticipation filling the room was the reality.

The World Series of Poker Tournament this definitely was not. Instead, twenty chatty women of varying ages, shapes, sizes, and backgrounds were seated around two big round tables which were covered with crinkly white paper tablecloths ready to learn the game of poker—No Limit Texas Hold 'Em, to be exact!

For three weeks, I'm taking a women-only class on how to play poker at the 92nd Street Y in New York—a great place that offers classes, lectures, and much more. And once again, as so many times before throughout my 52 Week journey, I came away with something other than what I expected. I've always wanted to play cards or be a part of a "group game," so suffice to say, this was the perfect opportunity to try something new this week, break out of my comfort zone, and get out there. What I didn't expect was the easy camaraderie I would feel with my fellow card-shark wannabes after just one class, the wonderfully diverse group of people I met, and discovering that playing poker isn't just about playing poker.

I am not a gambler. I don't go to Atlantic City and never have been to Las Vegas. Other than Go Fish, Spit, and an occasional hand of Gin Rummy, card playing is not something I do. I knew about straights and pairs from childhood games of Yahtzee, and as far as I was concerned, a full house meant the TV show with Bob Saget, John Stamos, and the Olsen twins when they were still sweet and adorable.

So I was totally out of my element. Ellen Leikind, the instructor of the class, was an amazing teacher. She's a fast talker, a real New York woman with her own style and flair, and from what I sensed almost immediately, a bona fide poker player who knows her stuff. Ellen left her job in the corporate world, tried her hand (no pun intended) at a bunch of different things—(kind of her own 52?), and found her passion.

I didn't expect to hear this story from my instructor but was inspired when she shared it. It was then that I realized the class wasn't just about learning the basics of poker. Ellen's teaching was also about helping women get what they want and move forward. It made the class that much more interesting for me, knowing that I was there as part of my 52. I plan on reading her book.

The class was challenging. It was fast-paced, our teacher didn't pander to us, and most of the participants, while there to have a good time, were also there to learn. The rules of the game, thinking about my opponents' hands as well as my own, strategizing, remembering new vocabulary and poker slang such as flops, rivers, backdoor straights, little blind, big blind . . . it was so much more than

I initially thought it would be. But I absolutely loved it! Once I had the basics down, I was eager to play. I was cautious and unsure at first, but as the evening wore on, a tentative confidence grew. And while there was definitely an element of competition by the end of the night, somehow the atmosphere stayed fun and relaxed.

As with so many other things I've recently tried, I have my work cut out for me in the next two weeks. There is much more to learn and a lot more to practice before I play in our own Texas Hold 'Em tournament at the end of the class. But I'm definitely not planning on folding yet. And as Ellen, my instructor, says: if you want to be in the game, you have to be at the table. Deal me in . . .

● ● ● ●

What is a Manhattan mom doing with a rifle in her hand?

What inspired another mom to drag her husband to tango lessons?

In this chapter, we explore, explain, and extol the value of trying something new. We were well into our 52 Week journey before we mustered up the courage to try many of these things. "New" is not always easy, but trying new things brought a level of energy and understanding to our journey—even if we chose never to do those "new" things again.

We've already shared how our blog was conceived and some of our trials and tribulations, but it wasn't until we began to focus on trying new things that we found *new* is not like anything else out there. That's not just our opinion and experience—many experts and others we've spoken to agree: if you feel bored, restless, or stuck, try just one new thing, and you will feel better. But that doesn't mean it's easy to do. It wasn't for us.

52 Weeks EXPERT ✓

Dr. Alex Lickerman, an internist who also is a practicing Buddhist, says that's not unusual. In his work, he has found that people often resist trying new things because they are afraid. Most people tend to stay with what they know—their established routine. Lickerman gives voice to many of our fears about trying new things. What if I don't like this new dish? What if the foreign country I am going to visit is dangerous? He believes we fear an unknown outcome more than we do a known bad one.

So how to embrace the new? We didn't expect ourselves to become experts; maybe you could say we just "dabbled." We took time for ourselves. And that wasn't easy. Carving out time for yourself is difficult—especially for many women who juggle family, kids, schedules, work, and all the rest of life—but we did it. We took classes and tried new things. Some things worked; some did not. All of them taught us something and helped us advance toward our goal of being happier and healthier, and moving again.

So why did doing something new feel so great? We wanted to understand why we felt the way we did. We wanted to understand more about our increasing desire to learn new things. We also wondered why this desire got more intense in our forties. We decided to talk to a few more experts we found along the way.

"Seventy percent of success in life is showing up."
—Woody Allen

52 Weeks EXPERT ✓

We spoke with Pam's poker instructor, **Ellen Leikind,** founder of New York-based POKERprimaDIVAS and author of *Pokerwoman: How to Win in Love, Life, and Business Using the Principles of Poker.* Ellen is an accomplished corporate executive who has been playing poker for many years.

She took a hiatus from the Fortune 500 world and rediscovered poker, a game she had learned as a teenager. The more Ellen played poker, the more she saw the similarities between the card game and the larger "game" of business and personal fulfillment. She founded POKERprimaDIVAS after experimenting with new things, rediscovering poker, building her confidence, and leaving a big marketing career for a while. She discovered that many of the skills she learned in poker help in the real world.

Now she runs amazing corporate events and team-building seminars, using poker to help women not just to try something new and play, but also to improve all areas of their lives. We decided to spend some more time talking with Leikind to understand how she approaches the prospect of trying something new.

"I think doing something new is critical because any time you get out of your comfort zone, you improve yourself. Anytime you do something you didn't think you could do, you are making a positive change in yourself."

Ellen shared with us a story about going to a spa in Arizona. She was part of an outdoor group activity that involved climbing up a *very* high pole, which led to a platform. She was then expected to jump! Petrified, Ellen at first felt she would never be able to do it. She told us, "I was sick just thinking about it, but I finally thought to myself, if all of these other women can do it—young, old, in shape, unfit—who were all probably just as scared—I have to at least try!"

In the end, Ellen grabbed a partner to figuratively and literally hold her hand. Ellen was incredibly scared going up the pole and in fact has no recollection of the ascent. She does, however, remember coming down. It wasn't until after it was over and her heart rate went back to normal that she realized how capable she is of trying something new (and even terrifying).

"Life is like a game of poker: If you don't put any in the pot, there won't be any to take out."
—Jackie "Moms" Mabley, comedian

Bringing it back to poker, Ellen explained that it's all about the idea of doing something outside one's comfort zone. She talked a lot about poker being an individual challenge, yet at the same time, you are surrounded by people. "Some people chat the whole time, and others just play quietly, but you're not alone. That helps sometimes," she said. "A lot of people know they want to play, but they are either afraid that there is no one to teach them, or they don't know how to 'get there.' It's about going to the class—it's not really about learning poker; it's about *showing up* and also participating in something that they were traditionally excluded from, since it's one of those 'guy-club' things. In general, it just represents a 'hurdle'—either psychologically or physically. Whenever you take on something new, just the act of doing it makes women bolder and braver for other things in their lives."

Dr. Lickerman also had great insight into why new things are so powerful, and we agree:

- When you try something new, you need courage. Even the act of summoning that courage is powerful. When you actually attempt the new thing, the power of that act engulfs everything in its path.
- When you try something new, you open yourself up to a host of new possibilities. New careers and even new life paths often are revealed when an individual "dips a baby toe" in the water and experiences a new idea. You may never know you love something until you try it.
- When you try something new, you battle boredom.
- When you try something new, you force yourself to evolve. No one grows by following the same path day after day. Growth requires a new action, a new attitude, a new thought process.

NEXT STEPS

Keep these things in mind when you start your own 52 journey.

Don't wait for an invitation

Life gets busy. There's not always going to be an embossed invitation (or even an evite) to go do something new. We have found that especially as we are getting older, friends are on different schedules. You often have to research, explore, and try new things on your own, and it's not easy. Walking into a class or a museum, or trying a new relationship in some cases takes guts, especially if you're the type of person who is used to having a buddy by your side. Of course, it's great if you do have a partner-in-crime, but even we, despite our best efforts, found we often couldn't coordinate our schedules. Even our blog, the52weeks.com, although conceived together, was really a solo mission; we realized fairly early on that we were on our own a good deal of the time, not just because our respective lists were so different, but also because our busy calendars just didn't make for easy schedule coordination. "If you can get past your fear of doing something new and tackle it on your own, you gain confidence to do anything," says Leikind.

If you don't like it, move on

There were new things we tried this year we didn't like. Golf? It was okay, but not enough fun to commit to on a regular basis. Kabbalah and dance lessons got higher marks—they moved into the "keeper" column. Boxing was a kick, but once was enough. And we don't think Manhattan's only shooting range will see us again anytime soon. But the point is, we tried them all. Try it to try it. Do it to do it. And then, after checking things off your list, decide which you want to keep and which to throw away. "You have

13

to know when to fold," Ellen said. "If you have a bad hand or it doesn't feel right, fold 'em."

If you're bored, you're boring

As you know by now, our blog was conceived one night when we were out having drinks and found ourselves grumbling (again) about feeling restless, bored, and "stuck." We were also becoming acutely aware of others who complained too much, which wasn't very appealing! Bottom line? If *we* were turned off by complaining, then of course others were likely turned off by us! Our blog made us stop whining and start doing. Leikind agrees: "If you feel bored, try something new, and you won't be bored—or boring—anymore!"

So if you're not good at it, big deal

People hate doing things they don't excel in. We needed to get over this psychological hurdle during our journey. Sometimes, we failed miserably at new things we tried. Sometimes, we surprised ourselves and discovered a new skill; it's all part of the process.

Leave the multitasking aside for a few hours

If you look around a gym, a restaurant, a supermarket, or even a museum these days, you inevitably will see people staring at their phones while they are trying to be present and enjoy the primary activity. Even when we were trying different things this year, it took practice to stop checking our phones on the golf course, in a class, or while striking a yoga pose. You've probably heard it before, but the key is to be present, focus, and concentrate. We all are moving too fast, and we need to slow down for a few hours a week at the very least.

When experts talk about the importance of doing something new such as taking a poker class or an art class, a good part of the reason to do it is to get out of your head and forget about your routine. If you find yourself texting your sister or husband or answering work emails during your "something new," then it's not resonating and it probably won't stick around for very long. Pat yourself on the back for trying it, and then move on to the next thing.

Get going

Trying something new is not always easy, but it's important to start exploring, trying, and learning new things to not only get going again, but also to be the best you can be—for yourself and for others. "In poker, like in life, the prize goes to the bold," Ellen said.

And part of being bold is trying new things.

 ## SOME TAKEAWAY ADVICE AND QUOTES TO GET YOU GOING

> ➢ "The person who never made mistakes, never tried anything new."
> —Albert Einstein
> ➢ In dance and in life, if you get tangled up, tango on.
> ➢ Get out of your comfort zone and take a risk.
> ➢ If you want to be in the game, you have to be at the table.
> ➢ Just show up; it's more than half the battle.
> ➢ Make time to fit in something "new" by pairing it with another activity or responsibility.
> ➢ If you are a night owl, get up early once in a while; a different time of day can equal a different perspective.

➢ Get out of your ZIP code, even if it's just for an hour, and explore.

➢ "We keep moving forward, opening new doors, and doing new things, because we're curious and curiosity keeps leading us down new paths."
—Walt Disney

IDEAS FOR THE READER

Here's a sampling of things we tried during our 52, and remember to check out Chapter 11, "Your 52," for more ideas.

- Learned to play poker.
- Took golf lessons.
- Tried tennis . . . again.
- Went to a shooting range.
- Went indoor rock climbing.
- Took nude drawing classes.
- Test-drove ridiculously expensive sports cars.
- Learned weaving.
- Took boxing lessons.
- Explored Kabbalah.
- Took dance lessons.
- Volunteered.
- Explored all things French.

Chapter Two

Wellness

"My grandmother started walking five miles a day when she was sixty. She's ninety-three today and we don't know where the hell she is."

—Ellen DeGeneres

They're Not Just Blueberries

Karen

Leave it to Oprah. Just as I was struggling to find the best words to talk about blueberries and write my first post, I picked up a recent issue of O Magazine *and decided to do some mindless reading. And there it was: A great article about food, featuring the perfect quote from* Winnie-the-Pooh *that somehow made it all come together: "When you wake up in the morning, Pooh," said Piglet at last, "what's the first thing you say to yourself?" What's for breakfast?" said Pooh. "What do you say, Piglet?" "I say, I wonder what's going to happen exciting today?" said Piglet. Pooh nodded thoughtfully. "It's the same thing," he said.*

And that's exactly it. Or at least, that is what blueberries have come to represent to me—exciting possibilities. For the past two years, I have told myself that I need to eat blueberries every day or at least frequently, because they are one of the most healthful foods—packed with antioxidants that counter bad habits (and I certainly have some), low-calorie, and easy to eat. In fact, experts say just a handful a day can do some great things. According to studies, blueberries have the highest antioxidant capacity of all fresh fruit, aid in reducing belly fat, and are natural anti-depressants!

"For me, they are not just a fruit; I imagine one huge blueberry as the mascot for feeling less 'stuck.'"

I have told myself that if I can successfully consume them daily, blueberries will be a powerful statement that I am starting on a new and different path. For approximately 24 months I have purchased them, even splurging for the organic variety, and they remain uneaten in my refrigerator. The best intentions are soon followed by an inevitable craving for carbs, eggs, or something else in the morning. Without fail, they sit in the fridge, taunting me, changing each day from a vibrant, bluish-purple hue to slightly brownish in color, shriveling symbols of failure. In fact, I cannot even tell you how many times I have disposed of a container of blueberries, uneaten, raisin-like, tossed in the garbage. For me, they are not just a fruit; I imagine one huge blueberry as the mascot for feeling a bit less "stuck." If I could eat and enjoy them, then for me, like Pooh, blueberries would represent something more—moving in the right direction, being "unstuck," sticking to goals. It would mean that something exciting could happen. So for this week, I bought blueberries on Monday and was determined to eat them every day for a week. There they were, sitting on the shelf at the store, those ubiquitous plastic containers holding dozens of those things at a time. I grabbed two containers and went to pay. Maybe it was my imagination, but I think the cashier was laughing at my determined expression.

From past experience, I knew this was only the first step; it would mean nothing if I threw them out again. I also knew I could not go "cold turkey" and skip carbs completely. So on the first day, I threw a handful on my half a bagel with cream cheese. I am not kidding. That's what I did. The next day I had a handful "on the side" with my eggs and toast—a colorful accompaniment. The following day, I smiled as I ate them simply with yogurt. Progress. I was getting there; all of a sudden, I felt the satisfaction that only happens when you say you are going to do something and actually stick to it. By week's end I was on the run, having a banana and a handful of those blue things on the way to the gym an hour earlier than usual. Hey, I was on to something.

Such a simple little thing that is good for you. I did it. This little, stupid change has pushed me out of the starting gate. I hope it will be the fuel I need for the next 51 weeks. I hope that on whatever week I set out on bigger challenges, I will be inspired by my blueberry project. Regardless, Week One is over. I hope I don't have to ask myself, "What's for breakfast?" going forward. I hope blueberries and other good things find their way into my meals without me even thinking about it. I doubt it will be foolproof but I can hope. But, I do live in New York City: home of the best bagels in the world. Thank God they will always be just a block away. I think I have even seen blueberry cream cheese . . .

A Change That Saved My Life

This is a guest post by Amie Valpone, HHC, AADP and author of TheHealthyApple.com. She is a Manhattan-based culinary nutritionist, personal chef, professional recipe developer, and food photographer and writer specializing in simple gluten-free "clean" recipes for the at-home cook. She writes for the Huffington Post *and numerous other publications.*

The 52 Weeks

The "best" doctors across the Eastern seaboard told me I was crazy. Mayo Clinic told me I was crazy. Even though I was lying on a hospital bed hooked up to morphine to relieve my intense, mysterious, undiagnosed bodily pain I had for years, my colleagues thought I was crazy, too. No one believed me. Did I give in, give up, or break down? No. I didn't give up. Instead, I took matters into my own hands. And changed my own life. And just like Pam and Karen sitting at that bar, when they decided they needed change, so did I (of course on a much more "serious" level, as Karen made sure to point out when I told her my story.)

I struggled for five and a half years with chronic leg swelling (twenty-plus pounds of water weight every day by 3 p.m.) and severe digestive issues while pursuing a "big" marketing and advertising career in corporate America: Vogue, Ralph Lauren Corporate, and the NBA. I never let anyone know what was going on other than my family. I felt gross, embarrassed, bloated, foggy-brained, confused, and frustrated. Instead of truly listening, doctors wrote me prescriptions for countless, useless pills. How was a 26-year-old woman to go on a date with swollen legs and chronic pain when all I could wear were spandex and gulp down water pills instead of cocktails?

One evening in 2007, I was rushed from my office to the St. Vincent's Cancer Center in NYC with chronic low white blood cells. Ten minutes later, I was getting a bone-marrow biopsy. Doctors told me to start making appointments at Sloan Kettering, that I had leukemia. I had exhausted all the doctors in the area and beyond. Countless tests revealed nothing. I ventured to Mayo Clinic in 2010. Still no answers. My health continued to deteriorate. My doctor told my sister I was insane and should take drugs to stop the madness. After having kale in December 2010, I contracted parasites, pathogens, and had bacteria overgrowth. I was put on steroids and painkillers—and went on disability. The worst part? My colleagues at the NBA thought I was kidding. Human Resources would call, questioning my truthfulness.

The leg swelling got so bad I could barely move. I found cysts on my feet. No one could figure out anything.

Clearly, the Western doctors, for all their degrees in the world, and my unsupportive corporate job weren't going to help me get better. So I changed doctors, quit my job—and just like the promise of a new direction that is 52 Weeks, I changed my own life. I sought alternative options.

It wasn't until I began working with an integrative medical doctor that I learned I was suffering from heavy metal accumulation in my tissues and that I was born without the gene to absorb folate—key in detoxification. I was confused as to why Mayo Clinic and all the hospitals didn't find the heavy metal problems. I soon learned that Western medicine only tests for heavy metals in your blood—not tissues. I started chelation (a process to draw the heavy metals out of your body through an IV) along with taking chelating agents.

And as "crazy" as it may be, my painful experience led me to one of my greatest joys in life: helping others heal. I went back to school to learn more about Eastern medicine and nutrition. Using acupuncture, yoga, meditation, herbal medicine, and fresh, organic, 100 percent whole, unprocessed foods, I healed myself and remain completely symptom-free nearly five years later. I am still unable to consume gluten and dairy (except an occasional Greek yogurt), as well as grains, oils, fruits, and sugar. These past few years, I discovered I am allergic to sulfates and cannot digest packaged foods. Therefore, I eat like a cave woman and follow a clean lifestyle filled with lean proteins, healthful fats, and lots of veggies. It has changed my life, and now it's my full-time job—helping others feel good and find the real solution to their ongoing pain.

For several years, I was positive and held my head high, even though I was frustrated and felt like no one listened to me. Do I still have days when I feel crappy? Yes, but my passion, my pride, my yearning to find an answer and help people just like me to not give up keeps me going.

Ready, Set, Run!

I downloaded an app from Apple's iTunes store this week. It wasn't just any app. It was something that represents a big "to do" for me. And then, I actually did it.

Pam

I went running. And I used a silly little app on my iPhone to help me get started. I suppose a little background is in order . . .

Committed exercise has always been an obstacle for me. I don't exercise on a regular basis, have never partaken in the latest trends—no spinning, Physique 57, or step classes way back when. The truth is, I just don't do any organized exercise on a consistent schedule. While my friends are training for the marathon, pole dancing, or going to Boot Camp, I am usually spending my energy thinking of excuses—"need new sneakers," "could use a personal trainer," "have no time." I guess you could also say I've been one of those "lucky ones" too, so it was never a huge issue. I am slim, live a "healthy-ish" lifestyle, and am able to stay fit doing the minimum—an occasional bike ride on the weekends, yoga classes, and lots of walking. I am able to put regular sugar in my coffee, eat Oreos, and still fit into most of my old jeans.

But it feels wrong not do something more formal in terms of exercise. It's embarrassing already and stupid, I know. I am being a poor role model for my kids, and it's just irresponsible that I am not taking better care of myself as I enter the "next demographic." And if I am being brutally honest, things are starting to "shift" a bit now. The mental and physical benefits are paramount—being stronger, happier, and healthier—but who am I kidding, I still want to look good, too! Trying to be consistent with exercise has always been something I want to do. Now it is time to finally really try.

So I bought an app. At $2.99 it was a lot cheaper than hiring a personal trainer. I don't particularly like running, so I'm not sure why I chose this as the "thing to try." But maybe I will change my mind.

Couch to 5K talks you through a 30-minute workout, slowly building up from walking and running to (theoretically) running a 5K in nine weeks. I put on my headphones, pressed play on my phone, and listened to my new virtual friend as she helped me begin something new. "Welcome to Couch to 5K; begin warm-up now," Cybergirl said. Five-minute warm-up, 60 seconds of running, 90 seconds of walking, 90 seconds of running. A half hour later, mission accomplished.

My husband came along for the first workout. Even though I had my cyber pal with me, a real live person is the only one who can make you feel sheepish if you don't follow through. Downloading an app is one thing, but pride, guilt, and embarrassment are also wonderful motivators! Here are a few of the details—my headphones didn't work halfway through the run (I was quickly able to plug my husband's headset in), the path I was on was filled with too many puddles after a huge rainstorm, I definitely need to buy a sports bra, and it was hard. I did not enjoy it—but I finished. I am not sure of the distance I actually went. The program works you toward a 10-minute mile or 30-minute 5K, but that doesn't really matter. What matters is that I exercised for 34 minutes and didn't cheat. I followed Cybergirl's instructions, completed what I set out to do, and will do it again day after tomorrow.

I live along the NYC Marathon route, and every year, I cheer the runners on from my balcony. I watch in awe when the Achilles Club athletes pass by, cheer in amazement when the runners swoosh past, and get choked up when that last walker is escorted through the streets and walks into the night to get to the finish line ,at Central Park. And every November I say, "I want to run the marathon one day." Within a day or two I snap back into reality, because I remember that I don't really like running and I can barely commit to an exercise routine. Perhaps that's part of the reason I tried running. I want to know what all of the hype is about. Maybe it's like thinking you don't like Brussels sprouts even though you've never really tried them. Maybe it's like Sam-I-Am finally trying the green eggs and ham. I am not planning on running the marathon, but I do hope to be able to run a few miles at some point. Honestly, did I feel rejuvenated and invigorated? Not really. I was hot, sweaty, had wet sneakers from the puddles, and really had to pee. I really didn't like it all that much—yet. But I'm going to do it again day after tomorrow and keep at it for a while.

Trying to Quit

Karen

I hate this blog this week. I am not going to lie. This was only Week 6 and I just didn't or couldn't seem to do "something big" that would be universally defined as "unique," adrenaline-inducing or even potentially life-changing. For the record, I am also on Week 6 of packing my daughter's knapsack each morning for day camp. Same drill every day: two bathing suits, two towels, two kinds of sun lotion—you get the idea. It's boring me to tears. Sorry, no "Mom-of-the-Year" award here. Routines can be comforting the experts say; this one is not working for me.

And then about Wednesday, it hit me: I was doing something on my "list" this week; in fact, I was doing something that is just as—if not more—important than the previous weeks (nude drawing, French cinema, golf lessons): I was "taking stock," regrouping, and taking steps toward bigger life changes. You see, like our history-making, battle-worn President, I have an addiction that I can't seem to shake and, like President O, I find myself sneaking cigarettes (yes they still sell those and now they are about $14 a pack). I know smoking is disgusting, so please reserve judgment and spare me the lectures. I am a smart, strong woman most of the time. I just can't seem to quit smoking completely on my own. I am not proud of this disgusting "secret." I can blame it on a predisposition to addiction, my tendency to be anxious, and my age group (if you're in your forties, you grew up around it, and college was a smoke-fest). But I am too old now to be smoking at all. The few people I know who still smoke don't really smoke. They have a few cigarettes a year when we venture to *a casino or go away on a trip. I envy them. I am not built that way. For me, it has to be all or nothing. I have tried the "cutting down" thing, have spoken with therapists about smoking, and I am exhausted from thinking about smoking. I need to quit already. I wasn't ready to "talk" about this yet but decided I needed to write about it or it wouldn't happen. It's out now. I can't take it back.*

So I called and researched one of the best. Known as "The Mad Russian," Yefim Shubentsov, based in Brookline, Massachusetts, is the guy who helped Billy Joel end his twenty-seven-year smoking habit. Joel, who had tried to give up smoking for years, read about Yefim in the newspaper. "He is intense and convincing," says Joel in a USA Today article. If this guy was being praised by the Piano Man himself he can help me, right? Further reading revealed Drew Barrymore and Courteney Cox and ex-husband David Arquette also made the pilgrimage to Massachusetts. Yefim uses bioenergetics during group or private sessions—"a healing life force that circulates within all living things."

The 52 Weeks is all about doing new things that sometimes have a "wow" factor that comes with maybe jumping off a cliff (with a parachute, please!). But this was a different kind of week for me. I turned inward. When a Ferrari test drive (on my 52 list) couldn't be arranged this week, I looked at my list again and picked the "biggie," the smoking thing. That's about as real as you can get. That's about truly getting "unstuck." Leaving your comfort zone is not just about bungee jumping.

I am now on the waiting list for my voyage to Brookline and the Mad Russian. I could almost hear my Mom saying, "Just do it Karen. You do everything else. Grandpa stopped cold turkey after a three-pack a day habit without any help!" I couldn't help thinking what a different world we live in now. We seek help from our trainers, our shrinks, our Yogis. If we have access to help, why not accept it? Writing about quitting made it real. I feel like I jumped off a cliff. My calls, my research, and my process are my "parachute," and I need to go through this process. My Grandpa was a strong guy, yes; but he also came to this country off a boat from Russia and had many other challenges I couldn't even imagine. I found it ironic that this stop-smoking guy is called the "Mad Russian." Coincidence? Or is my wonderful Poppy helping me from "the beyond" through this guy? Hey, ya never know.

Running to the store now for Nicorette gum and more sun lotion for my daughter. Tomorrow I need to pack her backpack again.

With a Little Help from My Friend

Pam

Lately, I've been looking for a new sport or exercise to explore (the running didn't last). I really want to check this off of my 52 list. It's just that trying something new can sometimes be a little daunting. So this week, Karen and I decided we'd help each other move beyond our comfort zones and lend each other moral support, expertise, and a chance to try something out of our element. Easier said than done? We'll see.

My idea of a workout? A Vinyasa yoga class. Karen's idea of a workout? A hard-hitting tennis game. My exercise comfort zone? Noncompetitive, and definitely not too sweaty. Karen's comfort zone? Very competitive, and preferably sporting a shiny glow by game's end.

I'm sure you know where this is going.

I played (and I use that term loosely) tennis this week. Karen planned to join me (again, loose use of the term join) in a yoga class next week.

- *I donned my yoga pants for tennis (the only "workout" clothes I own); Karen will don her "tennis" sweats for yoga attire (they look a lot like "yoga" pants, if you ask me).*
- *My sneakers went on; her sneakers will come off.*
- *My heart raced for a solid hour (hard hitting workout or just out of shape?); she—in theory—will take deep, relaxing breaths.*

- *I reached for the shots; she will reach and stretch.*
- *Lots of noise and laughs during tennis; a keen sense of quiet and hearing one's own breathing during yoga.*
- *She was my coach; I will be her silent cheerleader.*
- *Adrenaline rush; internal calm.*

In their own way, both can be the perfect mental and physical release.

I expected to feel intimidated. After all, I hadn't picked up a racket since the third grade. Instead, I was offered kudos for my solid attempt at playing. No pretenses, no "one-upmanship" or bravado; just one friend encouraging another to try something my mind and body were so unfamiliar with.

Karen pushes herself to play tennis regularly even when she's "not in the mood" because she knows her mood will change once she's on the court. I admire that. I hope I can offer the same inspiration to her when it is my turn.

This week's 52 wound up not being about playing a game of tennis for the first time in many years, but rather, I found myself realizing that reaching out to others, to both help and be helped, has as much to do with getting unstuck as getting off your own ass. You don't have to go it alone. Sometimes you need a helping hand when you are trying new things and striving to find what's right for you.

Breaking Up Is Hard to Do

Karen

It's over. I just can't continue with you on a daily basis—even a weekly basis anymore, at least for a while. I want you every day, and I just can't have you anymore. I've had enough of you to last forever, and I want to stop craving you. "It's not you, it's me," I thought to myself.

I broke up with cheese this week. I can't eat it anymore. If I continue eating it I will constantly be struggling to lose that "extra" weight. If I continue, cheese will have won. I eat it too much, usually accompanied by crackers. But I seem to find a way to eat cheese with every meal—cheese and crackers, cheese on my sandwich regardless of what I am eating, cheese omelets. I am a cheese addict. I can't stop eating it, especially this winter as I fight the frigid temperatures, snowstorms, and the cravings. Even when I have "cut back" in the past, I still purchase the fat-free cheese as a substitute. Why any human would want to eat fat-free cheese is beyond me; rubbery, slippery, no taste, and doesn't melt.

For the record, I am not a candidate for the Biggest Loser or anything. I just constantly want to weigh ten or twenty pounds less than I do. This winter has brought that number to a new level. Put simply: my jeans don't fit anymore.

Day 1: I couldn't go cold turkey. I tried to be proud of myself as I carefully measured one tablespoon of shredded cheese and scattered it over a piece of whole-grain toast, which I then melted in the toaster. I remember Weight Watchers had said that measuring cheese by a tablespoon was better than slices, etc. At least I wasn't picking mindlessly.

Day 2: I made the mistake of cooking Chicken Parmigiana for my family. The good news is it was a hit. I actually even had the willpower to make a piece, on the side, sans mozzarella cheese. The bad news? I was starving at 10:30 at night when the house was finally quiet. Or maybe it was just emotional eating? Not sure. I found myself eating Wheat Thins and cream cheese, watching Millionaire Matchmaker on Bravo. Not funny.

Day 3: Newfound determination. I am really mad at myself. I'm throwing out all the cheese in the house, and the family will have to deal with it. The fact is, I don't think they really care. Here I go; I am throwing out the cheese. Had my first cheese-free day in ages.

Day 4: I think pizza will be making an appearance here later. My husband was working late and I had plans to go to dinner with the girls—i.e., eat a big salad. I usually order a pizza for the babysitter and my daughter. It's a routine. I wondered whether the leftovers would tempt me when I returned home, but I did it. The leftover pizza went untouched, and I went to bed.

The week continued without cheese consumption. I am not sure whether I will avoid cheese forever. My goal is to just be in control of my cheese consumption and enjoy it as something special rather than look for it daily like an addict. Like I said earlier, sometimes baby steps are important to move forward and trying to eat better this year is one of my goals. I know it's just cheese, but like the blueberries, it became symbolic of the things I need to change. I know if I try to change too much or all at once, I end up crashing and going back full force to whatever bad habits or patterns I have. The last thing I want to do is find myself "friending" Kraft's Fan Page on Facebook. So I choose this week to just continue working on my food habits a bit. I hope I have the willpower to stay out of that relationship for a while, or at least until my jeans fit again.

• • • •

When we conceived our blog that cold night, we talked a lot about wanting to shake it up, especially when it came to exercise and health. We were both really stuck. Karen went to the gym regularly but didn't go much further than the gym in her building—an unattractive, basic, dungeon-like space off the lobby. Each time she went, she did the same thing—some cardio and weights. It wasn't very inspiring if you wanted to move forward. Karen was bored and her body showed it. Pam, genetically-blessed to be thin and "in shape" without doing much, just didn't really work out at all. She was mad at herself. She wanted to change that.

Then there were unspeakable old habits that had to go, and an embarrassing addiction to cheese for Karen that probably kept the dairy farmers in business. It was a bit overwhelming. Had our busy lives gotten in the way of taking better care of ourselves? "When did we get to be forty-something?" we would whisper to each other, as if no one could really tell. Karen longed for the days that she could eat countless chicken wings, keeping pace with her 6'3" husband, and not gain a pound. Those days were long gone.

It was as if we both saw one person in our heads and someone else staring back in the mirror.

It was also a mental game. We needed to accept where we were right now and try to do something about it. Our patterns and habits were deeply ingrained at this point. How would we start making changes? What would we put on our 52 lists that would make us feel better, look better and be healthier? It was going to be tough. Could we do it?

The next day we officially started creating our 52 lists. That same morning Karen woke up and, not surprisingly, craved her carbs again. She ate blueberries for breakfast that first week instead. What was great about that experiment is that it was do-able. She didn't say to herself, "I can't eat anything I want again." She simply wanted to see if she could do it and it was an easy, light way to kick-off her 52 Week adventure. Karen even looked at her egg-bacon-cheese-eating husband and had the willpower to say "no!" Men often lose weight more easily: they just stop eating bread for a while and that's it. We had to stop fighting that and just accept it.

Pam was determined to really start exercising. She was focused on trying and finding new things she liked to do. She ran (didn't love it); she played tennis (probably not pursuing); and she tried new classes, including Bikram and Body Ballet (liked them better!). That's a big message we want to get out there: the52weeks.com was all about trying new things, making changes, and getting out of our respective comfort zones. We didn't have to like all of our challenges, what mattered was that we were getting unstuck.

We also found that it is easy to fall back into patterns and routines that are familiar but not necessarily good for you. After our initial 52 Weeks, we could see this happening at times. Now, there is something to be said for the familiar. The important lesson in the end is you can't know what really should stay the same until you change things. Explore, try, fail—see how change feels and then, find the right balance. After a while, the "new" isn't new anymore; you just become a better version of yourself.

Finally, let's talk about life's curve balls: health, major family problems, relationship challenges, whatever. We learned you can't beat yourself up if you need to stay "emotionally in place" for a while. These are the times you have to look within, be strong, and deal with stuff. There are bumps in the road and many times you just can't possibly think of running to a new class or caring about blueberries. Try. If you fall down, pick yourself up. Sometimes you will get up quickly and sometimes you won't.

So how do you get out of a wellness rut? We reached out to two great experts to get some advice for readers and ourselves.

Dr. Jennifer H. Mieres, a leading expert and patient advocate in the field of cardiovascular disease in women, also has been a dear friend and neighbor of Karen's for almost two decades. "Our girls are friends, too," says Karen. "I am always amazed watching Jennifer go about her life as a mom, friend, and top doctor. She sets the bar high!" When we thought about this chapter, Mieres was the first to come to mind. It wasn't just because she is an advocate for women's health and an award-winning cardiologist, she's the real deal and a great role model for all of us, especially when it comes to making simple changes.

Karen

I remember working with Jennifer on a project a few years ago. We would often asked each other for advice and she's an amazing sounding board. This time, she asked for some marketing help with her book launch. Now, of course I know the phrase "take baby steps"; it's not new and has been used by various professionals for a long time. But, when Jennifer said it aloud when we were editing something together it really stayed with me. It wasn't just because of my age; it was because she was incredibly passionate about how important even small steps can be. She gave me hope that some of the seemingly insurmountable hurdles I faced could be overcome. I often forget to congratulate myself for little accomplishments. I often wouldn't start or try something unless I thought I could do it one hundred percent. For example, if I wanted to run a mile I would think it wasn't worth it unless I "became a runner" and trained for something bigger—like a marathon. I needed to work on changing my mindset. I wasn't going anywhere like this. After that project with Jennifer I started to see and believe that small changes are fine. Most important, they often lead to bigger changes.

When we sat down with Mieres to ask for advice about wellness, her words never once felt preachy or made us run the other way. She focused on ways to get going again and feel better overall.

"As women, we need to realize that lifestyle choices are critical to ensuring our overall health and wellness," said Mieres. "Recent clinical studies have shown that women are different physiologically and emotionally than men." Even as laymen we knew that—intuitively and from experience. When our husbands ate a cow and still stayed thin, we didn't need a scientific study to tell us we have some differences!

"We need to promise ourselves to make simple lifestyle changes. As women, we have a tendency to put ourselves last on the 'to-do list,' and in doing so, very often we fail to get to the simple steps for us to maintain ideal health." We knew we had find time daily to exercise, eat right, and de-stress even if we felt we didn't have, or want, to find the time. We knew all this but hearing it from a doctor—especially a renowned expert on women's health—was important. We also think it is about changing your mindset. Karen still struggles with completely embracing the idea of tough changes not feeling like deprivation, but she's getting there.

"If you just choose two things a day to get started with, you are on your way," said Mieres. Little changes can help women prevent chronic illness such as heart disease, Alzheimer's, and cancer. It's also important to recognize the link between lack of sleep and stress, and chronic disease. "Thirty minutes of brisk walking, a colorful plate, and ten minutes of laughter can have great effects in ensuring a longer and healthier life."

The importance of going for screenings as we approach midlife came up a few times when we were talking. For some, the experience truly is nerve-wracking. As we approach and enter our midlife years, health issues, required screenings, and menopause can occupy our daily thoughts, but Mieres explained that health risks mostly depend on three factors: genes, age, and lifestyle habits. If you take the time to review family history and discuss your health risks with your doctor, you can plan a strategy to optimize health and wellness. "One major study highlighted the fact that the four simple lifestyle changes of being active, stopping smoking, reducing blood pressure, and controlling blood sugar can greatly reduce a woman's likelihood of spending the last part of her life in a nursing home."

Meditation was on Karen's list for 52 Weeks. As a first move, she downloaded a simple app on her iPhone. She knew she needed to incorporate meditation in her life to manage her anxiety. A recent scientific publication from the American Heart Association (November 2012) demonstrated the heart healthy benefits of meditation, including a reduction in blood pressure. Also, with meditation there is a decrease in the death rate, heart disease and stroke.

"One major study highlighted the fact that the four simple lifestyle changes of being active, stopping smoking, reducing blood pressure, and controlling blood sugar can greatly reduce a woman's likelihood of spending the last part of her life in a nursing home."

We were curious what Mieres would say when we pressed for some ways to improve one's health beyond nutrition and lifestyle choices. She talked about the benefits of volunteering (which we cover more about in Chapter 7, "Giving Back"). We loved that matters of the heart have heart-healthy benefits too.

Mieres joined the American Heart Association as a volunteer in 2000. "There was great synergy with my personal mission to educate and empower women about their heart health and the organization's Go Red For Women campaign," she said. She became a national spokeswoman for the movement. It was an

"Understand that health is a state of complete physical, mental, and social well-being and not merely the absence of disease or illness."
—*Dr. Jennifer Mieres*

easy fit, because the organization is committed to reducing the number of women dying from heart disease. But Mieres didn't start volunteering in 2000. She grew up in Trinidad where community service was part of her everyday life. "My family was committed to community service and volunteerism," said Mieres. "My dad always said, 'Do not be an observer of life; no contribution is too small.' So, volunteerism and giving back to the community has been one of the basic tenets of my family." A recent study confirms that volunteering provides both social and individual health benefits, strengthens communities, solves problems, and brings people together. A report entitled "The Health Benefits of Volunteering: A Review of Recent Research,"[1] described the significant connection between volunteering and good health. The report shows that people who volunteer have better longevity, higher functional ability, lower rates of depression, and less incidence of heart disease.

Lisa Lillien, also known as "The Hungry Girl," is the author of best-selling cookbooks and a well-known television personality who just seems to have it together when it comes to food—a big topic for women in their forties, and really every decade. When we were researching experts who could share simple, easy changes to get unstuck in the nutrition, food, and wellness areas, we knew we had found the perfect *52* expert. She considers herself a typical woman battling the same food issues most females struggle with. When we read on her web site that she considers

---

[1] Corporation for National and Community Service, Office of Research and Policy Development. *The Health Benefits of Voulnteering: A Review of Recent Research*, Washington, DC 2007.

herself a "foodologist"—not because she has a fancy degree but because she is obsessed with food, how wonderful it is, and how much of it she can eat and still fit into her pants—we knew we had to see if she would answer some questions for us.

Like many of our experts she was quick to point out that women tend to spend more time taking care of others than they do taking care of themselves. We knew that. That's why it was so important to make changes, any changes, to get unstuck.

Lillien is all about food swapping and making small changes. We've included just a sampling of her suggestions in this chapter. What do they all have in common? A clear message: go to the produce aisle instead of the snack food. Even for just one week. Try it. To be honest, we didn't have a "formal" swap plan on our 52 lists. The funny thing is we were doing it at times without even realizing it. When Karen stuck blueberries in her cream cheese, she was finding a creative way to get them in. That's the idea.

When Karen "broke up with cheese" she did feel a sense of accomplishment. It's also about working in substitutes or finding ways to get that same feeling without the food you are overindulging in. "Women really fear change and they shouldn't—especially if you approach it as a challenge and feel better," says Lillien. "I try to make it easy, because many of the foods I make are still comfort foods. My philosophy isn't about saying no to foods— it's about celebrating food, finding ways to eat what you crave and have fun with it."

We wanted to dig deeper and find out if she ever felt "stuck" or had any fears. "I had always been intensely afraid of public speaking," she explained. "It was a terrible fear of mine. However, once I started doing book signings and speaking to hundreds of people at a time I was able to overcome it. It is the best feeling in the world to move forward and tackle a fear."

Knowing fear of public speaking was a hurdle that Lillien had to overcome made watching her on television that much more inspiring. "When I saw Lisa on Dr. Oz I was really drawn to her," Karen shared. "Her comfort food swaps made me hopeful that I could eat macaroni and cheese again. She took a love for food and made it into a career about helping people."

Many of our attempts to create healthy lifestyle changes didn't make it into the book, but in the end we realized what is most important is to **just keep trying.** Sometimes change isn't easy. Sometimes you will fail and you have to just try again. It's also important to remember that novelty is important but routine (when it works) can be comforting and reduce stress. When we think about it, in the end this may be the most important contributing factor to overall wellness: combining the new with the old. And, if you add a new, "Hungry Girl" version of macaroni and cheese to your diet, you will hit the jackpot.

Karen now watches her husband eat chicken wings weekly and doesn't partake with him except for the occasional "I will just have two" moments. She is even considering becoming predominantly a vegetarian with quarterly steaks at the famous Palm restaurant—her favorite. Pam used to forget to drink enough water and would constantly be dehydrated. Now, more often than not, she is drinking plenty of water and sipping green tea instead of sugary juices. She still reaches for her fix of Reese's Peanut Butter Cups but there is more wellness balance in her life. We both like yoga and try new things more than we used to. Yes, we are still figuring it all out but we are determined to permanently adopt the things that work. Last but not least, don't skip breakfast. We've all heard this before, but do it. A 52 reminder: a trip to Dunkin' Donuts doesn't count as breakfast!

NEXT STEPS

Keep these things in mind when you start your own *52* wellness journey. Thanks Dr. Mieres and The Hungry Girl!

Avoid cigarette smoke

Karen continues to try each and every day to fight smoking cravings. It's embarrassing for her to admit it. There is such a stigma now associated with smoking, but she is not alone. Many people still "sneak" cigarettes, but do whatever you can to beat that habit. Remember the movie theaters, restaurants, and airplanes with smoking sections many years ago? Crazy! Pam is lucky. It was never an issue for her.

Swap, swap, and swap!

We're sharing a few of The Hungry Girl's great food swap ideas at the end of this chapter. She has many more to check out. Or create your own. Just swap.

Choose to be active, and keep moving

Get off your butt and be active. Dr. Mieres recommends taking a minimum of 10,000 steps every day. Shake it up and try new things; you won't find Pam running all the time, but she continues her practice of yoga. Karen really loved yoga but still finds herself drawn to the "boring" treadmill—her comfort zone. But, hey, 10,000 steps are 10,000 steps. What we love about this advice is that Mieres counts *all* steps for the day— including walking to the movies, the diner, and even perhaps, running away from irritating family members!

Eat a Mediterranean diet

A Mediterranean diet includes plant-based foods such as fruits and vegetables, whole grains, legumes, and nuts; and replacing butter with healthy fats such as olive oil and canola oil. It also means using herbs and spices instead of salt to flavor foods, limiting red meat consumption to no more than a few times a month, eating fish and poultry at least twice a week, and drinking a little red wine (optional). The diet also recognizes the importance of enjoying meals with family and friends.

Maintain an ideal body weight for your height

This is tough and gets harder after a certain age. But it's not just about appearances, you also need to keep your weight in sync with your height for maximum wellness.

Lift a glass, but only one

We love our wine. Fortunately, there are health benefits to having "just one," but once you exceed having one glass, there are health risks. Cut back. Start adding ice to your drinks. Self-medicating is too common. Karen is the first to admit that controlling her anxiety with an extra glass of wine is not uncommon for her. You have to continuously try to take steps to avoid this, and do what you have to do to control it in a healthy way: yoga, meditation, therapy— whatever it takes. She is still working on that but certainly making progress. Check out, "Facing Fears," in Chapter 6 for more on managing anxiety.

Get enough sleep

According to Mieres you should get at least six hours of sleep a night. It's tough. Women especially often worry about a million things while their significant others (especially men!) snore loudly through everything and anything. Add perimenopause and menopause to the equation and you may as well just clean all of your closets out at 3 a.m.—which we have both done! Karen is reluctantly trying to go to bed earlier and has even cut back on her evening, television habit.

Be a partner with your doctor and be your own best advocate

When you don't connect with your doctor, change doctors. Keep journals, speak up, and don't allow them to say you are just "stressed out and tired" if something is bothering you. Unfortunately, doctors are more likely to say this to women instead of taking their symptoms seriously.

Keep connected: stay in contact with family and friends

Even a top cardiologist like Mieres told us how important it is to stay connected to family and friends. It's also critical to reduce stress, learn to forgive, and foster and treasure your relationships.

Control stress

Eating certain foods can increase your serotonin levels, which help you sleep better, control appetite, boost metabolism, and decrease levels of the stress hormones cortisol and adrenalin. Good foods to include in your diet include complex carbohydrates, almonds, avocados, and fatty fish (omega 3 fatty acids). Exercise, learn proper deep breathing techniques, and try a few minutes of meditation each day.

Strength train at least twice a week

Yes, cardio is key, but don't forget to strength train. It helps with weight control, minimizes bone loss, and helps prevent middle-age, metabolic "sluggishness," which can lead to a big middle-age belly!

Make better dietary choices

Use a natural sugar substitute, and avoid artificial sweeteners and soft drinks. Limit salt intake and go for colorful plates with five servings of fruits and vegetables every day. If you can't get them in, try veggie smoothies. Karen finally bought one of those blenders they advertise at 3 a.m. Yes, she was having sleep issues, but at least she made good use of the time!

SOME TAKEAWAY ADVICE & QUOTES TO GET YOU GOING

➢ "A bear, however hard he tries, grows tubby without exercise."—Winnie-the-Pooh

➢ "Today is your day! Your mountain is waiting so . . . get on your way!"—Dr. Seuss

➢ Get out of your comfort zone, and you may just discover new passions or perspectives.

➢ Don't forget to breathe.

➢ Don't have things around that will tempt you. If it's not there, you can't eat it. Don't pretend "others" (i.e. your kids!) will eat it!

➢ Don't fool yourself. Sometimes, you are who you are no matter how much you may try to be someone else. Know your weaknesses and deal with them; get help when you need it.

➢ Enjoy each day—with or without cheese.

➢ Keep trying lots of new things until you find the right fit. Sometimes you get it right the first time; other times, it takes many tries.

IDEAS FOR THE READER

Here are some things we tried. For a complete list of more specific ideas see "Your 52," Chapter 11.

- Put the soda down. Try drinking only water for a week.
- Forget the elevators, escalators, and mass transit or your car. Walk!
- Toss the bread. See how you feel. Our experts tell us you'll likely want to keep going; that's typically what happens when people skip the carbohydrates.
- Try eating fruit each morning for a week.
- Quit smoking. If you fail, try again.
- Change to an organic dry-cleaning service.
- If you always take fitness classes or run on a treadmill, start running outside. If you always run outside, take a class.
- Vow to never again eat white rice.
- Face fears head-on: do the one thing that you are afraid of when it comes to personal wellness.
- Make a personal pledge to make two wellness-related improvements every day.
- Volunteer. Go out and help someone. It's good for you.
- There is an app for everything. Find the one you need.
- Grab a friend for support. It makes it all easier.
- Forgive and forget.
- Meditate.
- Try new things.

• • • •

Food Swaps from "The Hungry Girl"

- If you love spaghetti, try spaghetti squash (zucchini sliced into ribbons) or broccoli slaw (it's just shredded broccoli, cabbage, and carrots cooked in a skillet with marinara sauce).
- If you love French fries, try baking butternut squash, carrots, and turnips to make "fries" (slice into spears and bake at high temperature until crispy and cooked through).
- If you love potato chips, try baking kale in the oven as a substitute. Just bake at a high temperature until crispy.
- If you love comfort food such as mashed potatoes, try mashed cauliflower instead.
- If you love potato skins, hollow out zucchini boats for low-carb skins.

• • • •

For additional ideas go to: www.hungry-girl.com.

Chapter Three

Just for Fun

"If you never did, you should. These things are fun, and fun is good."

—Dr. Seuss

Driving My Dream Car Away from Routine

Karen

"I need conditioner," my daughter reminded me as I dropped her at school last week. Her hair looked frizzy. She grabbed her book bag, kissed me goodbye, and ran into school. I mentally added, "buy conditioner" to my list of things to do, and thought about the day ahead filled with mundane errands and deadlines. Duane Reade, check. Stop at the supermarket, check. Bring play date home, check. Squeeze in time at the gym, check. Spend three hours coordinating family schedule, check. I was feeling stuck again. It was time to finally take my fantasy sports car test-drive. It had been on my 52 list for a while now.

For years, experts have used the sports car as a symbol of the typical male mid-life crisis: a selfish, impractical purchase men make when freaking out at a certain age—you know, the "little red sports car." Well, here I was feeling the same thing. I wanted to push the pedal to the metal. And I did.

I am not alone. Hard data shows that men and women are not so far apart in their car-coveting habits after all. I read that 41 percent of women who will buy a car this year will consider buying a sports or luxury car, versus 47 percent of men[2]. And trust me: these women are not using them for carpooling.

My fantasy ride was not easy to arrange. In August, while out of town, I tried unsuccessfully to test-drive a Ferrari. In New York City, it was still impossible. As it turns out, there are only thirty-four Ferrari dealers in the entire country. I had no idea. Many of them are also strictly showrooms, and test driving is impractical in places like New York City.

And that wasn't my only concern: I was nervous about the manual transmission thing too. I know it's lame, but I am an automatic transmission girl. Vague memories of trying to drive my high school boyfriend's car (a beat-up Nissan) with a manual transmission came flooding back to me; if I couldn't do it at "fearless-seventeen," I was definitely more hesitant many years later. When I mentioned this to my husband he said, "They all have paddles now on the steering wheel. Anyone can drive them with the paddles." Paddles? I was envisioning boating oars jutting out of the dash or from the side of the wheel. I was psyched to feel like a real driver with a stick shift and a sports car. The paddle revelation was a bit of a bummer. Wasn't the stick shift part of the allure? Where have I been that I didn't know about the paddles? I'll tell ya'. I've been cut off from fancy car fun in my boring "Mom" SUV with its automatic transmission and Disney Radio playing Selena Gomez or

---

[2]   *Dr. Pamela Gerloff, Psychologytoday.com, June 21, 2011*

Justin Bieber! My research revealed that Bieber himself owns a flat-back Ferrari 420. How ironic. How annoying. He's a teenager!

After making numerous calls, I finally found a dealer in Spring Valley, New York, that was ready, willing, and able to assist me (brave guys). The showroom sparkled and was filled with red Ferraris of all kinds. There was even a Ferrari clothing section near the front—proof that women had to be coming in at least once in a while!

I only got to look at the Ferrari California (it was being repaired!), but I couldn't take my eyes off of it. It is billed as the "more feminine" Ferrari. I sat in it, stared at it, and fantasized for a few moments. I then bee-lined to the F430. Loved it. It had that engine in the back that you can see through fiberglass. I imagined speeding along in this amazing-looking car. "Nope, can't take that one out either," the Ferrari salesman said. "It's just for show." Maybe he wasn't so nice after all? Maybe this wasn't meant to be. But then he said, "What about that Maserati Convertible over there? You can take that out and get a feel for the paddles and have a great ride. Try it." I reluctantly agreed, dreams of my Ferrari drive dashed. It was a Maserati GranTurismo Convertible. Could I feel, for even a few moments, like a "bad girl" in this car?

It was pure luxury. I read later on a car blog that celebrities love to be photographed whenever they are stepping out of one of these cars, and "the interior will match any smile and swag the celebrities might have." Okay, I can definitely see that. Gary (the Ferrari salesman) sat patiently in the passenger seat as I hesitantly pulled out of the lot and onto the road. A few minutes later, we were on the highway, and I was getting more comfortable. And there they were: the paddles. Gary showed me how to shift and I felt the power of the car. It was a hot day and the convertible top was down and I never wanted to go back into my SUV again. And you know what? The paddles were kind of cool. You feel the shifting and your hands don't leave the wheel. "That's why professional race car drivers like them," my husband added later. "You don't lose time shifting." I really didn't care about that. I loved the dash (it was almost a little retro) and it felt like a sports car without being a typical, male, mid-life-crisis-screaming, sports car.

"Did you know this is the car featured on that HBO series Entourage *this season?" Gary asked me. No I didn't know that—pretty cool. Some Googling later revealed some famous owners including Vanessa Williams. Nice. Unfortunately, it also revealed that Lindsey Lohan owns—or more likely, owned—one.*

Feeling "bad" without actually being bad is what driving one of these is all about. Yes, the Maserati ate my Ferrari dream today, and that's okay; that Ferrari is still waiting for me at another dealer somewhere. But today, it just wasn't meant to be and I loved it anyway. Maybe the red Ferrari was a bit too "guy with the trophy wife" for this woman anyway.

Reaching New Heights

Pam

Moving forward is what this project is all about. While people may interpret that in different ways, for me it is all about pushing myself to just "do" in all sorts of ways that I have never done before and hopefully motivate others, too. So far, some weeks have been about emotional growth, other times it's just been about having some fun, and in the coming weeks and months it might be intellectual or spiritual. Then, of course, there is the physical aspect. For this week's "52," I committed to get out there both physically and mentally and still managed to have more than a few laughs (as well as some bumps, bruises, and a really sore shoulder) along the way.

I decided to go rock climbing. It was on my list for a long time. Well, I was about to make good on it! It's just another thing I've always thought about trying but just never did. Why not? Who knows?

Rock climbing, while a physically demanding sport, is also a mental game, I quickly learned. Strength, endurance, and agility are all needed, but it is the use of your brain that is really the most demanding part. Not only do you have to push your body to go just "one more step," you also have to know where that step is. Strategically mapping out where to place your hands and feet as you hold on for dear life is a bit different than running, biking or doing a downward dog in yoga class. Since it was unlike the limited physical exercise I push myself to do on a not-so-regular basis, this was a true "wall" for me in more ways than one.

I corralled my friend, Stacy, to join me this week. City women that we are, we visited an indoor climbing wall at a local Sports Center. There would be time later for the great outdoors if we ever mastered this! We donned our climbing shoes and stepped into our harnesses; we buckled and clipped ourselves in (thank goodness Stacy is a former flight attendant and knew her way around a seatbelt and buckles), and then we were ready. Next was chalking up the hands. Like two schoolgirls, we giggled our way through the early part of the evening. Stacy's sweaty palms, the distraction of our cute climbing instructors, and the dancers and gymnasts auditioning in the gym next door for an upcoming Broadway production of Spiderman: The Musical, *all added plenty of levity to our night.*

We were there to learn and try our damnedest too, but we were also determined to have a good time.

During the first round of climbing exercises, I hovered toward the back of the line and went last in my group. I started to worry: I really wasn't such a big shot. Would I make a complete fool of myself in front of total strangers? They all seemed to be in better physical shape than me. Oh yeah, and a lot younger than me too. I definitely did not want to be the one in the bunch that couldn't do it. I tried to make some jokes with our instructor, but he would have none of it. He maintained his composure and was quite serious. A real mellow dude. The anxiety of this could have gotten the best of me, but I reminded myself I was there for a reason. GO! I. Made. It. To. The. Top! YES!

But that was just the beginning. It definitely got more challenging. After each climb, my instructor calmly told me that I did great. I think that was part of his training—tell the forty-something woman who comes to try rock climbing for the first time that she's doing great when really she looks like an idiot. As the night wore on, the routes became more demanding, but I gained confidence and courage as I ventured up the face of the wall. While I still wasn't rushing to the front of the line, I was no longer hanging back. I really did find myself ready for more with each new course. I began to map out my steps, looking ahead for the next hold or feature in the rock wall, thinking of where I should place my foot or hand in order to reach higher or take that next step.

By the end of the night, I was really proud of myself. Stacy was also amazing! It was great to have the support of a friend. Would I do it again? Absolutely. Do I need to work on getting stronger? Definitely. Will I ever go outdoor rock climbing where there is not the security of knowing that the matted floor is beneath me in case I slip? Not sure. Was it scary? Nope, not really. It was a lot of fun—but hard, sweaty fun. The experience was more satisfying than I would have thought. The triumph was real when I made it to the top of some of the more difficult courses, but the satisfaction that I successfully tried something so off my usual path and took that "next step" was really what made me feel happy and then content. Can I scale a wall for a spy adventure now? Perhaps. But I now know for sure that I can still get up a tree to retrieve a lost Frisbee, or climb the fence when my kids lose a ball. More importantly, I can confidently push myself mentally and physically in taking that "next step."

It's all in the (Tarot) Cards

Karen

This past week I had a Tarot card reading. What made it even more unusual is that I had it done in an unexpected place—a spa! I was away with some friends for an annual girls' getaway weekend, sans family. I am sure other moms can relate when I say that while women around me had pedicures, facials, and massages, it was quite strange for me to be sitting and having a reading with someone billed as a "special guest"—a professional Tarot card reader. It was a chance to do something out of the box and just for fun. I arrived at the spa after making thirty-five brownies for my daughter's Halloween party at school. Maybe I felt orange frosting under my nails made the whole manicure-pampering thing almost pointless!

For some reason I have always been curious about the occult and the paranormal. I am intrigued by psychics, astrology, and the possibility of supernatural forces making things happen in life. I have never done much about it other than read the occasional horoscope and secretly watch a paranormal special or two on cable. Maybe it's my controlling personality that really wants to believe that there are bigger forces at work in our lives and that no matter what we do it's all about energy and the universe and absolutely not about what we can control despite our best efforts. That would really take the pressure off, right?

The occult, which involves tarot card reading, is defined as "something that either deals with or relates to supernatural influences or phenomena." Some sources say that the word "occult" evokes thoughts of devil worship or other dark practices. In reality, however, occult does not mean anything sinister whatsoever; it literally means "hidden" or "secret" as in hidden knowledge beyond the scope of most people's perceptions. I wanted to have the hidden knowledge and find more inner peace, and I thought one of the things on my list this year could be to begin this exploration—not as a time-consuming quest or obsession, but just to see what is revealed. I want to explore things like Kabbalah and mysticism. My Tarot card reading was just a fun little experiment to see if I can shake my Type A personality, relax, and see if there really is a bigger force at work.

So while I watched women in white terrycloth robes enter rooms for treatments I went, nervously, dressed in my old sweat suit, and entered the room of Paula, who was a psychic and clairvoyant, according to her business card. I immediately felt comfortable with her. She was warm, mellow, and had "been around a bit"—I liked that. At first I had to remind myself that I wasn't entering my therapist's office. I was so comfortable I wanted to tell her my life story. And then I stopped myself and realized that I was here to see if she picked up on things about me, my life, where I had been, where I was going and what was "in the cards" for me. It was actually a relief not to talk that much. I am not going to detail what Tarot is all about here; what I will say is that Paula was pretty "right on" with her intuition about me, and where I was in my life despite me offering very little information. According to my research, Tarot is more of a guide than a map. It shows the flow of energy and events and helps direct you toward bringing about desired outcomes.

Since our time was limited, she did ask me to focus on a question or two. I chose to ask her about this blog (yes, I wanted to know if my passion about it meant anything and where it was going) and more importantly, my personal relationships. The cards were dealt fast and furiously and I tried not to react too much as I saw the images laid out before me: the Hermit, the Wheel of Fortune, the Devil (agh!), the Tower, the Seven Cups, the Ace of Swords, and others were all laid out in a pattern before me.

"It's an important time to go inward," she said, pointing to the Hermit card. "Stop looking outside for inner peace and find it within yourself." I was scared of the Devil card of course (why was that card there?!) and asked her what it meant. I didn't really understand her answer but I looked it up a few days later: the lesson the Devil teaches us is one of simple awareness and human empowerment. Once you begin to realize that darkness is a natural part of life, you can begin to gain mastery over it. All human beings have the capacity to become properly self aware to the point where we are no longer controlled by any seeds of darkness. We can gain freedom and not dwell on the forces that are always at work in the world at large. Whoa! That was a little much for me but I think I get it. We just have to let go; we just have to accept that we don't have much control over the bigger forces at work. Easier said than done, but I am glad I met Paula.

Celebrities often turn to psychics. I learned that Brad Pitt turns to one to gain insight on his life. "The Hollywood hunk apparently asks for readings when he is struggling with a problem and is keen for the fortune teller's guidance," says an article in Life & Style magazine. I read about other celebrities and regular people, like me, who go to psychics routinely—almost as often as I go to the supermarket. I *just can't shake that image of the Devil card though. Maybe it's better to just talk a lot with a therapist. The Hermit, the Devil, the Tower, the Seven Wands...*

I am ready for my massage now.

• • • •

It's easy to forget to laugh and play. When we started the52weeks.com we made a pact to take time for ourselves each week. Yes, we wanted to try new things with a purpose—get in better shape, give back to others, and so on. But we also just wanted to play again. We wanted to make sure we carved out time for ourselves to have fun. It's not that we didn't laugh together. We did. But lately it was almost a laughter fueled by the absurdity of our predicament. We realized we were complaining about the same things over and over and, frankly, it was a bit pathetic. We had finally reached a point when we said enough is enough. Let's change. It was time to start playing and doing instead of complaining.

> *"Life is too important to be taken seriously."*
> —Oscar Wilde

Girls Just Want to Have Fun

Like many women our age, before starting the52weeks.com we frequently found ourselves getting our kids to and from all of *their* fun activities without ever scheduling our own playtime. That was one of the things we complained about most when we first conceived the idea for the52weeks.com; when was the last time we had taken time to really play? And we're not just talking about going out to dinner or lunch with girlfriends or couples, even though that was "fun," we're talking about shaking it up and doing things out of our comfort zone. We're talking about simply playing or signing up for a class that has nothing to do with your career; taking a whole day off just to explore; trying something you've always wanted to do "just because" or literally remembering to simply laugh more.

While writing this book, we discovered a startling statistic: the average four-year-old laughs 300 times a day; a forty-year-old, only four! Definitely some food for thought.

Do other women in our age group feel this way?

We believe that all women can use more laughter in their lives. Of course, we get that everyone has a different personality and many women in their forties somehow "make it all work" (or so they think). But even these women—the ones who juggle all the balls in the air with ease and confidence—could perhaps benefit from taking a little time to play without purpose. Would the world end if you skipped your Pilates class, parenting group, or book club just one week to do something spontaneous? We know these are great activities but if you are doing the same things week after week isn't it time to try something new, or simply play with no "end-goal"?

We reached out to comedian **Michele Balan**, a finalist on NBC's *Last Comic Standing*, to get her take on the whole thing. "Women deal with so much stress and need to release those endorphins that you can only get from laughter, sex, and the gym," Balan said. "However, I think it's a lot less work to laugh." She's right. "Can you imagine if you are not laughing, having sex, *or* going to the gym?" one of us commented. Now *that* made us laugh (don't cry if you fall into this category—there is hope!).

> **"Trying new things is an important part of play. I want to learn how to play piano this year but first have to figure out how to get the thing up my flights of stairs and through my door! Maybe I should try guitar?"**
>
> *–Comedian Michele Balan,*
> *Finalist of NBC's "Last Comic Standing"*

Michele makes people laugh for a living. "If adults came to my show, they just may laugh twenty times a day instead of four," she joked. "People think that I find everything funny and laugh all the time. That couldn't be further from the truth." She was quick to point out to us that even comedians get stuck and they have the same stressors that we all have. "We get in the same ruts! When I do, I make it a point to go out with my friends for a night out. If I just want to laugh on my own, I watch a movie or show that makes me laugh. I even watch other comics to feel better."

Michele is right on target; reaching out to friends to join or motivate you is typical of the women that inspired us. While we were writing the book and continuing the52weeks.com, we heard from women all around the world doing exactly what we set out to do. One group in Massachusetts was started by a woman named Peggy Barons who found herself feeling stuck in her mid–forties and was dreading another long, cold Boston winter. She reached out to her friends and others and decided that on the third Friday of every month they would do something fun: horseback riding, ice skating, Segway riding, biking through Boston, race car driving, rock wall climbing, rowing on the Charles River, hiking, foodie tours, snow shoeing, cooking classes, a 50-mile dog sled ride, and simulated sky diving. Her group is called B.O.D.S. (Babes Out Doing Stuff).

> *"Do something everyday, regardless. Nothing will happen unless you first initiate a process of cause and effect. This starts with an action. Reawaken the possibility of possibility. Reawaken it with play."*
> —David Horvitz, artist

A little closer to home, right in Brooklyn, we discovered an amazing group called Mice at Play. We decided to take time to talk to the founder, **Nadia Stieglitz**, now a true "play" expert, to find out more about her inspiring group.

Stieglitz is a true believer in the importance of play. "Play has always been an essential part of my life. I delight in making everyday life fun and pleasurable. It's a way of living. It has been my way of coping with the ups and downs of life."

We were curious as to what inspired Stieglitz to form Mice at Play. Was she feeling like us when we started the52weeks.com? She had just given birth to her third daughter, and her husband worked away from home for months at a time. Between taking care of the kids and her big job at a publishing company, Stieglitz found herself unhappy and with little or no time to laugh and play. When we heard her story we realized it really doesn't matter what age or stage you are at, you can always get stuck. It wasn't just about approaching midlife. It really can happen—and does—at any age.

There are "stuck" cycles and cycles where you feel momentum, right? One thing we know for sure, there are many times in a woman's life when you need to take action to make change happen. It's just not always easy. The key difference for us was the challenges we are now facing in our forties: midlife, long-term marriages, children growing up, aging parents, and more. Each cycle, stage, and age is different and presents unique challenges and opportunities. Yes, this book is really intended for our peers, but the more we looked around the more we found women of every age group feeling the same way.

*"The most wasted day is that in which
we have not laughed."*
—Sébastien-Roch Nicolas, playwright

Stieglitz told us that she didn't mind her workload and responsibilities, but the problem was that she just didn't have time for fun, and it was impacting her wellbeing. Like us, she was craving time with her friends to do new, creative, adventurous, and "playful stuff" away from her kids.

So she began planning adult playdates and, with her husband away on business a lot, her friends started teasing her, saying, "When the cat is away, the mice will play."

"That's how we came up with Mice at Play as the name for the group," she said. She loved the mischievousness it implied and it brought her back to her childhood. Perhaps that is why Dr. Seuss—his simple quotes and important life lessons—became a jumping off point for the52weeks.com. There is something about going back to things from your childhood—a simpler time—that can help put it all in perspective.

Stieglitz started doing some research when she formed the group and read that 26 percent of all American women were taking some kind of mental health medication for anxiety and depression related problems. That was another critical moment for her to formalize the adult playdates into Mice at Play—she was inspired to help women live a more balanced life. We're not suggesting that playing always replaces mental health support or medication (see Chapter 6, "Facing Fears") but there is stuff you can do to change your mood and make changes. Play is important. We had forgotten that.

When we took time out to go play it really did make a difference—especially when we look back. It also took some practice.

Karen

I remember when I put aside a day to test-drive sports cars. I was trying to find the location—about an hour north of New York City. I was driving there in my boring SUV, looking for the remotely located dealership, and the whole time I was thinking I really should turn around. I had so much to get done. Who was I to be taking an afternoon to do something with absolutely no purpose other than to relax and play just because it was on my 52 list? That was the hardest part; I wasn't used to doing things without an "end" goal even if it was just checking off "bought toothpaste" from my to-do list. To relax a bit, I momentarily thought about combining the outing with errands, but I stopped myself. A million thoughts were racing through my head. I am so glad I didn't turn around. It was definitely one of the best 52 experiences I had for no reason other than to try something new and have fun. I had a renewed sense of confidence after mastering the gear shift paddles and driving at an obscene speed. I didn't think about any deadlines, any errands, or any problems. It had been a while. I even forgot about the toothpaste.

Pam felt similarly guilty when she went rock climbing with her friend and target shooting at a rifle range as well as probably every single time she decided to do something just for fun or to relax. When we look back we agree that these were the best 52 days. It proved a point and kicked-off some research that confirmed what we—two ordinary moms—already knew: every time we did something we wanted to do just for ourselves, it made a major positive difference for us and for those around us. It lifted our spirits and made us more fun and interesting to be around, too. The take-away? Play, or your well-being will suffer.

During the whole 52 week thing, I was also occasionally blogging for The Balancing Act, *a national morning show on Lifetime Television. Pam and I had been crossing off our 52 lists individually. We definitely needed some fun friend time. The show asked me to write about a new Cuervo product. That's how our "escaping to Mexico" day happened, and we wrote about it on our blog. "We can't just drink Tequila for one of our 52 weeks," I said vehemently, feeling like it would be totally disingenuous and a cop-out for our blog. "We started this blog to really tackle our own 52 to-do lists," I added. "I know," said Pam. "But we can have fun and spend time together." I thought about it. She was right. Having more fun—alone and together—was one of our 52 goals. The show invited us to do this for them so why not?*

We taste-tested margaritas. We tried new recipes. It wasn't really about the TV show or the margarita mix. It was about having fun. I took the assignment and made it work for me. I took lemons and made lemonade. In this case, we took limes and turned them into laughter. It worked.

Months ago, before discovering Mice at Play, one of us stumbled upon The National Institute of Play—an organization solely focused on play—in a *New York Times* article. We were quite amazed there was an entire organization dedicated to the science of play. It was founded by Dr. Stuart Brown. According to his bio, his years of clinical practice affirmed the importance and need for healthy play throughout the human life cycle. Coincidentally, it was only when Stieglitz discovered a talk given by Dr. Brown that she confirmed what she, like us, already knew intuitively about the benefits of play. With that information and further research, she took Mice at Play to a whole new level. The National Institute of Play has endless information about the science of play for anyone interested. And like Stieglitz, it confirmed we were on to something when we started the blog.

A few of the tangible benefits of play listed by the National Institute of Play include:

- **Play & vitality**

Play generates optimism and inspires us to seek out novelty. It gives the immune system a bounce, fosters empathy, and promotes a sense of belonging and community. Each of these play by-products are indices of personal health, and their shortage can lead to health problems and personal fragility.

- **Play & stress**

Play reduces stress and depression. A life with little or no play is a major public health risk factor. The prevalence of depression, stress related diseases, interpersonal violence, addictions, and other health and well-being problems could be linked to the prolonged deprivation of play.

- **Play & personality**

Everyone has a unique play personality. When one remains in touch with his or her playful personality, it empowers and brings pleasure to life.

Our "Relationships" chapter, touches upon the importance of healthy relationships in one's life to feel better. The National Institute for Play confirms that play benefits these connections.

"Play is a way to keep us engaged in life," Stieglitz reminds us. When we dug deeper with Nadia she also talked about how important it is for your interaction with those around you. Play has incredible benefits for all relationships and situations at home, work, with our spouses, kids, friends, and colleagues.

Getting Rid of the Guilt

> "Society has to change its view on play as a necessity and NOT as something indulgent."
> –Nadia Stieglitz

Lots of people feel guilty spending time on play. We know for the52weeks. com we initially felt that way. It was "easier" and felt more purposeful to work on our 52 lists when it involved helping others or even ourselves. To just take a few hours or a day to play felt self-indulgent. It was a relief to hear that we shouldn't and couldn't allow ourselves to feel guilty when we played. The stress of modern and urban life has a negative impact on our well-being. Play helps us to deal with stress in a more positive way. "I believe that play is a critical survival mechanism. It's part of all the things (nutrition, movement, breathing, friends, family, and love) that make us physically and mentally fit . . . and happy," she added.

Even when it comes to success at work, play is critical. When we inject play into our lives we are more productive. According to Stieglitz, the French achieve their high standard of living by working 16 percent fewer hours than the average world citizen. "Success is not about working hard. It's about managing a balance between working and playing."

"It's even harder for women," said Stieglitz. "It's behavioral and cultural. As girls, we are raised to care for others. We learn to put the priorities of others before our own. We often feel guilt when we go out. Society is quick to harshly judge a woman who puts herself first. That has to stop."

Enda Junkins, MSW, licensed clinical social worker, is known as the Laughing Psychotherapist. Who knew they existed?! She had the following quick tips to share with us at 52:

- Give yourself permission to have fun. Women especially are conditioned to be caretakers, but we need balance.
- Fake it 'til you make it. Even if you don't feel like it, smile and laugh. It shifts your mood and thinking. The body doesn't know you are faking.
- Playing and laughing relieve anxiety. You can't laugh and be afraid simultaneously. It's physically impossible.

We came up with our respective 52 lists and started out with the best intentions: we were going to make time to play—alone and together. Did we always succeed? No way. We certainly did not play as much as we wanted or needed. There were also times that our priorities shifted and things were crossed off or added to our respective 52 lists as the weeks went by. But it all made us more aware of how important it was to play and laugh. It also made us take time to play and not feel guilty about it. Our comedian contributor, Michele Balan, told us that it is a challenge, even for her, to not take things so seriously. "For me, I have to look around and see that as bad as I feel, I have more than most people. When I remember this, it helps me to snap out of the 'poor me' syndrome." We think she is so right.

"If you obey all the rules, you miss all the fun."
—*Katharine Hepburn, actress*

Remember to play.

NEXT STEPS

Keep these suggestions in mind when you are scheduling playtime, and remember to laugh!

Keep Learning

We would have liked to have crossed more just-for-fun items off of our 52 lists, but learning new things definitely made us feel better and it was fun. "Once I got over the guilt I felt when doing something just for me and just for fun, I realized how good it made me feel," says Pam. "In the end it was actually beneficial for everyone around me. They benefitted because I was happier." Play is part of our development at any age. Our capacity to learn never stops as we are aging. Don't stop playing just because you are an adult.

Breathe & play

It was interesting for Karen to learn that play is located in the same part of the brain that controls breathing. Breathing is a big thing for her. Anxiety and shallow breathing in fact go hand-in-hand and are a challenge for many people. Check out "Facing Fears," Chapter 6, for more about breathing and anxiety!

Find (and nurture) your playmates

Writing the book took us a bit "away" from each other. It was a strange paradox and we often felt a bit sad about it. We set out to have fun together and to grow as individuals. We did. We learned. We grew. We laughed. We argued. It was only after we faced deadlines and a book deal that we stopped "playing" together. That was not supposed to happen. Perhaps though, there was a reason: maybe it was up to us to get the message out there and inspire others. Just make it happen no matter how busy life gets. Make a deal with your significant other to each take equal playtime away from the home; plan your "me" times in advance, and put it on your calendar.

SOME TAKEAWAY ADVICE & QUOTES TO BRING FUN INTO YOUR LIFE

➢ Remember to laugh often—at yourself and at other things as much as possible.

➢ "When you laugh you change, when you change, the whole world changes."—Dr. Madan Kataria, founder of Laughter Yoga

➢ Surround yourself with people and places that make you laugh.

➤ "We don't stop playing because we grow old; we grow old because we stop playing."—George Bernard Shaw

➤ "I think of life itself as a wonderful play that I've written for myself, and so my purpose is to have the utmost fun playing my part."—Shirley MacLaine

➤ "It is a happy talent to know how to play."—Ralph Waldo Emerson

IDEAS FOR THE READER

Here are some "Just for Fun" ideas. For more see "Your 52," Chapter 11.

- Take your dream car for a test ride. Make sure they are impractical, super expensive, and ridiculously sexy.
- Rock climb just because you never did it before.
- Remember to laugh: on the golf court, tennis court, or even in traffic court!
- Karen spent a day "in" France by immersing herself in all things French.
- Take a plunge—literally! Nadia and Pam both did a Polar Bear swim!
- Go to a comedy club. If no one in your life is making you laugh, be proactive and find someone who will.
- Make yourself laugh; rent funny movies, read funny books, and watch your favorite sitcom.
- Explore your dangerous side. Pam indulged in her "spy" fantasy for a day.
- Browse the web for inspiration.
- Explore music, and find songs that make you smile. Find some of the newest artists.

- Try an Erotic Scavenger Hunt.
- Play hooky!
- Clear your mind. You can't laugh if you are weighed down with thoughts!

Chapter Four

Arts & Culture

"Every child is an artist. The problem is how to remain an artist once we grow up."

–Pablo Picasso

Twenty Years and 10 Minutes to Get to Carnegie Hall

Karen

I don't know why it took me so long. Twenty years to make plans and then a ten-minute cab ride, and I was standing outside of Carnegie Hall. I have always been drawn to classical music; it silences my overactive brain and calms my nerves. But I rarely make time to enjoy it, especially live. Hence the reason it made it onto my 52 list.

I went with my husband and some friends. Skeptical at first, I wondered if my mood would be in the right place or whether I would be better off at a mediocre movie or going out for a nice dinner. That's the downside of buying tickets in advance; you never know how you will feel that day. The upside of buying tickets in advance? You're less likely to cancel and wind up doing the usual, routine things.

Carnegie Hall is an incredible place. Despite being a New Yorker for more than two decades, for some reason I haven't gone since I was a kid. Upon entering, you feel transported to a time of elegance and grandeur. And if you ever forget why you love New York City (or are trying to figure out if you ever did), it will remind you that there is a world beyond the Second Avenue subway construction, school drop-offs, and long lines at Starbucks.

The program for the night was the St. Louis Symphony Orchestra, playing a number of programs with Tchaikovsky's Symphony No. 6 in B Minor, Op. 74 as the highlight. But that's not really the point. It was more about just being there, experiencing the evening and listening to music beyond my daughter's top 10 picks.

Our seats, perched high above and to the side of the orchestra, were incredible. We were in prime box seats given to us as a gift, sitting on decadently comfortable chairs that reminded me of plush bar stools. What I loved most about where we sat was watching the conductor—from the side—instead of staring at the back of a moving tuxedo. You couldn't help but feel his passion for the music. His amazing gray hair flew back and forth in tandem with the music as he expertly guided the orchestra through the program.

I loved the entire experience. I loved the elegant intermission complete with coffee and champagne. I loved the intimate environment filled with an eclectic crowd of people. I loved that I didn't look at my phone for almost two hours. I loved the romance of it all; the detail and the architecture of Carnegie Hall and all the new sights and sounds. I loved that my blog this year forced me to do this (with some tickets from my neighbors, thank you very much).

I thought about the Lady Gaga concert I went to last year with my daughter and her friends (don't ask). I thought about what I listen to on my iPod—everything from Elton John to Beyonce—and then I thought about the upcoming Stevie Nicks-Rod Stewart concert I was going to next month. Where will classical music fit into my life? I didn't know. It certainly won't replace the other stuff. It's just a totally different thing, like moods that vary for food, fashion, and even friends. I just know I have to find a way to fit the New

> *"Everywhere in the world, music enhances a hall, with one exception: Carnegie Hall enhances the music."*
> —Isaac Stern, violinist and conductor

York experiences of classical music into my schedule. And for that, I am grateful to be on this often challenging, difficult, and fun 52 Weeks journey.

It's No Longer Looming

Pam

I wasn't sure I would ever walk in.

It is the brunt of many jokes in my family—how I often say I am going to do something and then don't. A perfect example is launching this blog. Just the thought of trying something new or different every week for 52 weeks, writing weekly, and having a deadline has got to be one of the craziest ideas I have ever agreed to. When I told my family, their looks said it all. They truly thought I was going off the deep end. Karen, my driven blog partner, sure has a lot of faith in me.

Let's just say I'm not always a doer. Don't get me wrong. I get things done and pretty damn well (if I do say so.). I manage my household, work part-time, take care of my family, am there for my friends, and remember to buy the cat food (and feed her too!)—but I've come to realize that I rarely "get it done" without a lot of thinking and procrastinating. I get "stuck" a lot.

So where did I go? Trapeze lessons, perhaps? Nope. While that is on my 52 Week to-do list, I wasn't quite ready. No, I decided to sign up for a weaving class. Seriously!

Here's the deal. Every day for a year, I have walked past a little storefront a few blocks from home. I kid you not—for a year, I've been walking right by it. At first, I'd just take a fast peek in the window. On another occasion, I picked up a pamphlet. Then I went to the website. Got another pamphlet. For some reason, this place always intrigued me. Was it the quirky underground space that reminded me of Laverne and Shirley's basement apartment? Was it the fantasy that I'd walk in to this weaving studio, have a Zen moment and start singing Kumbaya with the others? After a few failed attempts, I finally made the appointment, determined not to think about how boring it could be or what I would do if my "artistic side" didn't carry over when weaving.

As I walked in, I was asked to take off my shoes and was led through a tiny doorway. The space was a little oasis of colors, creativity, and serenity in the midst of the city—it didn't seem to belong here. The owner, a quiet woman dressed in one of her beautiful creations, showed me to my loom and explained how to begin. Her calm demeanor and few words forced me to hold in the nervous chitchat that often gets the best of me. I listened and tried not to ask too many silly questions. Very soon, I realized that there weren't a lot of rules to this. It was actually quite simple to do. Almost too simple, *I thought. Just like getting out and trying something new every week.*

The little girl next to me, who was there with her nanny, graciously shared her "beginner's basket" of beautiful yarns and fibers. The Australian grandmother sitting across from me, working on an intricate piece, wove side-by-side with her four-year-old grandson. It was his third time here, he proudly told me. As I started to weave by moving my feet on the wooden pedals of the loom and pulling the colorful yarn through my fingers, I became more confident. Soon the rhythm took over. Hey, this was fun! I thought about telling the woman next to me why I was here but resisted and realized it didn't matter. I was here. Just enjoy! It was out of my comfort zone yet oddly comfortable. And when it was time to go, I left feeling proud.

It is funny that a simple little thing such as weaving on a loom for two hours could have lifted my spirits for the day. But I felt good—for agreeing to journey with Karen, for making a cute little tapestry, for using colors in my design that I usually don't like, for just doing it. Later that night as I showed off my masterpiece to my kids and my daughter's piano teacher, it was great to see their interest and I know I was able to spread the word and the good vibe I had carried with me all day.

Taking a weaving class is not earth shattering by any means and definitely not for everyone. But it was a step—a small, simple step for me in the exciting direction of "doing" and not just thinking. Will I go again? Who knows? But those few small steps can only lead to sure-footed bigger ones. 'Til next week . . .

Nude Inspiration

Karen

"Very few people possess true artistic ability. It is therefore both unseemly and unproductive to irritate the situation by making an effort. If you have a burning, restless urge to write or paint, simply eat something sweet and the feeling will pass." —Fran Lebowitz

This quote made me laugh as I recently set out to take my first art class (or at least my first in years). And not just any art class. A nude drawing class. A live model, charcoal, and an adorable studio on the Upper East Side that has been there for twenty-five years that I hadn't known existed. I was psyched.

Why did I want to draw? I am not sure. All I know is that for the last five years I keep buying those professional-looking art kits sold in various places. I am pulled, as if by magnetic force, to those all-in-one "Learn to Draw" kits. I have four, sitting unopened on my bookshelf.

So I decided to go to a professional. It's like when you try to work out every day but you really need a trainer, or a buddy, because you just don't really stick to it alone.

I found one of the few studios that offers classes á la carte classes instead of requiring a long-term commitment. This was critical as I set out to find a class; I wanted to experience a real art class but I was hesitant to do it long-term. I was also a realist: Fran Lebowitz's words were in the back of my head, and I knew that I was unlikely to uncover some inner Picasso that has lurked beneath for years. Taking her advice, a pint of Ben & Jerry's New York Super Fudge Chunk® was waiting in the wings in case I had to face reality.

Dino and Patricia, husband-and-wife studio owners, greeted me warmly as I entered the studio. Immediately, I sensed their passion for art. It was a cozy room. About ten stations were set up with stools and professional, tilted art tables. I liked how the room felt. I loved the supplies. Easels were available upon request, and I liked that I didn't have to feign competence. Dino sat with me and explained some drawing basics as we waited for the nude model to arrive. A Romanesque-like bust sat on the "stage" for us to draw while we waited. I couldn't imagine being able to be still long enough for someone to draw me (add in the nude component and that brings the anxiety to a whole other level!). I do want to master the art of stillness. But for now, I have trouble sitting long enough to just get my nails done at the corner "ten-minute" place. I learned that basic shapes such as a circle, square, cylinder, triangle, and so on form the basis of almost every figure drawing. Pretty cool. Dino was patient and knowledgeable. If I saw him on the street I would think he was my neighborhood butcher or a friendly retired pharmacist. But when he showed me how to hold the charcoal and how to become "one" with the pencil, I was truly in awe of his love for all things art.

Students of all levels were at the other stations. Some, I was told, came regularly. It was a diverse group—all ages, all types. I loved the group feel coupled with the truly private, independent experience.

Then she walked in. I am not sure what I expected. The nude model looked like a dancer. Petite, slim with a pleasant demeanor, she had a quiet confidence and ease and appeared to have done this before. I quickly learned that there would be a series of poses. "Do a '5', a '5' again and then a '10' and a '20,'" Dino said to her as she shed her simple summer sundress. I quickly learned that the numbers he was shouting out referred to the number of minutes for each pose; from simple to more complicated stances. A large drawing pad was in front of me. Charcoal was in hand. My first attempt was actually not too horrific. I was encouraged to be "loose" with the charcoal and "follow-through." I was surprised to hear that phrase in a drawing class; long-ago memories of hours on the tennis court came back to me; I also heard it at my recent golf lesson. I didn't expect to hear it here. My next few attempts were pretty bad. Dino told me just to keep drawing. Then, surprisingly, on my fourth try, I actually felt the rhythm, and Dino exclaimed, almost proudly, "There ya go; you're finding yourself now!"

Drawing, for me anyway, was relaxing. I was actually able to sit still. I liked the quietness of the room—the ability to focus and try something new. I took some photos, chatted with the model during her break (sundress included!), and even had a few words with Patricia as she painstakingly helped a student with a sculpture model of some sort. I loved the place. I liked drawing. I want to go back. I think, instead of Fran Leibowitz, I should remember the words of the great Van Gogh: "If you hear a voice within you say 'you cannot paint,' then by all means paint, and that voice will be silenced."

Tickling the Ivories . . . Again

Pam

"Put your left hand here and play D and A," Barbara said to me. I hit the notes tentatively, feeling the eyes of my husband, my two kids, my daughter's friend, and the piano teacher on me—all holding their breath. While I was a bit unsure about playing the piano, I felt differently than I did the last time I was learning how. I was probably about seven or eight years old when my parents enrolled me in piano lessons. I suppose it seemed like the natural thing for them to do. We had a beautiful piano in our living room; my older sisters were taking lessons, and my cousin was an accomplished and classically trained pianist. I don't really remember whether I expressed an interest in taking lessons or whether it was one of those things my mother thought was "the right thing to do." What I do remember is that my piano teacher's name was Ann; she always would sit next to me in a metal folding chair, *and I was **always** called in for my lesson when I was in the front yard playing with my friends. I don't think I practiced that much, but I do remember playing a childhood version of Ode to Joy (doesn't every kid learn that?) and a few other catchy tunes that still pop into my head on occasion. Then, at about age eleven, I went to gymnastics camp, sprained my shoulder while attempting a vault, and couldn't take lessons for a few weeks. For some reason I never went back to the piano. And that was the end of my piano career (or so I thought). But as I got older, I would often try to remember how to play something, secretly wishing I was one of those people who could just sit down and have the music spill off my fingers. In college, I even signed up for lessons as part of some required music credit but I was either put on a wait list and never got into the class, or didn't want to get up for the eight a.m. practice sessions. Who can remember?*

I suppose I've been toying with the idea for a while now, thinking about things I'd like to try again as an adult, things I wish I had followed through with. My daughter expressed an interest in piano a few years ago, so now my husband's old childhood upright is being used for her lessons. There it sits, in my living room, taunting me. Sometimes I'll try to tickle the keys, hoping I can make a little music and let loose, but I remember very little.

So I added this to my 52 and finally decided to take some lessons to see if I really want to pursue this again. I asked my daughter's piano teacher for a trial lesson. Although I was a bit apprehensive at first, Barbara's teaching style suited me. She takes an individual approach with each of her students so no two lessons are the same. She put me at ease as she had me try a piece she brought for me and then read some music. I think I surprised both of us when I was able to get through a Beatles song she selected for me. I can't say that it all came right back, but it was obviously buried somewhere in me. I'm hoping it gets uncovered more. Throughout the lesson, Barbara gave me words of encouragement and said I have the potential to be a "piano player." I believed her.

I once heard someone describe the piano as a "friendly" instrument because it is so inviting and just about anyone can sit down, hit some keys, and make a relatively pretty sound. Other instruments take enormous amounts of practice and learning— proper holding, blowing, or positioning—before hitting just the right note. That's what I like about the piano and about moving through my list of 52. It's accessible and inviting. Doing something for personal satisfaction but also something to share with others. It's a good thing to try something new . . . again.

• • • •

No doubt one of the things that excited us the most during our weeks of exploration was finding time for the arts and culture. Every single time, during the course of our 52 Week experiment, whenever we ventured out to do something artsy or "crafty," or cultural, or musical, or what-have-you, we always returned with our endorphins pumping. It wasn't just upon our return either. These outings not only left us with a great feeling but were highly anticipated. We always looked forward to these jaunts. From museum gazing to drawing classes to concerts, we always enjoyed these *52's* the most. Even missed opportunities, such as when Pam kept attempting to get to a specific exhibit at The Metropolitan Museum of Art in New York City, were outings that lifted our spirits.

For Karen, not taking advantage of living in New York City was perhaps one of her biggest frustrations when we launched the52weeks.com. Pam lost track of how many times Karen bemoaned that she dropped her daughter at school *every* morning literally right next door to the Guggenheim Museum, but could not remember the last time she had walked inside. It actually infuriated her and she knew she had no one to blame but herself. As we have said before, every day seemed to be filled with work, errands, and things we just "had to do." For Karen, this left a cultural void and a made her feel a bit

"I like to go to art museums and name the untitled paintings . . . Boy With Pail . . . Kitten On Fire . . ."
—Steven Wright, comedian

restless. Pam, on the other hand, recalled that she retired all of her drawing and art supplies to the back of her closet for no apparent reason and then forgot about them. It wasn't until the 52 Weeks idea came up that she realized she really missed art and wondered why she had pushed her creative pursuits aside. Like many things we talked about changing, the solution was simple and right in our own backyard: start filling our lives with more culture, art, beauty, and anything that enhanced our lives.

Although we had different interests, and often had the desire to pursue different experiences, the end results and the feelings they evoked were always the same: we both always felt happy, content, and rejuvenated after doing something intended to lift our artistic spirits. These types of *52s* invigorated us and made us feel good.

Perhaps that's why when we sat down to speak with our experts, **Daniella Ohad Smith** and **Andrea Blanch**, we found them to be so inspiring. Their sound perspectives and outlooks on the arts and culture really solidified what we both felt but were often unable to articulate.

Daniella Ohad Smith, Ph.D., is a design historian and critic on twentieth-century contemporary design culture and history. Her passion for life and the arts is infectious and uplifting. When we spoke with her, it confirmed that she was truly an ideal *52* expert; not only did she appreciate the importance of bringing art, beauty, and culture into one's life to get unstuck and feel better, but she also believes in the "try it and see if you like it" approach to identifying your true passions.

"Culture and the arts have the power to transform life and bring people together. Art can minimize difficult situations and stimulate solutions," said Ohad Smith. The power she attributed to arts and culture was a little surprising to us at first but it made sense. She even expressed that she believes that by bringing art into your life you can gain new perspective on all kinds of life issues.

Perhaps one of the most interesting things she shared was how filling your life with more art, beauty, and culture could actually contribute to one's emotional growth. "When you foster new relationships through the arts, these new relationships can become an important part of your life going forward," she said. "The arts open up new horizons. In our busy and stressful world, having appreciation for the arts and engaging with culture forces us to stop, enjoy, and explore the creative side of our brain." As Ohad-Smith continued, Pam remembered thinking to herself that she was already so calm just listening to her. Ohad Smith had an incredible ability to transmit her love and knowledge of her work just by talking to us. Her level of passion from exploring and engaging with the arts was contagious.

Even though we had personally experienced bursts of happiness from some of our art and culture 52s, we pushed Ohad Smith to tell us more about what bringing art and culture into our lives really would change.

"First of all, it's about beauty," she said. "It doesn't matter whether it's music, dance, art, or literature—it's about beauty. And beauty has been such an important part of human life since antiquity." She explained that even for people who are always dealing with numbers and linear thinking, exposure to art stimulates the senses and sparks creative thinking.

"Art enables us to find ourselves and lose ourselves at the same time."
—Thomas Merton,
No Man Is an Island

Ohad Smith fully embraces the power of art, beauty, design, and culture, even attributing it to expanding one's ability to judge many aspects of life, including music, theater, architecture, and fashion.

Our interview with Ohad Smith took us in many directions but an important idea that came from her was something that we definitely felt throughout our 52 Week journey: by bringing more art and culture into your life you will discover that other doors open. She shared stories of people in her path who found fulfillment in other areas as a result of initially opening their world to the arts. We often remarked that it wasn't so much what specific activity we were doing but that the act of doing it brought us to something else. Some will argue that art is art and should be appreciated for what it is, but we agree with Ohad Smith that art and culture can help you to achieve and succeed at other things. It is the process that is meaningful, not just the end result. Clearly that was the case with Karen's nude drawing experience. She was forced to be still and draw, take it all in, and step out of her comfort zone which led to new relationships and trying something new.

We wanted to get back to the idea that pursuing creative endeavors and exposing yourself to more art and culture can improve your mood. For some, communication is a problem, especially when you are stuck. "Once you experience the arts, it gives you more tools to improve communication," said Ohad Smith. "I think it's all really a crucial foundation of renewal."

Ohad Smith's perspective really hit home. 52 Weeks is all about renewal and trying to be better versions of ourselves. Experiencing renewal through beauty, education, and experience always had a positive effect on us.

"I found I could say things with color and shapes that I couldn't say any other way—things I had no words for."
—Georgia O'Keeffe, artist

Our conversation with award-winning photographer **Andrea Blanch** was rousing, funny, and inspiring, too. Blanch's remarks reinforced that simple pleasures gleaned from bringing more art and culture into life—in even the smallest of ways—can be a catalyst for a range of emotions and can elevate your mood. "Being exposed to art or beauty or photography, for example, absolutely makes you feel better," she said. "Art elevates you."

Granted, it was not a designer gown, but when I dusted off my sewing machine and made a costume for my daughter, it brought me such a sense of satisfaction. It was all about simple pleasures. I used to paint, draw, was crafty—even read more—and when you move away from that, you lose a sense of contentment as well as delight. When I ventured to the Metropolitan Museum of Art to get my ticket to climb the Big Bambú exhibit, and it started to pour, I was so defeated. As an outdoor sculpture atop the roof of the building, it would shut down if the weather was inclement. I had really wanted to see this sculpture. I had read about it and even marked it on my calendar weeks before. I had gone to the rooftop and walked underneath the canopy of the sculpture two times before and was enthralled, but hadn't toured it from above. Just the idea of going elevated my mood. Thankfully, I was able to go on another day and enjoyed it beyond my expectations. I feel the same way when I get out to see a new play or show. Or when I went to the weaving studio. When I escape into a new world and stimulate different senses, I always feel better.

Karen

One of my favorite arts & cultural outings for the52weeks. com was my night spent at Carnegie Hall. The title, as it appeared on the blog at the time, said it all: "Twenty Years and Ten Minutes to Get to Carnegie Hall." Perhaps twenty years was a slight exaggeration, but it had been way too long since I had been there. I love classical music. I know I want to make listening to classical music a more regular part of my life. It transported me and, as our experts in this chapter have said, it's about surrounding yourself with beauty—whatever that may be for you as an individual. Though I fear sounding a bit too hokey, it filled my soul. I need more of that in my life. My nude drawing class was another favorite 52. It also falls into the category of trying something new but it was about creating art, taking time to look at things, slowing down. And for many students, it is about creating beauty (I am not sure to this day what I created but let's just go with the beauty thing for now!). Another 52 outing was simply going to museums more often. I know this is not earth shattering—many people go to museums regularly. But it was about planning the outing, making the time, and then following through just to gaze at art. Even though I remember not liking the exhibit, that wasn't the point. It was about the act of going. It was about getting unstuck. Sometimes, you just have to make a conscious effort to bring something back into your life.

Blanch spoke to us about how she approaches "getting unstuck" in her own life as well.

"I handle it in different ways," she said. "There's the pragmatic ways of dealing with it—taking a walk, thinking things through, doing something I don't usually do to break the pattern. Then there's the indulgent way of dealing with it—doing anything that makes me feel good. I'll have a drink, talk to someone whose opinion I value, get a massage, go see art, buy clothes, or get a haircut." She ultimately brings it back to the arts. She makes it a habit to go to galleries, museums, lectures, movies, and plays.

"Art is much less important than life, but what a poor life without it."
—Robert Motherwell, painter

Whether you are an aspiring poet, writer, or dancer; a painter, musician, or art history buff; a sculptor, scrapbooker, or fashion designer; a patron of the arts (or would like to be) or want to take a more hands-on, active role in creating art, bringing it into your routine—even just a little—can bring about a sense of calm, and contentment and open up your world. Take a dance class or just watch a performance. Listen to music or take a piano lesson. If you aren't a culinary master, watch great cooking demonstrations at a local culinary school.

Whether you choose to be an interested observer or an active participant, surround yourself with beauty and explore the arts and culture all around you. The benefits and rewards are infinite.

NEXT STEPS

Both Blanch and Ohad Smith offered up some practical, simple suggestions to bring more art and culture into your life.

Passion

Develop a passion. Passion is not something you are born with. Finding it can be a process, but don't get discouraged. Try your hand at new things, and test the waters. Then work at refining that passion. It is not something that happens overnight. Think about what gives you pleasure and then work toward taking it to a new level; nurture it so it goes from being something you like, to something you love. Eventually it will become a passion. This will open your world, make you look at things in a different way, and help you move forward and grow.

Curiosity

Karen always wondered what went on during a nude drawing class. Pam was intrigued by the quaint entryway leading to the Saori weaving studio. Curiosity didn't kill the cat. The rest of the old saying actually is "satisfaction brought it back!"

During her interview, Ohad Smith talked about how curiosity can innocently yet greatly expand one's world. She relates a story about her friend's interest in Africa. Ohad Smith's advice? Take a trip to Africa; go to a lecture about Africa; visit an art gallery showing African works; see an African dance troupe; take African dance lessons; start

> *"Passion is not something you are born with. It's something you develop."*
> —*Daniella Ohad Smith, 52 expert*

collecting African masks; create your own masks; find out about African show openings; Skype with someone living in Africa; even find a relevant Facebook group. The possibilities are limitless. Curiosity opens your world and takes things to a new creative level.

"To be creative means to be in love with life. You can be creative only if you love life enough that you want to enhance its beauty, you want to bring a little more music to it, a little more poetry to it, a little more dance to it."
—Osho, professor of philosophy

Go with your gut

You may not know exactly what you like to do, but when you have *that feeling*, listen to it. Exposure to arts and culture can strengthen these instincts. After familiarizing themselves with the arts in a variety of settings, both Ohad Smith and Blanch found their artistic calling because they finally just *knew*.

Blanch's story is particularly magical. Although she was a painter, she never before had picked up a camera, and never had any aspirations to do so. But it just so happened that she offered to house-sit for a friend, and the house was being used by photographer Richard Avedon for a photo shoot. As she watched him work she knew instantly that this was what she wanted to do. She became Avedon's unpaid "trainee," and he soon became her mentor. *American Vogue* was her first client.

Ohad Smith had a similar experience. Coming from a family that had a very strong background in literature and music, she was exposed to the arts but still didn't have a clear direction of what she wanted to do.—that is, until she took an art history class in college. This, she says, is where she found her calling. She credits an

"Culture is the passion for sweetness and light, and what is more, the passion for making them prevail."
—Matthew Arnold, poet

inspiring, amazing art history teacher who helped her look at art in an entirely different way. She knew this was where she belonged and what she loved. She knew she needed to pursue this feeling.

Try new things

We've said it before and we'll say it here too. Trying new things is what it's all about. This could not be more true than when experiencing the arts. Both Blanch and Ohad Smith agree it's important to sample new things—go to a museum or gallery and think about what gives you pleasure—music, dance, a good lover! They even have their own list of things to try including a new art project, an upcoming book deal, and traveling to new places.

SOME TAKEAWAY ADVICE AND QUOTES TO GET YOU GOING

➤ "Music washes away from the soul the dust of everyday life."—Berthold Auerbach

➤ If you listen to Bach, try the Beatles. If you listen to Beyonce, try Bach.

➤ Trust yourself: sometimes you just know who you are and what you like.

➤ "I don't like to say I have given my life to art. I prefer to say art has given me my life."—Frank Stella

➤ Try new things—even if only to remind you of what you like and what you don't.

➤ "Creativity takes courage."—Henri Matisse

➤ Look closely at other people's passion for food, music, and life—passion can be contagious.

➢ "Without poets, without artists, men would soon weary of nature's monotony."—Guillaume Apollinaire

➢ Remember, sometimes a ten-minute cab ride can change everything.

➢ Make a plan, stick to it, and go no matter what your mood.

IDEAS FOR THE READER

Here are some things we tried. For a complete list of ideas see Chapter 11, "Your 52."

- Take a drawing lesson.
- Weave, paint, or learn to play an instrument.
- Change your view: take photographs.
- Visit museum exhibits.
- Explore French cinema.
- Discover or rediscover live theater.
- Read classic novels.
- Write.
- Go to a concert.
- Dine, bake, cook, and eat.
- Dance.

Chapter Five

Relationships

"... the most exciting, challenging and significant relationship of all is the one you have with yourself. And if you can find someone to love you, well, that's just fabulous."

—Carrie Bradshaw, *Sex and the City*

Seven Days of Smiles

Karen

This week I discovered that Dr. Seuss was actually wrong once. He said, "Be who you are and say what you feel because those who mind don't matter and those who matter don't mind."

The fact is we all say too much sometimes. We complain too much and say the same things a lot—especially with those we love. I call them conversational ruts and patterns. And you know what? The people that matter most do mind. You just may not realize it; they may not always say anything.

A few months ago I heard myself saying the word "annoying" for what I estimated was about the hundredth time that week. I was annoying myself! My voice, tone and words bothered me. It was like when you learn a new word or hear a song that you think is new only to discover it's been out forever; then, all of a sudden, you hear that word or song everywhere. I started being hyper-aware of the word "annoying" and how much I used the word "tired" or complained about something. Not attractive. Not good. It had to change.

When I had this realization, I added, "Stop complaining so much" to my 52 list, and vowed to try to be more interested and interesting—especially during day-to-day conversations with my husband of eighteen years. Loving husband that he is, he will tell you he doesn't even think about it. He will tell you he wants to talk to me during the day, regardless of my mood or his. Unlike me though, he doesn't complain as much.

Like most busy couples, our quick calls during the day are often about daily matters that just need to be addressed. However, I feared my comfort level with him (and vice-versa) had made us take these quick moments of phone time for granted. I was simply "dumping" sometimes because I felt so comfortable with him. I had to stop that. He was busy and stressed at work and the last thing he needed was to hear me complain about being stuck behind a school bus trying to get our daughter to school. I mean our interactions did not scream "we're broken" but I felt we needed a tune-up. Would my new awareness and effort change the dynamic of our daily conversation? Would it improve our interaction and fan the flames of something? I had to find out.

With the intention of trying this experiment for a week, I was conscious of my tone, words, and manner. I listened more; I was sweet. I didn't complain. I encouraged him when he started telling me about his challenges that day. I paid attention. It was strange (ha!).

One of the surprising outcomes was my own mood. I was happier. It reminded me of what author Gretchen Rubin says in her popular blog and book, The Happiness Project. Her Third Commandment of Happiness is "Act the Way You Want to Feel." She is definitely right. A post from her blog says, "Although we presume that we act because of the way we feel, in fact, we often feel because of the way we act."

The impact on my relationship with my husband? He was more affectionate (little gestures, little compliments); he seemed happier! He had an epiphany about the third day (men are a bit slow sometimes, or maybe he was afraid to rock the boat). "Is this what you are doing this week for that 52 Week thing?" he asked. I played dumb. "What do you mean 'this'?" I asked. "What's going on with you this week?" he responded. "Nothing," I said. "Just enjoy it." And like most members of the male species, he chose to leave it be. Smart. A woman would have analyzed it, dissected it, and dug deep for the motives. He laughed at me from time to time during the week. He saw me using all of my willpower not to complain, yell, or have a "tone" (even with others). My breaking point was on the sixth night: we were trying to figure out iMovies on my daughter's Mac computer. We had to send a video to a cousin who was compiling a DVD for my uncle's birthday and we were late. Without going into detail, neither of us knew what we were doing with the editing technology on the Mac. Homework was still not done. House was a mess. Daughter was a royal you-know-what. Couldn't help it: days of complaining came pouring out. I hate to admit it, but it felt good, or maybe just familiar.

But I still think my experiment was a success. I'm better now at holding back and am intent to try to smile more—especially with the people I love the most. My husband noticed for sure, and I certainly got more kisses.

Don't always say everything you feel and don't always be totally who you are all the time—it might make for more smiles. Sorry Seuss . . . they do mind and they matter most.

Makeover Madness

It's ironic how you can set out to do one thing and it can take you in an entirely different direction. Sometimes things change course and it all winds up working out in the end, but sometimes not . . .

Pam

Karen, and I spend a fair amount of time together chatting, laughing, debating, commiserating. In fact, that's how our 52 Weeks journey began. We talk, we text, we e-mail. But ironically, since we've committed to this project, we have not been able to do as much together. I guess we've each been working on our own 52. Lately, we've also talked a lot about how our project is moving forward and the exciting directions it is taking us. But actually "getting unstuck" together has taken a back seat.

So we decided we would spend a little time with each other for our 52 this week. Sounds so simple, doesn't it? But how? During a routine late (very late) night conversation we talked about some "blog" business, the day's events, and then finally that we both needed to finish up some more holiday shopping. Somewhere between Jimmy Kimmel and a re-run of a random late night show, I began to bemoan to Karen that at forty-something years old, I was having a skin breakout that would rival that of any teenager. I came to the conclusion that it was probably because I haven't bought new blush for years, and my cosmetics are probably full of "cooties." Karen chimed in that she was having the same "crisis." She admitted she hadn't changed her make-up routine since her pre-wedding makeover. And there it was. We would get some quick gifts and then visit the make-up counter at a department store for a fix-me-up! It seemed like a good idea—at the time. At that moment, I was game. I should have realized it was two a.m. and I was half asleep when I agreed.

Trite and frivolous, I know, but this 52 Week commitment is tricky and getting it all in takes some juggling and creative maneuvering sometimes. We've all seen people walk by those beauty counters peering out the side of their eyes pretending they are not looking when you know they really want to stop and sit in the director's chair to get all made up. Or maybe they are walking by laughing. Not sure.

Karen and I met up at Bloomingdale's for some shopping and a makeover. Well, Karen had a makeover. My day went a little differently.

Let's just say I couldn't wait to get home and wash away the entire experience. Lots of cream, too much foundation, sparkly purple eyes, wrong color choices, and the makeup artist who tried to guess my age but miscalculated by a few years (in the wrong direction!). It was all too much for me. From the people stopping to watch, the amount of makeup slathered on me, the prices of the cosmetics, to the holiday music being pumped in through the speakers, I was not feeling it.

What was I thinking? I don't love shopping (no, really I don't) and getting my makeup done in the middle of a department store the week before Christmas? Come on! While it was fun to be with my friend and we had a few laughs it was not the quality time I was looking for. Of course, we had advice for one another, gave our insights on the good, the bad, and even the ugly, but I quickly realized that this was not my idea of trying something new or fun. Admittedly, I was preoccupied with other things—maybe I should have cancelled—but I thought it would be time well spent together. Wrong again. I wanted to go to one counter, Karen wanted a different one; I got the novice make-up artist, she got the cool girl; I was poked, prodded, and annoyed; she was cleansed, massaged, and relaxed. The final straw came when we "lost" each other in the store. I stand firm that I was where we were supposed to be! All I could think was "exit door."

The next morning I awoke with another huge zit on my face and then Karen and I had a disagreement on the phone, in part about the previous day's events. Not one, but two eruptions! The date with my friend didn't work, the makeover didn't work, the shopping never happened.

Now don't get me wrong. I am always glad to spend time with my friend and I was so happy she had a good time. And she looked great! As Miss Piggy once said, "Beauty is in the eye of the beholder and it may be necessary from time to time to give a stupid or misinformed beholder a black eye." I'm not planning on throwing any punches, but she was right. Beauty is in the eye of the beholder. Sometimes people see things differently and what works for one person might not *for another. It wasn't the best outing together and we may disagree at times but we'll try something else another time. That's what friends do.*

Mother's Day

Karen

The years go by so fast. Mother's Day was always, rightfully so, about my mom. Growing up—and thankfully still—we would all be together. Most of the time it was an assortment of moms from the immediate family. Of course, once I walked down the aisle I inherited my husband's mom—adding to the pile of moms on Mother's Day. A few years later my sister got married. That brought her mother-in-law and sisters-in-law to the club. In 2001 we both celebrated the births of our daughters. I became an aunt, and became a mom. Powerful.

Flash forward ten years: somewhere along the way I forgot that Mother's Day—the holiday—was also about me. I am not suggesting that I don't think about being a mom every second of every minute of every day. I just sometimes forget I am a mom in the celebratory sense.

It's also a time-warp thing: the way many of us still look around for our mothers or "older" women when someone says, "Ma'am." The years fly by. When did we become our mothers? Why didn't we ever realize that Mother's Day is also about us? I thought about all of this recently and put my 52 hat on: I wanted to take a moment to remember that I am a mom too. It's not that I don't enjoy the Hallmark-inspired gatherings. It was just time to reflect a little on motherhood: my daughter just turned ten—a milestone. I deserved

"I love being married. It's so great to find that one special person you want to annoy for the rest of your life."
—Rita Rudner, comedian

to celebrate by squeezing in a few things just for me. So this week, even before the official day arrived, that's exactly what I did.

It was also the ideal time to be with my fellow busy mom and blog partner, Pam; we embarked on this journey together and although we always knew from day one that we had different 52 lists, we expected and planned on doing some fun things together along the way.

Culinary Therapy

Expanding my culinary horizons has been on my 52 list all along, and I had read about a Mother's Day breakfast demo at Williams-Sonoma. Pam (being a better and more proactive cook in general) did not jump up and down with excitement but agreed to accompany me. "It will be fun," I promised. So we went.

Ryan, a store employee and food aficionado, deftly demonstrated an amazing waffle iron and made incredible blueberry waffles. Pam and I asked Ryan a few questions and chatted incessantly with one another while sampling. I thought about the crappy frozen waffles I often make my daughter. I love this store. For some reason looking at non-stick pans, gourmet sauces, and amazing cloth napkins always relaxes me. We talked about knives. We talked about nothing. We talked about family. We talked about Mother's Day. We both decided to buy a stuffed-pancake pan. We were determined to make these pancakes for Mother's Day.

Never Underestimate the Power of Underwear

I think I was about sixteen when I first read that you feel better when you wear great stuff underneath your clothes—this has been drilled into our collective female brains forever. We stopped in at Victoria's Secret. Look, I know this was only about replenishing my lingerie but there is nothing like new underwear—some lacy, some plain—to make you feel a bit better. Mission accomplished, I walked out with my pink, shiny Victoria's Secret bag in hand.

Lots of Lattes

Finally we plopped down at our favorite Starbucks and sat in the sun. We talked about the blueberry waffles and a million other things. We forgot, for a little while anyway, about our errands, routines, and our hurdles that we still need to overcome. We even forgot about the 52 Weeks for a while. It was like old times or B.B. (Before Blog). We reminded each other that it's okay to do this kind of stuff today. We had already crossed off some "big" 52 Week stuff. We did silly, "girl" stuff today. We needed it.

I had no firm plans for Mother's Day this year. I was relieved that I hadn't had to commit to any version of a "moms-all-in-this-together gathering" and could, just this once, have a day free of social commitments, a day to just go with the flow. And just when I thought I would be the only mom around that day, my husband looked at me and said, "Ya know, we really should visit my mother at her new place."
I sighed to myself and said, "I guess you're right. We should." And just like that my I-am-the-only-mom-here-day evaporated into thin air. It was still a success though. Most importantly, I made time for my friend and blog partner and had some great blueberry waffles. Knowing that made it easier to appreciate the time spent with family, without feeling resentful that my "me" time had been usurped.

Sometimes nonstick pans really can help you get unstuck. I still plan on making filled pancakes for my family. And, if I get stuck under the Style Section in bed, so be it. It's time to remember I deserve a break, too.

"It's not easy being a mother. If it were easy, fathers would do it."
—The Golden Girls

Love and Marriage:
A Carriage Ride in Central Park

Karev

One of the many things on my 52 list was to jump-start my twenty-year relationship with my husband. Whenever I walk, hurriedly, by Central Park and see the tourists going on leisurely carriage rides, I watch from afar with envy. So I arranged to take a horse-and-carriage ride together in Central Park with my husband. But first I had to make sure that my daughter's homework was done and that she ate dinner. The babysitter arrived and we bolted out the door with some cash, our camera phones, and some info I had hastily printed from the Central Park web site. Wound-up from the day and a little irritated that I couldn't just leisurely get ready for my date, we started walking. I looked at the time; we were going to miss the "perfect carriage ride hour" so we hailed a cab on 5th Avenue. Bad move: the cab driver talked incessantly on the phone and blasted some pretty awful music the entire ride! We continued to Central Park in stop-and-go traffic while my husband returned emails and stared at his BlackBerry trying to finish his day. In his defense this was earlier in the day than we both usually "relaxed" and the transition was difficult, but I was determined to make this happen. Did I mention I screamed at the driver? Very attractive.

Thank God for Paul. As soon as we departed from the nightmare cab ride we were greeted by a charming man from another era with a sexy Irish brogue and a top hat! Although there were numerous carriages to choose from (who knew there were different styles?) I was immediately drawn to Paul and his hat; he really sealed the deal when he took out some carrots and directed me to feed the horse. "Her name is Dream," he said with that amazing voice that reminded me of Colin Farrell. Despite some irrational fears, I was pretty comfortable taking a carrot from Paul and feeding the horse before we pulled ourselves up and into the white, half-top "Cinderella"-style carriage with the red, slightly worn plush interior. We chatted with Paul as he held on to Dream's reins but also knew when to stop talking. He took us at a nice pace going west on Central Park South to the nearest park entrance. Despite being a veteran New Yorker, I immediately was caught up in the experience—it was something new and so different for me. There was no horrible music, Paul didn't talk on his cell phone or look at any type of electronic device and neither did my husband (nor me for that matter!). The leisurely pace of the carriage ride was a welcome escape from the usual speed of life, and of New York City in particular. It was also surprisingly quiet perched atop a carriage. We saw places I don't recall seeing in the past on foot or bicycle, and we passed places I have been but had never seen from this vantage point. We talked about nothing and just enjoyed the ride. We both marveled at the fact that we had never done this and vowed to do it again with perhaps a bottle of champagne in hand for the second ride. We took some photos and said good-bye to Paul and Dream and made our way to dinner in a whole different mood—emails, homework, bad cab rides all distant memories.

I sometimes think the New York of yesteryear would have been a better place for me: the slower pace, the horse-drawn carriages for getting around, the gentlemen in top hats. Men like Paul are hard to find and just their presence can lower your blood pressure. As it turns out, my husband and the ride, in the end, had the same impact as Paul, unfortunately without the sexy Irish brogue but I'll take it. I don't think of Sinatra or corny songs very often (okay, maybe I do!) but I certainly couldn't help remembering one song that night: Love and marriage, love and marriage . . . go together like a horse and carriage.

Friends

Pam

In the past three weeks, I've been lucky enough to see two very dear and usually far-away friends. My bestest friend from college, who moved to Australia too many years ago, was unexpectedly in New York for only a few hours before catching a flight when she gave me a call. I dropped everything and raced to Queens to visit her. It is not often that we get to see each other these days and it leaves a hole in my heart that she is so far away. But the distance and the limited times we get to be together always seem to melt away the minute we are together. Although she was back in the States because her father passed away and grief surrounded her, our short visit was filled with the usual laughs and giggles, non-stop chatter, and smiles that we so easily give to one another. I'd like to think it was a comfort and a needed distraction from the sadness and the tears shed over the loss of her dad.

Several days later, an old friend of mine from childhood, who I recently happily reconnected with, also came to town for a short visit. Again, I dropped everything, rearranged my schedule, and headed down to Tribeca. I had an amazing evening with her. She now lives in Kentucky, so we don't often get to see each other either.

But a third visit this week was a little different. While I dropped everything and fit my old friends into my hectic schedule, I've been finding lots of excuses with this one. Let me explain. Several years ago, a very special friend of mine passed away suddenly. It was unexpected and tragic. While it sounds so cliché, truly not a day goes by that I don't think about her. She wasn't a friend who had been in my life for many years—we were in the infancy of our friendship—but she was someone that I knew I'd be friends with for a long time to come.

A charming, old fashioned green park bench with a sweet, shiny engraved plaque on it that her loving husband and daughter adopted through the Central Park

Conservancy has been dedicated in her name. This is her memorial. I've been to "the bench," as her friends and family affectionately call it, many times but I've never visited alone. So this week, I put a date on my calendar to do just that.

It was the perfect autumn day—crisp and sunny, birds chirping, the wind blowing, a few trucks honking in the background (this was in New York City, after all). I sat for a while, watching the joggers and bikers, mothers with strollers, and dog walkers go by on a beautiful October afternoon and quietly picked at my sandwich. I'm not sure what I was expecting. My thoughts drifted to snippets of times spent with my friend; I saw us holding hands as we ice skated around Wollman Rink like two little school girls, while our daughters watched in horror and utter embarrassment; sneaking Bloody Marys in her kitchen one chilly November afternoon; listening to her tough love when I needed a kick in the butt; remembering she had been there for me and so many others, sharing her unconditional love, no matter what; and just thinking how she was that rare person who lit up a room and made you want to be in her presence.

I probably could have stayed there all day. The park is glorious this time of year, and I miss my friend. But my bittersweet mood and happy memories would have soon turned melancholy and confused. It was time to go.

The day awaited, and I intended to embrace it. That's exactly what my friend would have done too.

• • • •

Let's face it: relationships are what make us complete. Relationships fuel our lives. Where would we be without them? We have our old friends, new friends, children, spouses, significant others; our mothers, siblings, neighbors, and co-workers. If you have kids, the list expands to the sometimes obligatory "mom" friends. In fact, it can all be a bit overwhelming.

Looking back, it starts early: by the time you have your first "best" friend as a toddler, you start navigating the complicated, often-frustrating yet wonderful world of relationships. Before you know it puberty, high school, college, and beyond brings it all to a whole new level of complexity: first loves, friends from school, camp, work, and others. There are weddings, divorces, deaths, friends who drift away, aging parents, children, husbands, and a few "forced" friendships. There are friends you finally break up with (or should), new friends, and now Facebook friends. It all seems too much sometimes.

Sometime in your mid-forties, you start re-evaluating your relationships and, like with other areas of your life, think maybe you need to take stock and decide where you should put your energy.

When we conceived our blog, we felt like our relationships needed a tune-up or even a total overhaul. Our lives had become so busy with day-to-day responsibilities that we often didn't nurture our most important relationships—not only our relationship with ourselves, but those with others. Some relationships were just stagnant; others had drifted and were hanging on by life support, and some were just sucking up our time because of a warped sense of obligation. It became clear to us that it was yet another area of our lives that needed to be reassessed, re-evaluated, and rebooted!

We didn't tackle all we wanted to in our 52 Week journey when it came to relationships but it certainly got us thinking and we got started. At the very least it inspired a new outlook: you can't take relationships for granted and they do need nurturing. It wasn't always easy to take a first step when it came to our most important relationships, but we did it. We didn't write about all of the things we did—some situations were perhaps too raw. But the truth is, the ones we started working on got us thinking and became significant. We were paying attention. That's what matters.

When we talked to women our age many felt the same way. Some had rifts with family members and wanted to at least start making an effort to repair the relationship. Some were hanging on to friendships that they had outgrown and just didn't know how to end; other relationships were more toxic and didn't work at all anymore. And the most common complaint? Women who knew their primary relationship needed the boot or, more often, a reboot! It was universal: finding time for your significant other can seem almost impossible.

The 52 Weeks is all about finding time for yourself without guilt. If you don't grow and aren't happy, your family will know it. Karen has a sign in her kitchen that says, "If Mama ain't happy, no one is happy." It is so true. Women often set the tone for the entire family—that's a lot of pressure. So the bottom line? Focus on time for yourself. Consider rebooting your primary relationship—it probably can use it—and figure out where all of your other relationships fit in.

We talked with **Dr. Debbie Magids, Ph.D.,** a psychologist with a thriving private practice in New York City. She also is the author of *All The Good Ones Aren't Taken: Change the Way You Date and Find Lasting Love* and has has appeared on countless television shows guiding viewers with no-nonsense advice about relationships. We spoke with Dr. Debbie to shed light on how to tackle some of these common relationship issues.

Before we asked her some of the more "pressing" relationship questions, we wanted to know what she does when she feels like she's in a rut or "stuck." She said that she makes very few plans, pulls back on work, and makes time to get enough rest, work out every day, meditate, eat healthy, and drink a lot of water and green tea. Okay, but you know what Dr. Debbie? We aren't the naturally green tea sipping, meditating kind of women. "I am more naturally drawn to Entenmann's cakes or a glass of wine!" says Karen. So what should women like *us* do?

"I find that doing a new activity or taking a trip is only a quick fix but doesn't really address the issue," Dr. Debbie added. "So the 'getting unstuck' feeling is short lived. I may go away to a spa-like retreat if I feel really stuck to do this inward search—but most often I do it in the comfort of my home. This kind of atmosphere allows me to be still, and get in touch with my feelings— the things that are hurting me. These feelings are what really fuels the rut to begin with. Once I find the truth, the rut dissipates, for real." *Wow*, she's really together about this kind of stuff. Pam and I weren't. So, all the more reason we wanted to hear what she had to say about relationships.

We asked Dr. Magids why women sometimes find themselves in a myriad of relationships that really don't work for them anymore. "We are all drawn to relationships for a reason," she said. "Whether it is a romantic relationship or others, we all have a blueprint or a pattern—often from childhood—that can explain our connections to one another."

According to Dr. Debbie, it goes beyond just your spouse or significant other. All of our relationships are affected by our past. Depending on your history, changing a difficult relationship may cause uncomfortable feelings to surface that you don't want to deal with: guilt, people's anger, not feeling good enough about yourself—it really depends. "The fact is though, if you stay in something that doesn't make you happy, there is some deeper issue going on," Dr. Magids said. "You really have to think about what you want out of a relationship and almost demand it."

Getting out of a relationship—any relationship that isn't working—is difficult. We asked Dr. Magids why women in particular seem especially challenged when it comes to ending those relationships we have outgrown or that are even toxic. "Many women have been conditioned to be "yes people," she says. "The first line of defense is making a decision that your own needs are going to start counting more or at least as much as the needs of the other person," You also have to make a commitment to live with some discomfort for a while. When anyone makes any changes, it never feels good. It's different, unknown, and you don't know what is on the other side," she added. We couldn't agree more. During our 52 Weeks an obstacle we often faced was feeling "okay" when doing something for ourselves and not feeling guilty about it. We also felt more than a little discomfort at times when deciding to try something new or unknown. It definitely wasn't always easy and fun.

Since *The 52 Weeks* is all about taking small steps to start reaching any goal, we asked Magids for just a few baby steps towards repairing a relationship.

Her advice? "Begin with setting small boundaries at first. If it is someone who calls chronically, start limiting the calls; if it's someone who speaks unkindly, start speaking up and telling him or her it's no longer OK; if it's someone who asks too much of you, start saying no to smaller things at first. With small subtle changes, you can then keep progressing so the relationship gets redefined. Ultimately, though you may have to have a hard conversation if someone just doesn't get it."

Dr. Helen Fisher, the author and journalist also featured in our "Flying Solo" chapter, had a few things to say about friendships and getting unstuck. Fisher said women often feel obligated to stay in friendships with other women that are no longer working for them. "It's OK to break up with girlfriends if the relationship is really not allowing you to grow," she said. "If your friends just like to sit around and eat or drink and you are at a point in life that you want to get out and exercise more, then move on to others for now." Okay, Dr. Fisher, how do we break out of our comfort zone with certain friends where "eating and drinking too often" is commonplace?

"As you get older, your interests and the things you want to spend time doing will likely change. You need new friends for these things," Fisher said. We don't think it's so black and white. We believe there are different friends for different reasons and you need to find the right balance. That's not easy. But we also see her point: if you really have nothing in common anymore, want more balance or need to break certain patterns, you need to make changes.

We also believe it's about normal cycles in a friendship—especially long-term relationships.

Karen

For Pam and me, the 52 Weeks was actually a bit of a strain on our friendship. Yet we know that despite the hurdles and the "I don't want to talk to you today" moments, we are life-long friends. You just know that kind of thing. We care about each other too much. Yes, we had different points of view on the blog and book but we know our friendship will survive and go through many phases in our lifetime. That's the difference between a friendship that you have outgrown or isn't "good" for you anymore and normal friendship "cycles."

Bringing it back to rebooting your relationship with your significant other or spouse, we thought about our lives; we often find ourselves tired from little sleep, kids, stress, and just day-to-day stuff we all have to take care of. But according to Dr. Debbie, if you want your relationship with your significant other to grow or you need to pay attention. Getting unstuck in your primary relationship is not necessarily something on everyone's 52 list but it showed up a bit more on my list when compared to Pam's. During my 52 I tried to complain less to my husband, do more romantic things with him (carriage ride in Central Park), and took dance lessons (tango anyone?). Without

*realizing it, I was already doing things recommended by the experts. Really,
though, it is about feeling better about yourself, and friends and family will
benefit by default. It obviously takes more than just carving time out for a few
things but it was all in the name of trying to give my twenty-year marriage a
kick in the butt. I suppose the key is to make it a part of your regular schedule.
I am really still trying to figure the whole thing out: how do you stay really,
really connected when you have a middle-school aged kid doing homework
until late at night, day-to-day stresses, and limited time? I think it is an
ongoing challenge for any couple. I guess it is about the little things, like
bitching and complaining a little less! That's a good start, because most
couples don't have the time or luxury to jet off to St. Barts or Paris any time
they need a boost.*

Dr. Magids suggests these initial simple tips to try as a way to bring the
"mojo" back to a relationship:

- Talk to each other about each other. There is nothing more intimate than
  telling your significant other how you feel when you are with him or her,
  what you love about him or her, or what makes that person so special.
- Bring sexy back if it's gone. Tell someone how "hot" he or she looks or
  send a sexy text during the day (instead of "don't forget to pay the electric
  bill!"). It will bring excitement back into the relationship.
- Take turns planning nights out together. Always keep in mind what the
  other person likes—not just what you like to do.
- Stay home without the kids. Plan to have the children out of the house
  and enjoy a night in together alone.
- Create intimate time. Forget about a sex agenda. Make time to just be
  together.

"Each person in a relationship wants to be desired, heard, and loved. Figure out what the other person needs and try to give it to them, even if you don't understand it." According to Dr. Debbie, the biggest problem she sees in her practice is each person giving what *they* want instead of what the other person needs.

NEXT STEPS

We got some great advice to try and better understand our relationships and how to reboot and move forward with your significant others, friends, and family members. Keep these things in mind when you start your own relationship-repair journey.

Sex

We disagree about the importance of planning for sex in a relationship. "I think life is busy, and sexual intimacy can easily fall by the wayside, and you need to carve out time for it like anything else on a 52 list," says Karen. "If you plan for it or talk about it too much, it's less likely to happen," counters Pam. Well, we didn't list "sex" as an item on our lists, but maybe it *should* be on some people's 52 lists. We found that most women in our age group—especially those married ten, fifteen, or twenty years—complain about sex, or the lack thereof. Dr. Magids is adamant about how important sex is in a relationship. "It is the most intimate connection you have with someone, and is what differentiates this relationship from all of your others," she said. After talking to Dr. Magids and doing some of our own informal research we did concur with her that it's not necessary to pay attention to how many times a week or month couples should be doing it; the barometer must be based on satisfaction. "If both parts of the couple are happy with once a month then you're ok. It's only when one is dissatisfied that trouble begins. However, if both are satisfied with no sex at all, then there is something deeper going on—and not a good thing," she cautions. Perhaps the best place to start is just reconnecting emotionally. Hopefully, it will lead to better sexual intimacy.

Make your own rules

When we asked her about couples that make their own rules—even if they are "unconventional"—Dr. Debbie says making unique rules is great. There really are no two couples that are alike, and as long as the people within the couple are in sync with each other and connected to whatever they decide to do, it can work. With this said, if for instance they are bringing a third person into their bed, they may not fully understand the emotional ramifications. So she would suggest counseling and deep contemplation before moving forward. And make sure one member isn't acquiescing in order to please or keep their spouse.

Feel better about yourself to be better in a relationship

Women would feel better about themselves if they paid attention to their own needs and sense of self-worth. We hear again and again that women should "act as if they felt better about themselves" and not stand for bad treatment. And in time, the new behavior will become habit and can change the whole dynamic of the relationship.

During our 52 Weeks, we also found that simple things like "just picking up the phone" after an argument with a sibling or repairing a relationship can be the hardest thing.

Own it

People have such a hard time because they are stuck in their emotions and being "right." The first line of defense is always self-awareness. People need to understand what is triggering them to feel so angry or hurt. The other thing is we all have to take ownership of our part of an argument. Everyone needs to take a piece of the pie. First step, figure out your part, take ownership, and say you're sorry. This will do wonders for the other person. Instead of being defensive, they will be more open to a real conversation and hopefully take responsibility for their part.

Evaluate

Think about or make a list of the value a relationship has in your life. Usually the signs are clear. If you never make the first move to be in touch, always take a long time to get back to the person, or dread time spent with him or her, then it's time to reconsider that relationship. If you don't enjoy your time with this person it is time to let it go.

Take action

It may be hard, but if you have evaluated the relationship and tried to repair it or make it work for you and it still feels the same, take small steps to end the relationship. Of course it is more complicated with family but for friends and others that just don't work for you anymore move away, even slowly, from the relationship.

This advice is not a panacea for all of your sticky relationship issues and hurdles. Our hope is that you felt a connection to our blog stories and are inspired to take stock. Do you see your mom enough? When was the last time you spent more than an hour with your best friend? Do you complain too much? It's all about paying attention and making the changes that will put you on a different path for your fourties and beyond. Don't feel guilty if you need to move on from certain relationships that simply don't work anymore. Start making your own list of things you want to do to make this part of your life better. Even if you only check off a few, it's progress and you will feel like you are moving in the right direction.

SOME TAKEAWAY ADVICE AND QUOTES TO GET YOU GOING

➢ "A friend is someone who gives you total freedom to be yourself."—Jim Morrison

➢ Invest time in your relationships.

➢ Don't keep doing the same things together.

➢ Always make time for Mom. It doesn't necessarily have to be on Mother's Day (as long as everyone is okay with that!).

➢ "There comes a point in your life when you realize who really matters, who never did, and who always will." —Unknown

➢ Remember to tell the people you love how much you love them, often.

IDEAS FOR THE READER

Here are some things we tried. Seems obvious, we know, but sometimes a little reminder can't hurt. For a complete list of more specific ideas see "Your 52," Chapter 11.

- Stop bitching and smile more.
- Bring romance back into your relationship.
- Nurture your friendships; make a plan and stick to it.
- Have a regular "date" on the calendar with your friends.
- Have a regular "date" on the calendar with your significant other!
- Try something new with an old friend.
- Stop emailing, texting, and sending messages to friends via Facebook; pick up the phone.
- Drop everything when a good friend comes in from out of town. Time together is so hard to find.
- Say you are sorry.
- Take dance lessons together.
- Try Tantric massage with your significant other.
- Go for a makeover with friends—even if, in the end, you have different experiences!
- Never underestimate the power of a sexy accent to completely alter your mood!

Chapter Six

Facing Fears

"You must do the things you think you cannot do."

–Eleanor Roosevelt

Camera Shy No More

Pam

Max is a confident, personable guy and well suited to be on camera. Good-looking and put together, he always seems to be "camera ready." I, on the other hand, while confident, not only am camera-shy, but also always get caught in my sweatpants or with my hair sticking up when I bump into the ex-boyfriend or my best frenemy at the supermarket. Generally, I am not "camera ready."

Max is also my real estate broker. I am in the process of selling my New York apartment and looking for a new one. In addition to brokering real estate deals, Max sometimes appears on a local TV show, The Hunt. In the show, realtors take their clients out and about to look at available properties.

A while back he asked me to join him on a segment. I politely said, "No, thank you." For some crazy reason, he thought I'd be a good fit for the show. I knew what he was thinking: Pam is friendly, poised, outgoing, and always quick with the witty retorts. She'd be great at this! At least that's what I hoped he was thinking. What he didn't know was that although I can command the attention of thirty first graders in a classroom and have been called a "Chatty Cathy" more than a few times in my life, I do not like to do any kind of planned public speaking. Center of attention? No way. He asked me again. "Thank you," I said. "I'm flattered, but I really can't."

A week later, Max emailed me to say that another segment opportunity was available. I guess the third time is the charm, because I finally agreed. I must admit—I was more than a little curious, and it also was time to face this fear. It would be fun as well (or so he told me). It was definitely something new. While "shooting a local TV show" is not on my 52, overcoming fears and having fun are big goals that I am trying to accomplish as part of my list of to-do's, and this covered both. All of this plus knowing I'd get a nice lunch and a day out finally got the best of me and I caved! Perhaps this would be my "fifteen minutes of fame." Reality TV here I come.

Our "film crew" for the day consisted of Alex and Adam—two affable, twenty-something hipster guys who served as our cameramen, sound and lighting crew, interviewers, and comedic warm-up coaches. As for hair and make-up, well, I was on my own there; This was local TV after all. While the operation was relatively bare bones, it was still interesting to see what goes into filming and creating the show. Sound and lighting were checked; my mic pack wouldn't stay where it was supposed to be; gaffes, giggles; flubs; retakes; camera angles; marks.

I was nervous in the morning and felt rather uncomfortable standing in the street in my heels and coat as I spoke directly to the camera with no prepared lines. Some people stopped and watched, others couldn't care less; and then there were those who gave that annoyed look because we were in the way of their rushed a.m. commute. Just a typical New York City morning. Okay, this wasn't so bad. Max and I visited the first apartment, filmed some "filler scenes" walking around the neighborhood the rest of the morning, and then broke for lunch. By the afternoon, I began to feel more at ease and even got a bit punchy. I tried to forget the cameras were there. A few more takes, some question and answer footage to shoot, and it was "a wrap"!

The final piece still has to be cut and edited, I wonder how much of my close-ups will actually wind up on the cutting room floor. But it was fun to be the center of attention for at least a little while. I must admit that even though I still don't like public speaking and am insecure about seeing the final piece when it airs, I got caught up in it by the end of the day. I came home exhausted and was dreaming that my assistant would be waiting for me at the door with my glass of wine and a foot massage. Instead, I was greeted by my family—my daughters needed help with their homework, my husband was ready for dinner and the litter box needed to be changed.

Ah, the life of a star . . . .

Just Breathe

Karen

I took my first yoga class in 2002, and I had a panic attack. I am not kidding. It wasn't funny. Of course, the main reason I took a class to begin with was to relax. I left the class and vowed never to take a yoga class again. I would stick to tennis, the gym—the stuff I was comfortable with. I needed to actually move to quiet my brain. The deep breathing, the calm atmosphere, the poses—ironically, everything about yoga made me anxious. Maybe I am just that kind of person, I thought to myself. Maybe I need movement, brain clutter, and shallow breathing to feel alive and productive?

Years passed. Friends, colleagues, and others would sometimes say, "You would be the perfect person for yoga. You would love it." I then would share my story and receive looks of both amusement (I tried to make the story funny over the years) and concern.

Then I started this blog project, and I just knew that yoga had to be on my list. I know it sounds crazy because yoga for many people is a treasured part of their daily lives. But for me, it had grown to represent many things:

- *Getting over my fear of yoga (would I have another anxiety attack?)*
- *Getting out of my exercise comfort zone (it was getting boring), and*
- *Doing something for myself that I knew I really needed to do.*

Most of all, I knew it was time to get better at breathing and relaxing. I was perpetually working on this lifelong, anxiety-reduction quest without much success (unless, of course, a martini or a piece of chocolate was in the room!).

So I went. Pam, my blog partner, encouraged me to go and her support was especially important when I called her from my cell phone, nervous, on the way to the studio. She coached me through it and said, "You'll be great, don't think too much about going or you'll psych yourself out of it." I am thankful I had Pam to call and that I told her that I was going that day. I am not sure if I would have made it if I wasn't accountable to her and 52 Weeks.

The yoga studio was small but appeared nice, calm, and, most importantly, close to my apartment. A long walk in the cold weather would have given me more time to change my mind. I signed up for a class with Molly, who was perky, friendly, and calm. I introduced myself. I told her I was a true beginner. There was a group of thirty to fifty-something-year-old women in the room. I tried to fit in with my outdated tennis sweats and a shirt, but it was 75–80 degrees in the room, and I felt myself start to sweat before we even started Soft, spa-like music was playing as everyone positioned their mats and got ready. I took Pam's advice to set up near the door in case I needed or wanted to make a quick exit for any reason.

Molly started the class by telling us all to chant "ohm" a few times. I felt kind of like a jerk doing this but I went along. Then we did some breathing exercises—we held two fingers together and closed alternative nostrils, then began inhaling and exhaling (I looked it up later and found that it has a name: Ujjayi or Pranayama breathing). It was hard to clear my mind at first; my heart was racing, and my breathing started out shallow. We then did poses, stretches, and more breathing. Molly was patient and calming and perfect for my "re-entry" into yoga.

Throughout the class she said things like "remove the clutter from your head, let good energy for the New Year enter your body and think about what you want to do this year." Good words of wisdom for the first week of the year. After about twenty minutes I was into it.

The class lasted over an hour. I returned my mat, put my sneakers on, and walked out. I thought about how I felt: I couldn't believe it, but I loved it. I was shocked. I loved the class, and how different it was from my regular stuff. I was also proud of myself for not freaking out and just getting through it. I called Pam after, amazed at my own reaction. I could hear her smile on the phone; she was also pretty shocked at my "yoga re-entry" mood but genuinely happy for me. I really had an "a-ha" moment this week. I plan on seeing Molly at yoga on many more Tuesdays going forward.

On a final note, I thought about a funny quote I read from Ellen DeGeneres recently. Her take on yoga makes me put it all in perspective. I had a hard time silencing my worries and thoughts during class but I was almost relieved when ridiculous thoughts started popping into my head rather than anxious ones. Ellen joked that a detergent jingle came into her head as she tried to quiet her brain during yoga one day.

Her remark? "I was in full lotus position. My chakras were all aligned. My mind is cleared of all clutter and I'm looking out of my third eye and everything that I'm supposed to be doing. It's amazing what comes up, when you sit in that silence: "Mama keeps whites bright like the sunlight; Mama's got the magic of Clorox 2."

Winning at 35,000 Feet!

Karen

I hate flying. I hate everything about it. I hate the airport. I hate the lines. I hate that I have to throw my full bottle of water or hairspray or anything else that is not three ounces away before going through security. I hate taking my shoes off and putting my crap in that plastic box. I hate the sensation of flying; it just completely disagrees with me in every way, in every cell of my being.

But I love to travel, if that makes sense.

I like landing safely. I like leaving my routine at home and being somewhere else. I just hate flying to get there.

Being a mom, I have mastered the art of appearing engaged, strong, and fearless when my daughter is on the flight with me. In fact, flying with her usually is a great distraction.

She did, however, catch on once when she gave me a weird face midflight after I asked her to repeat something three times. I think I was focusing on the engine sounds. It just so happened recently that we couldn't get seats together on the way home from a family vacation, and I thought sitting alone was a good first step to start conquering my aversion to flying. I would fly "solo" again. I would fly alone, without the distraction of my daughter. And, I would be away from Mr. Big Shot flyer husband who would patiently look at me when needed with reassuring eyes and secret code words (so daughter wouldn't notice) letting me know that the bumps we were feeling mid-flight were "normal." Patient? Nice? Enabling?

I am not sure when exactly this fear of flying really took hold. I remember going on a trip to Italy in high school that I had convinced my parents was critical to my education. I was fearless, confident, not a care in the world. Back in those days there was actually smoking in the back of the plane (imagine!). I remember sneaking to the smoking aisles with my best friend Sharon. No fear. No thinking. Different world, different time. There were, of course, many, many trips after that. I don't remember thinking about it. I was different then. Maybe I was just young and clueless.

I don't want to hate flying so much. I want to learn to let go, accept that we have no way of controlling everything in the world or the "master plan." I want to relax more when I fly and not look to my husband for secret code reassurances. He gets on a plane the way I get in a cab. He can fall asleep on the runway before take-off. It's irritating.

I think it got worse after 9/11. No-fly lists, enhanced security and our new world. So be it. I am jealous of my husband's ease with the whole thing. Like George Clooney in that movie, Up in the Air, *he glides through the whole process, as I figure out how to survive until I land.*

"There are so many people that hate flying," he said to me one night, trying to make me feel better. I did a little research: Jennifer Aniston and Cher supposedly don't love flying. But finding other, more famous people with the same issue just doesn't make me feel better. I want to beat this.

So there I was on a five-hour flight without my family close by. I blasted my iPod when I first took my seat, watched comedy on the little TV in the seat in front of me, and had my "emergency" vodka bottle in my bag. There was no small talk to distract me. The flight was fairly smooth, but of course I was still aware of every sound and movement. I looked at the flight attendants here and there ("if they are not worried, then all is fine," a friend once told me). There was no opportunity for my husband to reassure me in code. No daughter distractions.

Had flying with my family all the time actually contributed to my prolonged anxiety? If I had continued to fly all over the country working would it have prevented my flying anxiety?

The fact is, we all have "our stuff," and a big part of it all is not so much fear but fixing how you react to those fears and hurdles. I want to fly all over the world with my daughter by my side, fully conscious and present, and enjoy it as much as what happens after we land.

Bare Awakenings

This is a guest post by Diana Spechler. She is the author of the novels Who By Fire *and* Skinny *and of stories in the* New York Times, GQ, O, Oprah Magazine, *the* Wall Street Journal, *and elsewhere. She teaches writing in New York City and at Stanford University's Online Writer's Studio.*

As an adult, I've overcome most of my old insecurities. I'll sing karaoke. I'll propose a toast. I no longer panic about whether to kiss on the cheek or shake someone's hand. But my negative body image, the demon I most want to destroy, still shrieks when I address my full-length mirror and taunts me in the presence of food: you're seriously going to eat that? What are you, a sumo wrestler?

I'm tired of lamenting the same stomach I lamented in high school. I will never have Janet Jackson's abs circa 1998. Why can't my brain accept that and move on to important things? Like global climate change. The unemployment rate. Kim Kardashian's baby.

Recently, when a friend told me about Naked Yoga, just the words juxtaposed— naked, yoga—sent a shock of dread up my spine. I thought for a moment about those arachnophobes who get locked up in rooms full of spiders, who scream and scream until they finally stop screaming, because they're no longer afraid.

I knew what I had to do.

In New York City, where I live, one may choose from an eclectic menu of yogas—laughing yoga, trapeze yoga, yoga for foodies, for gay men, for children. Because I've been practicing yoga for years, I'm familiar with the local scene: in this city of eight million, classes are packed to capacity. I've been kicked during warrior three, smacked in the face during spinal twists. When the whole room chants, "Ohm," the floor shakes. Picturing those crowds gave me courage: in a crowded Naked Yoga class, no one would notice the ingrown hairs on my bikini line. No one would notice my imperfect body. I'd be one imperfect body in a sea of imperfect bodies.

The day before class, I spoke briefly on the phone with the teacher, a friendly woman named Cindee who equipped me with an Upper East Side address and answered my astute questions, including, "What should I wear?" That evening, I showered, applied eyeliner, and blew my hair out smooth, as if I were primping for a hot date. I dressed in black, the hue of concealment. When I looked in the mirror, my insides quaked.

I was surprised to find that the address Cindee had given me was an apartment building, and that when she let me in, I was standing in her home. I hung my coat among her coats and followed her through a beaded curtain into a room large enough for no more than six yoga mats, where incense burned and wall hangings of the Buddha surrounded tapestry-covered windows. My pulse began to race. What about the sea of yogis I'd envisioned? The lighting wasn't even dim. The only other people in the room were two silver-haired gentlemen, their mats rolled out on the hardwood floor. They each extended a hand to shake. I looked around, as if the rest of the students might be hiding.

"Is this it?" I asked. I didn't add, It's just me and two dudes?!

"This is it," one of the men said cheerfully.

When Cindee instructed us to disrobe, I accidentally saved my socks for last, and was, for a horrible moment, the woman in nothing but striped socks pulled straight up her calves. In the next moment, I was fully naked, shoving my clothes into the corner, and then Cindee was telling us to sit, my single most offensive naked position.

I tried not to focus on my rolls, and felt relieved when Cindee, naked and unfairly gorgeous with her toned arms and wild mane of curls, told us to begin in child's pose. At least for a minute, I could hide my stomach. I was less relieved to flip over onto my back and simulate riding a bicycle, elbow to opposite knee in slow motion, my breasts spilling into my armpits.

The 52 Weeks

Throughout the floor series, I kept my eyes closed. As long as I didn't look at anyone—scanning their bodies for tattoos and piercings—didn't glance between their legs to see what their penises were up to, maybe no one would look at me, either.

"We come into the world naked," Cindee said. "We go out naked. But while we're here, we tend to hide inside our clothes." She walked through the room, adjusting our hips and the angles of our feet, unfazed by our gaping butt cracks. "You'll see that you don't have to hide anymore," she said. The heat was cranking and sweat beaded up on my arms. By the time I rose for the first Vinyasa—plank, chaturanga, up dog, down dog—I was less worried about sucking in my gut than I was about failing. As any New York City yogi knows, yoga is quietly competitive. I wouldn't dream of sitting while my classmates stood in tree pose. I wouldn't pant while my classmates breathed easily. I would keep my face calm while my heart raced.

Cindee was working us—one posture flowing into the next. By the time she told us to stand on the left foot, grab the right big toe, and open the right leg straight out to the side, my self-consciousness was all but forgotten. My left leg trembled from exertion. "Good morning, sunshine!" our genitals cried.

I kept fluctuating between wanting to laugh—everyone was naked!—and wanting to weep—my waist would never be cinched like Cindee's—but as I lay in final Savasana, my eyes fell closed, my body tingled, and I eased into my blissed-out yoga buzz. This is what I love about yoga—the post-class sensation, reminiscent of relaxing in front of a fire after a hard day of skiing.

As I dressed, I was all smiles.

"Not everyone gets it," Cindee said. "Why we do this."

One of the men nodded. "We're a subculture. But just wait. It's like when you discover skinny dipping," he told me. Soon you'll wonder why you ever did yoga in clothes."

I'm not sure that skinny dipping has ever made me want to burn my bathing suits, but I saw his point. The world had shifted: the scarf I wound around my throat was a noose, the underwire of my bra a cage. I didn't want to zip my coat. Most interestingly, my "rolls" felt like "curves." I opened the door to go and waved goodbye to the men, smiling at their faces, erasing their naked bodies from my mind.

• • • •

When we started the52weeks.com, we wanted to take more chances and overcome some hurdles that were holding us back. In retrospect, maybe we were a bit scared that we weren't living

"If black boxes survive air crashes— why don't they make the whole plane out of that stuff?"
—George Carlin, comedian

up to our potential, or scared to be forty-something and losing a bit of our momentum when it came to checking things off the proverbial "life list."

At the time, we identified it as restlessness but, looking back, it was likely mixed with some anxiety: why had we gotten stuck? Had we stopped taking chances? Other than feeling like we didn't have the time, were there other reasons we stopped trying new things?

There were many reasons we launched the blog, but certainly the underlying, nagging sense of "we could be better" made us move forward and start compiling our respective 52 lists. A little anxiety can be a great motivator. If we did feel a little anxious about our situations it inspired us to take action and launch the52weeks.com. That's a good thing.

Karen's 52 list especially was sprinkled with tackling a number of anxieties and hurdles. Yes, it also included things like taking art lessons, exploring Kabbalah, and complaining less, but there were also to-do items such as "chill out on airplanes" and "embrace yoga without panic."

It was a bit harder to find those types of things on Pam's list, beyond her fear of public speaking, but if you looked closely you would certainly see a common theme of stop procrastinating and get moving again. Something was holding her back at times too.

So, yes, this is a chapter about facing your fears, but really, when we thought about it, taking steps to move forward in your life overall and tackle your fears is really a unifying thread throughout the book. The reality is, getting out of your comfort zone and trying new things is inherently scary. We know it can also be exhilarating but shaking it up can be frightening once you've grown accustomed to certain patterns and routines. In the end the message is simple: create your own 52 to-do list that is honest and real. Create a list that will push you out of your comfort zone.

So why do we talk about the "big" stuff (panic attacks!) and the smaller stuff in the same chapter? It's hard but they definitely have one thing in common: they all can hold us back. There are the small hang-ups and then there are the big hurdles and bumps in the road. Some have probably been in your life as far back as you can remember. Others seemingly come out of nowhere, like all of a sudden feeling anxious while just shopping and you don't really know why. Then there are fears and anxieties that are triggered by major milestones or life events, such as:

- The birth of your first child (or second, or third!)
- The moment you realize you are almost "middle-aged"
- You have your first real health scare or diagnosis.
- You lose a parent.
- You can't pay the bills.
- You lose your job.
- You get divorced or separated.
- Your children leave the house.
- You lose someone you love.

And, of course you can just get scared in the less serious sense of the word but scared nonetheless if all of a sudden you realize:

- It's really thirty pounds you need to lose, not just "ten."
- You no longer fit into anything in your closet.
- You can't play tennis, the piano, or speak Spanish anymore, and you used to be better than average—in fact really good—at all three.
- You find a random gray hair somewhere unexpected on your body.
- You will never be fifteen, twenty-five, thirty-five again.
- You are married, for better or for worse, to that person sitting next to you.
- Your sex life is boring or you have no sex life.
- You are boring.
- You are still doing, smoking, or drinking whatever it is you think you love or need.

Didn't see anything you could relate to on the list? What about specific phobias, like fear of enclosed spaces, fear of snakes, fear of heights, or fear of public speaking? How about being a little scared when, all of a sudden, you feel "stuck."

Then, you ask yourself, "How did I get here?"

Then, hopefully, like us, you make a plan to get going again. You start rebuilding your confidence. You try new things. You face some fears. You realize you just have to "get over it." You reach out and open up your world.

But sometimes you need help. Sometimes you need support, advice, and help from friends, family, or professionals. And that's okay. We've all been there. And, even if you are the kind of person who thinks you can do everything alone and are "never scared" or stuck in fear, you will one day hit a bump in the road and you will need more than just a day of "retail therapy."

In the end, we probably all have the "little" stuff mixed in with the big stuff. So when we thought about this chapter we knew it was important to point out this distinction—the little things and the big hurdles. Our expert addresses both.

Lauren Kantor Gorman, M.D., is a psychiatrist in New York City. She specializes in psychotherapy and psychopharmacology for adults dealing with a wide range of psychiatric issues, including anxiety.

"If you have anxiety and fear that matches the circumstances, you're not talking about an anxiety disorder," explained Gorman. "An anxiety disorder is a fear that doesn't match what is happening in your environment." Karen has personally struggled with this. Having a true panic attack in a yoga class, for example, is obviously coming from somewhere other than trying to do a downward dog! "If you feel anxious from events that take over the population, such as a severe hurricane, terrorist attacks, and traumatic personal events, it is only normal to feel your body and mind react. It is reactive anxiety and you are being threatened, you're vulnerable."

We talked with Gorman about what people, especially women, can do to alleviate true anxiety. She spoke to us about the importance of a support system, seeking professional help, and changing your lifestyle. We detail some of her specific suggestions at the end of this chapter. It was good to have clarification and confirmation about real fear versus feeling uncomfortable simply from trying something new.

For some people it is in their DNA to push the envelope, when many others might hesitate to even try. Everyone is different when it comes to his or her ability to handle stress. Everyone is unique in how they process his or her worlds and emotional life. Genetics and environment play a key role. What's important, though, is to step back, assess where you are on the spectrum, and try. You need to push beyond where your comfort zone is. Feeling uncomfortable is, well, uncomfortable. It prevents people from doing new things. "How we are built as individuals and our

"That seemingly scary condition, whatever it may be, is not the problem. It's your reaction that has you shaking. And that's why, if you'll become conscious of a fearful condition instead of afraid of it, you'll change forever your relationship with fear."
—Guy Finley, self-realization expert

own unique backgrounds explains why people are afraid to change, especially when it comes to bad habits. Quitting smoking is a good example. Of course it is highly addictive but it is much more difficult for some people because of personality, genetics, anxiety levels, tolerance for change and discomfort," Gorman added.

"Look, it's not going to feel good to make changes sometimes," Gorman continued. "But, the long-term benefits are so profound that you are going to want to get through that uncomfortable feeling." We could relate. The more you do it, the easier it becomes. Therapy is great for this, especially Cognitive Behavioral Therapy. Ultimately, though, you just need to deal with the discomfort.

We recently read a *New York Times* article about **Kilian Jornet Burgada**, the most dominating endurance athlete of his generation, and is a quintessential example of someone on the extreme end of the risk-taking spectrum. He appears to have no boundaries to his personal comfort zone, and is almost fearless when it comes to great physical and mental challenges. The article details his incredible world running records, Some are for distances that, according to the interview, would require most of us to purchase an airplane ticket.

The writer looked at Jornet's environment and unique physiological makeup. Scientists believe that these unique factors contribute to his astonishing abilities. He doesn't appear to have any apprehension about risk. Born into a Catalan family, Jornet grew up in the Spanish Pyrenees at 6,500 feet, and his gifts are literally in his blood. "When you are born and bred at altitude, you tend to have a higher blood volume and red-cell count for oxygen-carrying capacity," confirmed a researcher at Stanford. This translates to better endurance. "Years of daily running and skiing up mountains have further bolstered this advantage." We know he is an extreme example but it demonstrates how different we all are. Like Gorman said, we each have a different comfort zone, and anxiety and fear "set-points."

So what about the rest of us that aren't scaling major mountains and breaking world records? What about regular women whose abilities aren't being studied by the top scientists in the world?

Pam has never liked being in front of the camera or in the spotlight. It was only because of the52weeks.com that opportunities emerged in the past year or two that pushed her out of her comfort zone. The first was an opportunity to be on a real estate television show because she was selling her apartment, and the other was an appearance at the 92nd Street Y with other writers and bloggers. When she was first approached by the television show she said "no" numerous times. Finally, she gave in. She later wrote on the blog that she finally accepted the invitation because she was "curious" and she wanted to face this fear head on. She enjoyed the taping that day and it was a big step for her. It gave her a bit of confidence that she can,

"What matters in life is the pursuit, and everything we learn along the way. The important thing is moving."
—Kilian Jornet Burgata, endurance athlete

in fact, be in the spotlight. In February 2012, she walked on stage at the 92nd Street Y in Manhattan, one of the nation's premier cultural institutions, and, with Karen by her side, literally sat in the spotlight and answered questions. It was a big thing for her that night and certainly brand new territory.

Karen

Going back to yoga for me was a big deal. As I wrote on the52weeks.com, the "stillness" for some reason brought on a full-out panic attack. Yes, I had been struggling with panic on-and-off for a long time, but I never expected an attack to rear its ugly head while surrounded by Zen-like music, yoga mats, and a calm instructor.

I remember when I spoke to my therapist about my panic attack. It's quite common actually for panicky feelings to emerge when you are relaxing and finally stop running around like a chicken without a head. This is a thought she offered me while the two of us sat in her office, surrounded by her expensive furniture and paintings. I wondered why I was there, paying for advice, when I could be at lunch with a good friend. Then I remembered that the professional objectivity, the expertise, the tolerance, was really needed. Inevitably, you jump from subject to subject with a good friend. That is what is good about therapy. You can stay on point long after it gets boring.

I guess it made me feel better that I was not alone when it came to panic, but I certainly beat myself up for a long time for "being like that," only making me more prone to having attacks! It wasn't until years later, working with a behavioral therapist, that I accepted I was prone to panic and it's simply the way some people (me!) are built. I now have the tools to better handle my anxiety.

Apprehension about flying, breaking old habits and patterns, and facing middle age all adds up to a lot of work on "self." The blog got me going again and I began to check off hurdles one by one. Some I am still working on, and that's okay. Of course there are also new challenges that emerge every day. Being able to work on one challenge at a time is more manageable for me than flailing about randomly. Otherwise it felt like too much of a mountain and, unless you are an extreme, "ultra" athlete you can get stuck, almost paralyzed.

I read an interesting article by **Carlene Bauer**, *a great journalist who spent time with a 95-year-old writer, Diana Athill, from England. According to Bauer, Athill is "not that well known in the States but is something of a national treasure in England." Bauer sat down with Atlhill to explore the meaning of life, writing, and what it means to accept whom you are, where you are. "It can be quite painful," she shared with Bauer. "But you do, I think, learn yourself. Which, in the end, is worth doing." That's really what we believe our blog, and now our book, are doing for us.*

How you, the reader, face fears and start tackling hurdles in your own personal life is a very individual thing. There is no one answer. We are the last people in the world to ever suggest the topic can be fully addressed in just one chapter. What we are saying is that life goes in cycles and that we are all working to be better versions of ourselves each and every day. Know where you have been so far, where you are now, and figure out where you want to go.

NEXT STEPS

Keep these things in mind when you are trying to tackle your fears.

Get support from friends and family

Reach out for support and encouragement. Facing fears, whether big or small, is more manageable if you have a team and are accountable.

Accept life changes and cycles

"Women, especially, are subject to hormonal changes," said Dr. Gorman. "These changes throughout life can make the body react in ways you can't anticipate and are unfamiliar. They can be challenging and spark unexplained fears. Just because you never felt anxious or scared in your twenties or thirties doesn't mean you won't feel differently in your forties and fifties. Accept where you are and deal with it.

Keep trying

Don't give up. We sometimes took one step forward, then one step back. Go easy on yourself, and celebrate small accomplishments. If you fall off the horse, get back on.

Big deal! So, you need a little help!

We know you have great friends and family to help you through rough patches. However, there is no replacement for an objective expert who can give you useful tools to start overcoming your stuff. Also, there is still a perceived stigma associated with taking medication for anxiety and depression. If you need it, take it. Once you get over the fear of taking medication, you will learn to see it as just an aid. No one cares. Just get over it.

Do one little thing

"My grandmother was a Jewish juggler: she used to worry about six things at once."
—Richard Lewis

If you are afraid of heights, go just one more floor. If you are afraid of elevators, get in with a good friend and take a ride. Avoidance is paralyzing. Just take a small step.

SOME TAKEAWAY ADVICE AND QUOTES TO GET YOU GOING

- ➢ Often the only one judging you is you.
- ➢ Most of us will never have perfect abs or perfect anything. Embrace who you are, not who you fantasize about being.
- ➢ Sometimes you just have to dive in and face your fears head-on.
- ➢ Don't be afraid to be afraid. It's normal.
- ➢ "We should not let our fears hold us back from pursuing our hopes."
  —John F. Kennedy
- ➢ Get out of your comfort zone and you may just discover new passions or positions.
- ➢ Don't forget to breathe.
- ➢ Your reactions are often worse than your fears. Keep 'em in check.
- ➢ "I have learned over the years that when one's mind is made up, this diminishes fear; knowing what must be done does away with fear."
  —Rosa Parks
- ➢ Everyone has something in their "bag of tricks." Do what you have to do to survive and thrive.
- ➢ "Fear gives intelligence even to fools."—Anonymous

IDEAS FOR THE READER

Start your Facing Fears to-do list. Here are just a few from ours. Hopefully they will inspire you to get going. For more ideas see Chapter 11, "Your 52."

- If you fear the spotlight, embrace an opportunity or find an opportunity to be in the limelight.
- If you fear being naked, take a naked yoga class.
- If you always rely on others for support on a plane, train, or automobile, try going it alone.
- Don't avoid places and things. Try again.
- If you get the chance, just walk on stage.
- Quit something for a day, a week, or a month. Just start.
- Expand your comfort zone. Try new things.

Chapter Seven

Giving Back

"I always wondered why somebody didn't do something about that. Then I realized I was somebody."

—Lily Tomlin, comedian

Lessons Hurricane Sandy Taught Me

This is a guest post by Jackie Moffett. She is funny, smart, a former public relations maven, and an amazing writer. Most importantly, she is a wife, mother, daughter, sister, and a great friend. We reached out to Jackie to write after months of following her inspiring journey helping Hurricane Sandy victims. Jackie lives in New York City with her husband, two boys, and her dog.

Yesterday I gave a thousand dollars to a woman who lived in a cave. That was what she told me, in a Russian accent, across a card table set up in a chilly Coney Island elementary school cafeteria: "I live in cave." She meant her home, dark and wet, a home like many others in this Brooklyn seaside town, ravaged by Hurricane

Sandy. The storm had broken through seawalls, barreled through houses and submerged every vehicle. Five feet of water stood on Ocean Parkway, the town's main thoroughfare. Every sublet basement, home to countless poor families with multiple children, was flooded and powerless, as was the supermarket, hospital, and nursing home. Price gouging abounded—ten dollars for milk—and utility trucks sat idle as bureaucrats fought over jurisdiction, while babies slept on cold floors in the chill of November nights, mattresses soaked, damp blankets rendered useless.

This Russian woman, one of many queued up on a winter day to receive a donation from a rich man who also once lost almost everything precious, spoke to me because I was a volunteer for the Cantor Fitzgerald Hurricane Sandy Family Support Program. I handed her a thousand-dollar gift card from my card table stack and tried to look her in the eye, but she would not meet my gaze. After three months volunteering in Sandy's aftermath, I had come to expect this. Often, the people who needed money most were most loath to accept it. Because the storm took so much, they held on to their pride like a life raft and maintained a death-claw clutch on their dignity. The storm took everything, their averted eyes said. Please allow me this. And so I did.

How I got to meet that woman and give away ten million dollars is a good story, a story of great tragedy and a story of recovery. In other words, it's a quintessential New York story. It began with Howard Lutnick. He is a famous New Yorker, a man best known for being the CEO of Cantor Fitzgerald during the 9/11 attacks on the World Trade Center. The company lost 658 employees, among them Howard's brother and best friend. In the wake of 9/11, Howard, his wife, Allison, and his sister, Edie, mobilized to take care of every family member left behind, in every way necessary. Their effort came to be called the Cantor Fitzgerald Relief Fund. And eleven years later, almost as soon Sandy came ashore, the fund was expanded to include New Yorkers and New Jersey-ites affected by the hurricane.

In early November, Allison sent an email asking her girlfriends to meet in the Cantor Fitzgerald conference room, located in midtown Manhattan. I arrived to see fifteen or so other close friends and acquaintances. Usually we met over lunch or drinks and talked about things such as kids, husbands, schools, and basic parenting stuff. But today, the conversation was of floating bodies and raging fires. It was the same day we learned the fate of two missing toddlers in Staten Island. Their mother had been trying to flee during the storm surge and lost her grip on her children's hands as she tried to get them in her car. Their bodies were found in a gully at the end of the road. They were two and four years old.

So there we were. Mothers of more than forty children, collectively. I, myself, had not been in a conference room for eight years, and I felt totally out of my comfort zone. I think the same was true for a lot of us. Around that table sat former power players from finance, law, media, PR, advertising, fashion, and real estate, and although our conference table days were long behind us, this brain trust showed no signs of rust or weakness. We were lionesses, all. In the days to come, we would hold each other and weep witnessing the storm's carnage, but today, we were strong, and the urge to help was palpable. Now we just needed a plan.

Allison ran the meeting with Howard beside her. The mandate, she said, was that Cantor Fitzgerald wanted to give one million dollars to ten hardest-hit communities in New York and New Jersey. Our charge was to figure out which communities should benefit and how to give the money away. Immediately, suggestions flew in from all sides. There were lots of ideas and lots of roadblocks. And so it went, until Howard spoke. "This is what I want," he said. "I want to give money to parents with children who lost a lot. I don't want to be paternalistic and tell them how to spend it. I just want to put the money in their hands and say, 'Here. I hope this helps. And that's it.'" The room was quiet.

It sounded too simple to work. Maybe I had been away from the corporate world too long and didn't remember how plans like this pushed through. I knew that becoming a mother had made me more fearful of things. Moreover, the practical part of me did not believe that such a simple proposition would succeed. I could think of countless reasons why this would fail. And I knew others felt similarly. But what I came to learn is that in a storm, where everything is upended, safe and practical do not fly. And so I let go. I believed that the plan would work. I believed that a small group of my friends could take on the biggest hurricane to date and help people we had never met in towns we had never been to. Because it seems that conviction, mixed with a little bit of New York chutzpah, is as powerful as any storm.

Two days later, I was in Coney Island, Brooklyn, with four friends, Councilman Domenic Recchia and a plan to distribute one thousand-dollar money cards at local elementary schools. Domenic, a big lug of a guy, was our ambassador, and someone who had a kind word of encouragement for every passerby. We walked with him through still-powerless, sand-logged neighborhood streets to a parking lot. The lot had been transformed to an open-air marketplace flanked by FEMA trucks, generators, and Red Cross stations. It was more akin to a Third World displacement camp than to the streets of Brooklyn. Hundreds of people queued for miles, huddled in whatever dry clothes they still had, waiting for a donated blanket or bread. "What they really want is bleach," Domenic told us. "Because of the mold inside their houses." We had seen these houses earlier with their regurgitated candy-colored insulation strewn about front yards, their interiors gutted to skeletal wooden support beams. "You mean people are staying in these homes?" we asked incredulously. And as he bounded off to shake yet another hand, he answered us over his shoulder. "Yeah, they're staying. They have no where else to go."

Coney Island became one of our ten communities. In short order, the roles each of us would assume emerged, and as news of our efforts spread, our volunteer numbers grew. So did we, becoming increasingly adept at managing the process of list gathering and money distribution. We became principal liaisons, translators, greeters, and problem-solvers. We gathered in that conference room again and again, bonding over the shared drive to help, and learning as we went. We learned to wear fingerless gloves to turn pages of names while we stood in the cold. We brought candy for the children forced to wait in long lines, and coffee for their mothers. And we learned not to expect eye contact.

Many of the people who came up to my card table asked to meet the Lutnicks, who worked at every distribution. They wanted to give them carefully chosen thank-you cards, or just shake their hands. One woman came with a Con Ed bill for one thousand dollars, attributable to the space heaters bought to keep her children warm in a house without heat. She cried as she asked to please meet Howard Lutnick, wanting to acknowledge the gift and the giver.

The storm knocked things down and out and made the powerless even more so. It has been heartbreaking to watch and life-affirming to participate. Helping people has made me stronger than ever and solidified bonds with my friends. For all of us, Sandy was personal. The storm didn't hit other people; it hit our people. There were nineteen schools in all, and nearly five months later, we aren't finished giving the money away because of snow delays. I will be happy when we are finished because we will have helped so many but sad not to have the camaraderie and the sense of making a difference. And to those who didn't meet my eye, not to worry: I still have your back.

A Tale of Two Haitis

This is a guest post by Jami Kelmenson. She is happily single, lives in New York City, and is continuously getting "unstuck" doing amazing, interesting things, including going to Haiti on a mission trip with an organization she volunteers with. You can read more from Jami in our "Flying Solo" chapter.

I'd seen the pictures in the newspapers and on television after the 2010 earthquake in Haiti. I've been to Guatemala, remote regions of Mexico, Costa Rica before it was fashionable, and Caribbean resorts that required going through the "real" country before being greeted with champagne at the entrance. But nothing could prepare me for what I saw in Port-au-Prince when I traveled there last year with Community2Community (C2C), a U.S.-based service organization working with teams on the ground in Haiti to rebuild, restore, and reunite a broken country.

Three years after the earthquake, there were still huge piles of rubble sitting on the streets. The roads were broken up, buildings were half standing (some on their way up, some on their way down), and there were spaces between buildings where others used to stand. There was barbed wire or broken glass bottles where roofs used to be, intended to deter looters. There were stands in the street with people selling fans, electronics, and blenders. Who were they selling to, I wondered as our van rolled through what remained of the streets. The air smelled like the inside of a porta potty. But we were outside.

What was I, a single forty-something Manhattanite who enjoys fine dining, Fifth Avenue museums, and Central Park, doing in Haiti? I asked myself that several times during the week I was there. Especially when I needed a bathroom. But there was no way I could have understood the answer then. When I travel, I find that much of the experience actually occurs after the journey—in the days, months, and years that follow. Often, my remembrances are more spectacular than the actual experience, and the good usually outweighs the bad. In this case, the bad still lingers for me just as much as the good.

What I saw in Haiti was worse than I'd imagined. And also better. That is both the sadness and frustration of this unique island country that shares a spit of land with the Dominican Republic. What is seen in the news is hard to internalize unless you see for yourself the squalid conditions people are still living in years later. Yet the unspoiled beauty of Haiti, rivaling that of any other Caribbean island, is rarely spoken of.

One of the projects C2C is working on is helping to foster economic development so that the country can sustain itself long after the non-governmental organizations and American Red Cross have taken down their tents. The beautiful coastal village of Aux Cayes is home to a wild shrub called vetiver, whose roots form the basis for 95 percent of the perfume made in the world. That's right—from Yves Saint Laurent to J.

Lo, the source is pretty much the same and found in Haiti. It takes savvy farmers, some of whom we met with, to seize the opportunity to harvest the vetiver en masse and send it to Port-au-Prince, where it is shipped to many countries, including the United States, to create our favorite fragrances.

While the team was busy capturing footage of how the vetiver is farmed, a few of us kept the local children busy with our smartphones. They were completely mesmerized by what the gadget could do—one picture moving to the next with a flick of their finger, to the action games they could play, to seeing themselves on the screen. Everything we had in our packs seemed to fascinate them, including water bottles that they played like instruments, and sunscreen, as each held out a palm to sample the mysterious white lotion.

The night we spent atop a mountain, Piton Vallue, which looked like something out of Lord of the Rings, *was a memorable experience. The "mountain people" who live there work hard. Much to our astonishment, they cooked us a feast of fried chicken, fried fish, fried plantains, fried dumplings called "marinade" (pronounced mahr-i-nahd), which is the Haitian version of zeppoles, du riz colez (rice with beans), and pik liz (spicy pickled cole slaw). It was a "fried" feast that would be unthinkable for me at home, but made with loving hands that looked like they were part of a knitting club, working together to scrub clean the chicken and fish and prepare the marinade filling. I pitched in to help beat the batter—comprised of flour, water, baking soda, garlic, scallions, and other magic spices that tasted something like souped-up Alfredo sauce—to make sure there were no lumps. They put their hearts in to this meal. And we put our hearts into enjoying it.*

We didn't actually eat until one a.m.! We had a little dance party to attend beforehand. Under the school tent, with a band leader who officiated the evening (the band was comprised of self-taught musicians using handmade percussion instruments as well as a guitar C2C brought them), we danced under the incredible galaxy of stars to "compa" mixed with traditional folk music, moving rhythmically from side-to-side along with the steady beat. I had a lesson or four from the local boys, all of whom can move like Ricky Martin. If I veered off beat, which, let's just say, happened more than once, they knew how to get me back. Like a dance instructor at Broadway Dance, except they were four feet tall.

We ended our visit to Piton Vallue by christening three kites C2C had brought as gift for the kids. Silly me, I thought we'd be showing them how to assemble and fly them, and I had no idea how to do this. Kite flying just wasn't that big in my hometown of Brooklyn. Like with so many other things, they were way ahead of me. They already knew how to fly.

Now, some time later and back in the hubbub of my studio apartment in NYC, I haven't forgotten what I saw in Port-au-Prince. Or Aux Cayes. Or Piton Vallue. I no longer freak out whenever my hair dryer breaks, because having water, electricity and light do not come free in this world, even though it often feels that way. And I still hold the faces of the men, women and children of Haiti somewhere close to my heart, despite their hardships, to access when I need a reminder of how lovely life is, how inherently gentle souls are, and how fortunate we all are to be part of this great community called humanity.

The Power and Pleasure of Giving Back

Pam

In the aftermath of Hurricane Sandy, my daughters and some of their friends have been looking for ways to help in any way they can. Our family was one of the fortunate ones spared any real damage other than day-to-day inconveniences—rather humbling when I see the devastation all around me. So I was happy to have all of their kids over last week, because I was lucky that I could.

Two days after the storm, they went through our closets and found coats and blankets that we could spare, shopped for any relief effort supplies that were still on the shelves, and debated whether to use our car with the little gas we had left to deliver the items to the drop off centers all around the city.

The storm covered a lot of ground. We at least tried to cover a little. A quick stop to drop off blankets and cleaning supplies for the Rockaways on the East Side. No coats needed. Then on to the West Side to work at a drop-off center at Riverside Church for those affected in Staten Island. The coats were needed there. My daughters and their friends "worked liked dogs," as my mom would say. By the end of the day, they had hauled bags of donated goods; taped up tattered boxes; sorted, packed, organized, and lifted cartons . . . and stayed outside in the cold November wind for many hours improperly dressed, because we hadn't planned on staying at this one place so long. Considering we were able to go home to our heated apartment, it was not such a big sacrifice. They even went on a "search and rescue" for boxes. Supplies are great but only if you can pack them up, and the church had run out of packing supplies. Since garbage day is everyday somewhere in NYC, the girls were able to find boxes on the street waiting to be thrown out and picked up by the sanitation department. It was a real lesson in humanity and humility for these girls to dig through garbage for others. But they did it with enthusiasm.

Later that evening, my younger daughter snuggled in close to me—it had been the first time in a few days we were back to being "nice" to one another. A long week of nervous energy, close quarters, and that heightened sense of vulnerability I remember feeling after 9/11 had been swirling. Tension and bickering were running high with everyone home from work and school. She leaned in and said to me rather tentatively, "I had fun today. It was a good day. Wasn't it?" And I knew exactly why she was so unsure about saying that, but also why she said it . . .was she allowed to have fun doing what she was doing when people were in dire need? I assured her that yes, it was a good day.

Last Tuesday, Election Day, they were back at it again. A gas line snaked 12 blocks down First Avenue and passed in front of my building. It comes and goes daily as limited gas deliveries arrive and quickly gets swallowed up. The school next door was a polling site, and knowing there would be lots of voters coming by and beleaguered passengers waiting on the gas lines all day, my city-savvy daughters set up a bake sale with their friends in front of our building and donated their proceeds to the Red Cross. They stayed outside into the evening and wouldn't leave their post until the last bag of cookies was sold. Another cold night! I was more than ready to go inside but they refused.

That night I got an email from one of the moms whose daughter helped. "Thanks for including us in the bake sale. I don't think Amanda realized how much she would enjoy something like that! It was a great idea! She didn't want to leave. She had a really good time with the girls." It was such a simple, wonderful message.

For whatever reason, volunteering, giving back, repairing, made my daughter and her friend feel good. Whether it was the camaraderie, the adventure, some laughs, enjoying the air, they had fun and they felt good—they were busy, they helped, they experienced, they were with friends and family.

They asked if they could do more. This weekend, they are heading out to clean up areas with the help of our local councilwoman's office.

Saturday in the Park

Pam

Karen and I have been progressing through our 52 for sixteen weeks now and while we've both had some similar experiences and outcomes, we've mostly been on our own. She does her thing and I do mine—until now. It's one thing to be there for a friend embarking on a journey in spirit but it's another to actually be there with that person. So this week, we ventured out as a team and tried something together. Whether or not we would have the same experience was yet to be determined.

And what better thing to do with your girlfriend than plan a day of beautifying together? However, this day of beauty wasn't about us, it was about our local park.

As a city woman raising two kids in the concrete jungle, Carl Schurz Park is my "backyard." Unlike the grandeur of famous Central Park, this park is truly a neighborhood destination and a bit more intimate. Situated along the East River *on the Upper East Side of Manhattan, the park has dog runs, playgrounds, and areas for all ages; a promenade, park benches, and chess tables; and lots of local happenings from outdoor movie nights to the annual Halloween Howl where dog lovers parade their beloved pooches in costumes.*

Since we've both put "volunteering more" on our 52 this was the perfect meeting of the minds, and what better way than to give back locally to a place that we love and that needs assistance to keep it going strong? The Carl Schurz Park Association is an incredible volunteer organization. So we signed up to help it do some gardening. And we worked! No pretty planting or pruning or even weeding. Nope—we mulched, we raked, and we turned soil. We shoveled compost and carted wood chips in wheelbarrows. Dirty, repetitive, sweaty hard work—and it felt great! Along the way, Karen took too many photos and I chatted up too many people and complained that my boots were getting ruined. Daughter number two, who came along for the day, held steady, was a busy beaver, and performed like a trooper. Of course, we met the usual characters that make New York City the quirky, wonderful place it is. But we also were fortunate to meet some unbelievably committed people who give so much of their time and energy to this wonderful cause and keep the park going. Inspiring and interesting folks—just to meet people like that is exhilaration for me in and of itself.

Working alongside my friend, my daughter, and the fellow volunteers in this small local way was a good thing. Was this the most earth-shattering, altruistic endeavor I could have embraced? Of course not—but a few laughs, a sore arm the next day, dirty boots, and knowing I did something to help not just my little backyard but the backyard of my neighbors, was a day well spent.

• • • •

Giving back and volunteering more was always on our 52 list. Once we went to a local park in our neighborhood and helped plant and clean up. Pam even brought her daughter along (usually a big 52 no-no!) to further demonstrate the benefits of giving back as she always tries to do. We had a great day together. Karen donated her time making calls on behalf of a family whose daughter had been tragically missing for days. Pam went to her monthly Saturday program

"When I forced myself to just be in the moment and really looked around at the volunteers, I remembered how cool it was to be a part of something bigger than my own stuff."
—Karen

where she makes sandwiches and packages meals for a local food pantry. We wrote letters and sent holiday gifts to children in need as part of the U.S. Postal Service's Operation Santa program, and we connected with the Parkinson's Foundation because both of us had family members affected by this debilitating illness.

Then, somewhere about week 26, we realized that it was not necessarily about committing long-term to a cause, spending a full day, or even a few hours giving back. You can give back each and every day in small ways. Pick up groceries for an elderly neighbor (1 hour), bring soup to a neighbor who is home with the flu (15 minutes), or send flowers to the children's ward at a hospital (10 minute phone call). That's when we finally understood it's just like everything else: start small and bigger things can happen. Begin with a little gesture and you may just identify a place that you want to dedicate more of your time giving back. Find a cause you connect with. Give back each day.

"No act of kindness, however small, is ever wasted."
—Aesop

As we set out to dig deeper and find what motivates people to give back and the obvious and not-so-obvious benefits, we wanted to understand what drives women to help beyond simply that it is *the right thing to do* or out of a sense of obligation. If you're like most women, you understand that you *should* give back but what we came away with was that while giving back is meant to help others, it unexpectedly helps you get unstuck too!

The women we talked to have their own stories. In some cases, giving back is simply built into their DNA, or they accidentally stumbled onto something that became a passion and made them feel better. In others, their drive was inspired by a loss or personal story. What do they all have in common? Their stories, their dedication, their contributions are all inspiring and will make you take pause, think about how you are spending your time and, hopefully, in the end, motivate you to make a move simply to give back. We promise you will feel better too.

Dress for Success Worldwide is an internationally recognized nonprofit organization that helps disadvantaged women enter the workplace. It began in 1996, providing women with professional attire for job interviews. We spoke with **Joi Gordon**, who joined the company in 1999 and now, as CEO, is credited with rebranding the organization. Thanks to Gordon, the group now offers networking and support services, career development tools to help their members thrive, and other great services. The organization is now making a difference to women in 124 US cities and 13 countries.

"I think people volunteer because they want to leave the world a better place than they found it," Gordon said. "Often, women want to fill a void in their lives and find a true purpose. Maybe their job, or family, or other things they're engaged in aren't filling that void, and they discover that volunteering can. At the same time, they are giving back and making a difference."

"The best way to find yourself is to lose yourself in the service of others."
—Mahatma Gandhi

Gordon says that almost every volunteer she's met through Dress for Success started by simply donating an interview suit for someone. Soon, they found a way

"Unless someone like you cares a whole awful lot, nothing is going to get better. It's not."
—Dr. Seuss

to do more. Some of their volunteers work directly with clients to provide support and counseling. Others sort clothing; some serve as speakers at professional women's group meetings, offering valuable expertise for women trying to get back out there. Gordon talked enthusiastically about the volunteers at Dress for Success, especially because many started helping with just a small gesture and now volunteer everywhere. "Marketing, human resources, and even as personal shoppers," she explained.

Another advantage to volunteering, Gordon said, is somewhat less outwardly driven but important for personal growth. "For people who are in between jobs or some other life transition," she said, "volunteerism can lead to the next phase of their lives. I've seen it time and again in fourteen years at Dress for Success; women who came to us to volunteer were able to discover their true talent. Whether they moved on to a job with us, or in the same capacity with another organization, it helped to create an opportunity for them that they might not ever have considered." This can be especially true for women in traditional jobs that required a lot of training but not always a sense of reward. Finding that reward in the form of developing your true or hidden talents can have huge payoffs, personally, as well as for the community, or even the world.

Several recent studies reinforce Gordon's point of view. Not only can volunteering be good for others, but the benefits can go much deeper, both physically and emotionally. According to researchers at the State University of New York at Stony Brook, volunteering helps to stimulate chemicals in the brain that can make you physically feel better and lower stress—even live longer. Researchers from the University of Pennsylvania, Harvard Business School, and the Yale School of Management back up this idea with their own studies which found that when we volunteer our time, it makes us feel more efficient, and less stressed and hurried.[3] That sounded a bit counter-intuitive to us, but wouldn't it be great if sometimes getting away from your to-do list was the best way to get things done?

Even if you're just testing the waters, you can discover your passion by volunteering at a variety of organizations, or joining a board of directors to understand the inner workings of an organization and where you may fit in. This is what happened with Joi Gordon. She was a broadcast journalism major because she wanted to "be on the frontline speaking on behalf of people who didn't have a voice." Following her broadcast career, she went to law school to be, as she said "a champion of social justice. Helping women overcome obstacles, face their fears, and see success however they define it is true justice for me." After law school, she heard the founder of Dress for Success, Nancy Lubin, talking on the radio. Gordon decided to donate a suit. Shortly thereafter she joined the Board of Directors, which led her to her current position as CEO. She loves being the voice of women who may be invisible to many people. "I've been able to utilize the skills that I got through my education to be exactly where I am supposed to be in my life. This wasn't accidental."

Many women may have the urge to give back beyond their immediate worlds. However, many have kids, aging parents, pressure-filled jobs, and other responsibilities that hold them back from donating their time to a cause. As we said in the beginning of the chapter, you can give back for ten minutes, ten hours, or ten days.

---

[3]   Post, Stephen G. "It's Good to Be Good: Science Says It's So," *Health Progress*, July-August 2009.

"The importance of happiness for women is too understated in our society," said Gordon. "I'm a big believer that when we're happy, our children are happier, our husbands are happier. Women should do the things we want to do *and* the things we know we should do."

What's more, she continues, "When I volunteer outside of Dress for Success, I bring my kids along with me. That's quality time, right? It's much better than going to a movie with them. If you're busy raising a family and working, try to fit it in. When you're doing stuff with your kids, not only is it meaningful, but it teaches them something."

"It's funny. I remember having that exact sentiment when I was writing about Hurricane Sandy on the blog. The experience my daughter and her friend had reconfirmed that volunteering and giving back can make you feel better. My daughter couldn't wait to do more. Being a part of a community, keeping busy, and helping others in need also helps you." —Pam

For **Marie-Yolaine Eusebe**, founder of C2C, her company's mission is deeply personal. Eusebe was born in Port-au-Prince, Haiti. She came to the United States with her family when she was five. She knows there's a community of dedicated people in this country who believe in the promise of a self-sufficient Haiti. "I want the world to see the people of Haiti as I see them. A group that's been hit hard but who are resilient. People who want a hand up, not a handout."

Eusebe believes people volunteer in order to *be a part of something greater than themselves*. In the spring of 2009, Eusebe was working in the marketing department of American Express in New York when she had a strong feeling that she was destined for something else. But what? She knew it was time to move forward and thought about leaving the security of her corporate job to explore her options. When the January 2010 earthquake hit in Haiti, it was no longer a feeling. It was a future.

C2C is "like fire in my bones," said Eusebe. "It's pretty much all I think about right now. It lights me up." And judging from the passion of her volunteer staff, it lights many others up, too.

Although we couldn't know how wonderful it must feel to start an organization like C2C, we understood how even the little acts of kindness or giving back in small ways made us feel during our 52 Weeks and to this day. It just makes you feel better.

"Like me," Eusebe explained, "people feel a need to get involved. Collectively, we are building something we can all look back on after completion and say, 'I helped make that happen. I was part of a project that built a reservoir that provided clean water to sixteen-thousand people, and the reservoir is still there today.'"

"My dad wanted my brothers (who were born in the United States), and me to have better opportunities than he did. When we'd say we wanted to be like him, he'd respond, 'I want you to be better. I want you to do more. And I want your children to do more than you.' Thus, at a very early age, the roots of C2C were born."

It's great to see amazing women like Joi Gordon and Marie-Yolaine Eusebe heed their calling and make a difference in the world. But what if you want to do more than volunteer, but, like us, aren't ready to start or run your own organization? You always could run a few marathons. Or 52 of them. **Julie Weiss**, a forty-two-year-old mom from Los Angeles ran 52 marathons in 52 weeks to raise awareness and funds to help cure pancreatic cancer, which took the life of her father. How's that for a 52 list?

For this "marathon goddess," running with a purpose gave her a reason to live more deeply and find a greater purpose and meaning in her own life.

"I realized my dad was passing the baton on to me, and I had a new purpose: to help find a cure and spread awareness for this severely underfunded and devastating disease, the disease that took my father, my number one fan," Weiss said.

While it started out as a means to help others, Weiss is taking her inspiration to an even greater level. "My long-term goal is to continue to tell my story with the hope that it can activate other women to seek their bliss. It's my turn, and, now that I know it, I will find all the ways I can to put that dream into a reality."

Her advice to other women seeking their bliss? "Don't ever accept your limitations as if they were in concrete. If you let your past define your future, you will keep making the same mistakes. I know now that there are always more options than you think there are, if you just don't close doors that you are afraid to pass through."

We couldn't have said it better ourselves.

NEXT STEPS

No one can tell you how or how much you should give, if at all. It's a personal choice. But if you've ever had the inkling to be part of something greater than yourself, volunteering can be a great way to feel good while you make others feel good.

Start close to home

You don't have to make a big, grandiose statement. Opportunities to give back are probably all around you in the normal course of your day. Does your town have a library? A park? A hospital? An ASPCA? A church or synagogue? Stop in and ask them if they could use your help for an afternoon. A little research can uncover more opportunities to help with soup kitchens, at counseling services, and national non-profit organizations like Dress for Success that always need assistance. If you want to find a volunteer opportunity, search the web and see what turns up in your neighborhood. Or try Meetup.com to find out what volunteer groups have been formed. You may be surprised at how many people are finding ways to combine unique interests with organized opportunities to volunteer. Or better yet, start your own community group to address something you are concerned or passionate about.

Train for a cause

Run, walk, or bike for a cause. For example, C2C holds an annual "Run for Haiti" in conjunction with the ING NYC Marathon. And don't worry, you don't have to run 52 marathons in 52 weeks like Julie Weiss did! When Pam participated in a New Year's Day Polar Bear Plunge it was to raise money for a local food pantry and she only had to "swim" for a few minutes! Just plan in advance, and make sure you're up to the physical demands required. Invite friends or family members to join you and make it a fun event.

Think globally

If you love to travel or have a sense of adventure, why not combine these passions with a sense of giving back? Like our guest wrtier and book contributor Jami Kelmenson, there are many organizations that offer volunteer vacations that let you discover a place like Peru or Nepal while teaching children English or helping with construction projects, or you can still volunteer on a global scale without leaving home by sponsoring a child in need. Jami sponsors a nine-year-old named Ana who lives abroad by sending monthly contributions for the clothing and supplies she needs.

SOME TAKEAWAY ADVICE AND QUOTES TO GET YOU GOING

➢ Make an effort to help in one small way every day.

➢ Even small things can make a difference.

➢ "To know even one life has breathed easier because you have lived. This is to have succeeded."—Ralph Waldo Emerson.

➢ You always have more time than you think you do.

➢ "Only a life lived for others is a life worthwhile."—Albert Einstein

➢ A seemingly small gesture can lead to big things.

➢ "Service to others is the rent you pay for your room here on earth."—Muhammad Ali

➢ "If you wait until you can do everything for everybody, instead of something for somebody, you'll end up not doing nothing for nobody."—Malcom Bane

➢ "You can have everything in life you want, if you will just help other people get what they want."—Zig Ziglar

➢ "From what we get, we can make a living; what we give, however, makes a life."—Arthur Ashe

➢ "No one has ever become poor by giving."—Anne Frank

➢ "The greatest good you can do for another is not just share your riches, but reveal to them their own."—Disraeli

IDEAS FOR THE READER

Here are some ways we gave back, along with some ideas from our readers and guest writers. For a list of other ideas see Chapter 11, "Your 52."

- Donated goods to hurricane victims.
- Distributed relief funds to those in need.
- Cleaned out a flooded home with its owner.
- Volunteered at a local shelter.
- Took the kids along. It's never to early to learn about the value of giving back.
- Cleaned up a neighborhood park.
- Donated food and packed bag lunches for the homeless and homebound.
- Made a financial contribution to a favorite charity.
- Offered professional skills to a nonprofit organization.
- Participated in a Polar Plunge event to benefit Special Olympics.
- Took a mission trip to support redevelopment efforts in Haiti.
- Donated shoes to a child in Guatemala.
- Made soup for a sick friend.
- Distributed water to marathon runners.

- Collected clothing for homeless teenagers.
- Helped an elderly relative shop for groceries.
- Sent books to a school library in need.

Chapter Eight

Reflection

"If you get the inside right, the rest will fall into place."

—Eckhart Tolle

Finding My Religion

Karey

Last week my father-in-law died very suddenly. One minute we were lighting the Chanukah candles on the East Coast and the next minute we received a horrible call and learned the sketchy details of his passing at his home on the West Coast. My husband was inexpressibly close to his father—that rare closeness, the foundation for everything that makes my husband who he is today. Remaining steady for him and my daughter is truly testing my strength as a wife and mother. I lost my own father in 2002 while still reeling with post-partum hormones. You can't understand the emotions of losing a loved one unless you have gone through it before. I still miss my dad terribly. I loved my father-in-law from the minute I met him over twenty years ago. But a foreign feeling overcame me with my father-in-law's passing; I felt the absence of a spiritual and religious person who could help us through the difficult time. It was a strange awakening.

I have to share a little background so that anyone reading this can comprehend why this was unusual for me. I am Jewish. I guess I would say I am culturally Jewish and had what I thought was a "Reform" Jewish upbringing. However, I have never felt a true religious connection to Judaism. I could blame it on many things, but I won't. The fact is I was just never inspired to delve into it. My daughter does go to Hebrew school (perhaps somewhere deep down I want her to have the connection I never had). I have been dropping her there, twice a week, for three years. I take full blame when I say that I never made any real effort to know the rabbi at our temple. And finally, yes, I love the holidays—both the serious and the festive celebrations. However, my inspiration on these special days is more about being with family and eating. Let's see . . . to lighten my mood right now a few facts: bagels and Chinese food on Sundays of course; I cook a great kugel, sure. Worry a lot? No question. But that's it. Until now. Now my father-in-law has died, and I don't have a rabbi to call. Not good.

I thought about why I didn't feel this way when my own father passed. Was it because I was still adjusting to motherhood and had other, new worries? Was it because I am now in my forties and more aware of the passing of time and mortality? Or is it simply because there finally comes a time when everyone seeks more of a spiritual and religious connection? Am I just late arriving for the services?

My brother-in-law and sister-in-law happen to have an amazing relationship with their rabbi, even though they are not very religious. He is a member of the Chabad, a Hasidic Lubavitch missionary movement, and they were drawn to this wonderful man years ago and have developed a deep, meaningful relationship with him. He performed the funeral service for my father-in-law and I was grateful he was around.

A few days after the funeral, I called my temple and asked to speak with the rabbi. We spoke for a long time, and he answered some of my questions, and was open and sincere about getting to know our family. He told us that this Friday they will say a prayer for my father-in-law at services: we plan on going. I even started researching the Chabad movement to see if that was the way to go, or maybe the Chabad rabbi was just the catalyst to get me off my agnostic butt. I am not sure. All I know is that this week, during this really tough time, I felt the need to connect to a comforting spiritual and religious voice. I felt the need to explore my religion like I never did before, and I vowed to make it a part of my life going forward. Religion wasn't on my original 52 list, but now it is. Finding my religion for the first time is going to take more than one week, but I felt less stuck. I don't think I knew how stuck I really was.

I miss you Abe and always will.

Moving On and a Visit to Ground Zero

Pam

I am in the process of moving. While my family is excited about this next chapter and the new possibilities that await us, we are going tentatively, with many, many mixed emotions.

I have been thinking about how many memories are attached to our apartment. This is where I was living on 9/11. Most of us remember exactly where we were and what we were doing at that moment of terror and destruction—and I was in my apartment—this apartment—that I am now getting ready to leave after twenty years. I was a new mom nursing my two-week-old daughter with her eighteen-month-old sister tugging at me—counting the minutes until my husband returned home from voting that morning (it was primary day in New York City).

How do you neatly pack up and put parts of you away for good? How do you put closure on a big chapter of life but not forget about the past? You don't. You ultimately unpack them again in a different place or in a different way. But you learn to rearrange them, place them differently, and fit them into your future in a way that will allow you to move forward.

Visiting the site of the former World Trade Center was something I've thought about doing for the past ten years, but for some reason never did. I had lived it in real time. I had watched from my balcony window as the billowing smoke rose to the sky for days and smelled the acrid air even way uptown. I didn't need to see the aftermath to make it real for me.

The last time I visited the Twin Towers, I was a second grade teacher taking my class on a school field trip. It was an exciting day, filled with new experiences. Many of my students rarely left their insular inner-city neighborhood, so this trip was a very big deal. We rode the subway downtown, took the elevator to the top with our ears popping all the way, and marveled at the majesty of the view. I've often thought about how, thankfully, there were no kids on a class trip that day on the 107th floor where my class had been just months before. I've thought about how my colleagues were at school comforting all the kids on the day of the attack while I was home on maternity leave. I've thought about all of these "what if's" that so many of us have.

Today, my husband works across the street from the site of Ground Zero. Thankfully, he was not yet working for this company on 9/11. He now has a front-row view to the daily progress of the work going on there and the transformation that has taken place during the past ten years. I've driven by the construction site when I've given him a ride to his office on rare occasions, but I've never visited the area known as "the pit," on foot. First, busy with my newborn and toddler, then back to work, and the days became weeks and months, then years . . .

The recent killing of Osama bin Laden combined with the impending ten-year anniversary of 9/11 brought up a flood of mixed emotions. I had no desire to go dancing in the streets when bin Laden died, as some people did. Soon after, though, with the upcoming opening of the 9/11 memorial, President Obama's visit to the site, my daughter's tenth birthday approaching, and our upcoming move, I knew it was time to check a visit to Ground Zero off my list.

I got up very early and headed downtown alone. I arrived before the horde of commuters swarmed into the narrow streets. The groggy construction workers were just starting their day, still working on their first cups of coffee. I was there before most of the tourists arrived.

Two things immediately struck me: the massive size of the "footprint" (the space where the towers were) and the fact that, all around me, life went on. The area is, after all, still a busy, thriving business center in the heart of New York City. Amidst the K-9 dogs, the cement trucks, the newspaper vendors, the visitors, and the security details, there were people just trying to get to work, rushing, pushing, and knowing that they had to move forward.

I will say that, as a New Yorker, I am used to crowds around me all the time, but as morning commuters began to spill out of a Path train exit, I started to think about all those people rushing away from the destruction on that unforgettable day. That didn't hit me until I went to visit. The enormity of it is also hard to imagine until you are actually standing outside the "pit." The site is massive. It was sobering to think of. But soon, the vibrancy comes back; it was a sunny morning on the day I visited, and there was life at the site, a real positive energy.

There is not as much to see as there is to feel, but there is now a beautiful tower rising above the rubble and ruin. The memorial pools are visible too. An American flag hangs proudly on a crane stating "We Will Rebuild"—sadly with barbed wire all around it. Lots of noise (it is not a quiet memorial), trucks, piles of building materials, and a few remaining makeshift memorials. But visually that's it. Yet I couldn't bring myself to leave. I walked to the 9/11 Memorial Preview site, a small exhibit located half a block from where the World Trade Center used to be. It was a simple yet truly profound experience to visit that exhibit. There really are no words.

Memories and emotions are triggered in strange ways. As I start to pack up for my move, I am reminded that beginnings and endings come in all sizes. We have to move on no matter how hard it can be to get going sometimes. Whether you are mourning a simple personal change or a massive world-changing tragedy, the important thing is to move forward, keep going, be hopeful, and stay strong.

A Walk in the Woods

Pam

There is a nature preserve and a trail beyond the backyard and past the deer fence of my weekend getaway house. I look out the kitchen window every time I visit and often see people in the distance hiking through the trail. I wonder why I have not, in the six years since I've owned this home, taken a walk on this trail. It just seems ridiculous that I am always doing something else—emptying the dishwasher, cleaning out the garage, raking the leaves, running errands with the kids, and making excuses. I wonder why I've never explored what is, literally, right in my own backyard.

There is also a calendar, hanging on the bulletin board in the same kitchen, filled with dates and appointments. Next to my bag on the kitchen counter is my 52 list filled with to-dos. "Get in touch with nature and take a walk in the woods" or "go for a hike" is not on the list. I'm not sure why. I decide now is the time to put it on that calendar.

I finished up what I had to do and asked the kids to come along. They said no, of course, but my husband joined me. I put on my boots, left my cell phone behind, grabbed a camera, and took a walk in the woods.

The walk was invigorating. I carefully followed the trailheads, looked at some of the unfamiliar, interesting trees and plants and listened to the sounds of nature. It was a gorgeous, crisp, chilly day and perfect for quiet reflection, a chance to share some time with my husband, and an opportunity to reap the physical benefits of some good, old-fashioned exercise.

The trail was deep enough into the woods to get away from it all for a bit but close enough to my house that I didn't feel like I had to hike far off on some remote trek. I knew if I tried really hard, I could faintly hear civilization from beyond or, if I squinted, I might even see the outline of my house way off in the distance, but I closed my mind to those thoughts.

I'm pretty sure if it weren't for our 52 Week project, I wouldn't have taken the hike when I did. Maybe someday I would have, but not now. Something mundane or routine would have gotten in the way. Putting a date on the calendar and committing did the trick. The best thing that came from this? I've since walked it three more times. What was I waiting for?

One of our guest writers, Jami, recently wrote about her adventures and getting unstuck as a single woman. She went to exotic lands that are far from my reach right now. My local hike took me just miles away without getting on a plane or even in a car. You do what you can to get unstuck.

Ahh . . . Kabbalah

Karev

I recently took my first Kabbalah class. It is something I have been meaning to do for a very long time. I have been seeking something more, in the spiritual sense, for too long. It has been on my 52 list since the beginning.

The strangest thing brought me to spiritual counselor Eitan Yardeni's Kabbalah class. How I arrived there was proof (even to me) that the universe works in mysterious ways. Let's just say it was strange because one seemingly random business introduction led to another person, which led to Kabbalah and Eitan. I contacted Eitan on the phone. We talked, and he invited me to an introductory class at the Kabbalah Center in New York City.

When I entered the lobby, it was filled with people of all ages, stages, religions, and races, all mingling. There was a great gift shop to my right filled with books and the ubiquitous red bracelets. I was tempted to shop but I certainly hadn't earned that bracelet just yet. I was directed to the third floor. Surprisingly, about seventy-five people were already seated facing a screen and podium. We all waited for Eitan.

He started with the history of Kabbalah and what this class was all about. He used examples to demonstrate how "blocked" we can be—that we experience life using only 1 percent of what we are capable of, the other 99 percent not tapped at all as we navigate through each day. He asked us to share stories. Most of all, he made me think.

Perhaps the most shocking demonstration was when Eitan distributed a piece of paper with just a few sentences on it. He gave us time to count the number of F's on the page and then turn the page over in our laps. Being a PR consultant and writer, I constantly proofread documents for work. I counted three F's. He then asked the entire class: "Okay, everyone who counted three F's, raise your hand." I raised my hand confidently and so did a handful of others. He then continued, "Everyone who counted four F's raise your hand." A larger percentage of the class raised their hands. I started to get worried and embarrassed! He continued up to six, which was the correct number. I was amazed. How did I not count the correct number in a simple, three-sentence handout? He went on to explain what it all meant which was something to the effect that if you didn't count six F's you were blocked and you didn't see what was always right in front of you. I was sold.

This past year I took some baby steps toward bringing more religion and spirituality to my life, especially after my father-in-law passed away. I need to slow down, breathe more, be present, and all that stuff. I was fighting it constantly, though. I was trying to get by with the wrong tools, the wrong habits, and in some cases, the wrong support.

The word Kabbalah means many different things to many different people. In a nutshell, it is an ancient wisdom that reveals how the universe and life work. It offers different way of looking at the world that can connect you to the kind of permanent fulfillment you may be seeking.

I loved the class. I loved how it started me on the road to react differently to everyday events, people, challenges, and opportunities. I am not sure how it will fit into the bigger picture for me but it was definitely a new experience and I hope somehow it becomes part of my routine as I enter a new year. Now, if I can go to a yoga class and a Kabbalah class in the same week, I just may start to slow down and get some answers. Or, as Woody Allen once said, maybe seeking the meaning of life is all a bit too much when you can't even find your way around town sometimes.

Remembering to Laugh

Karen

I don't feel like writing today. I am mourning the loss of a childhood friend who died after battling breast cancer for a year and a half. I found out on Friday and the funeral was Sunday. I just had lunch with her a few weeks ago when she ventured into the city with her two amazing boys, aged 11 and 15. I am mad. I am angry. I am so sad. Life is so unfair.

A week or so before her unexpected passing, I was in one of my moods, which of course, in retrospect makes me incredibly mad at myself now that I am reminded, once again, about what's important and what's not. Procrastinating about something, I decided to get a quick manicure. I went into a "new" neighborhood place and regretted it within five minutes. The woman doing my nails was irritatingly slow and incompetent. My mood worsened. Just as I was about to start crying, a big, burly guy walked in, and the entire place lit up with his energy. He had come in for a pedicure and a manicure and was amused to see there was another guy in a chair getting his nails done. "I can't believe there is another guy here today," he exclaimed in a big voice. He was larger than life and just happy. Despite my mood, I couldn't help smiling—he was just funny. I was still getting my manicure when he finished his pedicure (yes, that's how slow my person was) and he plopped down next to me and said, "Well . . . you've been here a while! Do you know you have nice hair? He really is crazy, I thought to myself. "What about me? Do I have nice hair?" he asked. I didn't know where he was going as he had almost no hair, so I said, "Not really, but you are funny." For the record, this was not a flirtatious exchange; it just happened innocently and naturally. "I am a stand-up comic," he said. "No way!" He made me laugh throughout our whole conversation. His name is Michael, and he told me he appears at the Comic Strip in New York City. I vowed to go see him in the coming weeks. My mood lifted and I, once again, was reminded of the power of humor and laughter. And then I remembered that one of the things on my 52 was to laugh more. Sounds simple but it was on my list. I never go to comedy shows anymore. Years ago I had loved comedy shows, but since then I had almost forgotten they existed.

Later I had my chance to laugh some more.

I had gotten tickets months ago with a friend for an event at the 92nd Street Y. There are certain friends with whom you do certain things: Helene and I go to lectures and events at the 92nd Y as a way to see each other. It turns out this time, we would see Whoopi Goldberg interviewed by Judy Gold, a comedian. From the minute I sat down, I didn't stop laughing. Whoopi was honest, real, and naturally funny as she candidly shared stories about her kids, fears, and life. She talked about her fear of flying (which I could relate to) and how she was so terrified that one time she took an anesthesiologist with her on a plane to literally knock her out until she landed (I fantasized about having a private jet and an anesthesiologist myself). The hour and a half went quickly and I successfully forgot about everything.

I read Gretchen Rubin's The Happiness Project blog a lot. She often writes about laughing (even at yourself) to successfully increase your happiness level. She's definitely right.

As I am trying to get through this week after my friend's funeral, I've been thinking about trying to appreciate each day and finding more opportunities to laugh. Why is laughing important? Why do we forget to laugh even when we are not dealing with sad or life-changing stuff?

During Stacy's illnss she was on Facebook a lot. She showed incredible bravery and candor throughout her battle against cancer. My weekly articles for the 52 Weeks are posted to Facebook and I often felt weird posting my weekly challenges, of trying to get out of my rut by going to yoga or trying to stop eating cheese, when I knew there were many people out there, especially her at that time, dealing with terrible challenges. Stacy commented on only one post I wrote, "Seven Days of Smiles" (see "Relationships," Chapter 5). Basically the post was about an one week experiment in which I intentionally tried to act the opposite of how I usually did, especially to my immediate family. I was a little nicer, more "in the moment." According to some studies you will feel the way you behave. Stacy "liked" the post. She commented how important it is to be nice, laugh, and smile, especially around the people you love. She got it. She knew. The thing about Stacy was that she knew this way before she got sick. She just got it.

The key is to try to remember to laugh and smile when you're just going about your daily stuff. So, the next time I want to rip the stupid nail file out of a manicurist's hand and start crying, I will remember the funny guy I met a few weeks ago at the nail place, I will remember to try to live the "Seven Days of Smiles" experiment for more than a week, and most of all, I will always remember that if Stacy ever found me in a "mood," she would have reminded me to find something to laugh about. We'll all miss you, Stacy.

From the Spotlight to Solitude

Karen

Pam and I appeared on stage at the 92nd Street Y in New York City, as part of a panel called Women on the Web. It was our blog's debut "in the spotlight." Pretty exciting, pretty surreal. If you've been following us, you know that our blog is all about shaking things up and doing new things, and let me tell you, this experience definitely fit the bill! I am sure anyone watching us would have noticed it was not something we have done before. But we forged ahead, simultaneously trembling and proud. When our names were announced, we walked on stage. The lights were blinding as we took our seats and looked to the audience for our significant others and friends. It's funny what goes through your mind sometimes. I remember thinking that we had been told we would be sitting in chairs with armrests. I think I had even thought about using the arms as both a physical and emotional crutch. I remember looking at the armless chairs as they silently mocked me, and thought "Now what do I do?" We were nervous but knew we wanted to be with the other bloggers and authors to spread our message and inspire others. This was truly a 52—the ultimate representation of what the52weeks.com is all about: you have to do new things to move forward. You have to get out of your comfort zone sometimes to grow. Well, we grew all right.

We talked about the importance of taking risks, how we started writing and blogging and just shared bits and pieces of our lives and experiences. I thought about what forces brought us together with these particular women, in a moment in time, to share and spread a message.

To be honest, when I woke up the next morning, I was glad it was over! I was also tired and looking forward to reflecting for a few days about the event, our project, and the past year. I was happy it was a long holiday weekend. I decided I wanted to do absolutely nothing except eat, think, take some photographs and enjoy quiet time to reflect—away from emails, phone calls and work. Here are some thoughts I wanted to share as I look back on our night in the spotlight and my weekend of solitude (with the exception of my husband and eleven-year-old around!).

Reflections: the spotlight

- There is such a thing as being uncomfortable and comfortable simultaneously. I would like to make up a word for it. I will circle back.
- Never underestimate the power of a good blowout at your neighborhood stylist to boost your confidence!

- *There is nothing like a stage to validate what you are doing.*
- *Chairs are a big deal. We probably don't think about them enough. Armchairs are underrated. My conclusion is that sometimes you have to quickly adjust to whomever or whatever is holding you up—literally and figuratively.*
- *Sometimes you can just be hanging with a friend, feel strongly about something together, have an idea, and a year or so later find yourself on stage. That's cool.*
- *Inspiration trumps nervous perspiration.*
- *Pre-spotlight nerves may, happily, lead to weight loss.*

Reflections: solitude

- *In my opinion, you can only appreciate solitude if you don't have it very often.*
- *Doing nothing is doing something.*
- *I don't look up enough. (I am not sure why, but I don't. I guess I could blame my phone addiction a bit.) Looking at the sky is important. This weekend I saw sunsets, flocks of birds confused by the weather, and a lot of stars. I don't remember the last time I really looked up. Mother Nature trumps the spotlight.*
- *There is nothing like the freedom of not doing your hair for a few days.*
- *Beds are a big deal. A good mattress, books, magazine, movies, junk TV— American Idol, Judge Judy, Top Chef—can be priceless.*
- *Post-spotlight solitude may, sadly, lead to weight gain.*

Forced to Do Nothing

Karen

Sometimes old friends can be prophetic. Somewhere about the middle of August, I was having dinner with a very good friend visiting from the West Coast. We've known each other since college. We don't see each other often but when we get together it always feels like only yesterday that we last spoke, and we totally "get" each other. She started talking to me about this blog. "I love the idea," she said. "How is it going? Isn't it hard coming up with something every week?" "Yes, it is!" I said. "I think you should do nothing one week," she continued, "Aren't we always so busy? So many women and moms our age are too busy and feel guilty for doing nothing and we run ourselves down." My initial reaction was no way. That would not be in the groove with The 52 Weeks. I mean, this was my blog about doing new things. People wouldn't get it if I wrote about doing nothing. "This blog is supposed to inspire people," I responded adamantly. "I disagree," she said. "I think you deserve to do nothing one week and write about it."

And then came Labor Day Weekend. It was a day after a hurricane that was supposed to hit the tri-state area. There were no batteries in the stores or clouds in the sky. Around midday, I glanced in my rear-view mirror and noticed that my eye was pink. Twenty-four hours later I had a full-blown cold. I am writing this sick in bed while the new season busily kicks off around me—frantic scheduling, back to school, the Jewish holidays, endless stuff to do, and summer clothes piled everywhere. Even without a major cold it would be challenging to go from the beach to brisket in a New York minute! Despite the fact that I couldn't move, I am fraught with guilt just staying in bed. I didn't want to do "nothing" this week. But here I am. No choice. I feel like crap.

I don't think this is really what my friend was talking about, but was kind of ironic and made me think about the blog. The52weeks.com was born from a real feeling I shared with a good friend. Feeling stuck, feeling like it was time to get out of our comfort zones, and wanting to get moving again, learn new things, and inspire others to do the same. But as I think about it now, sometimes we need our comfort zones. Sometimes we need to stop running errands, working, moving again, and planning. Sometimes we need to just watch TV and stay in bed. As they say, getting sick is often your body's way of telling you to slow down.

And as I try not to look at my guilt-inducing list, I am watching television and feeling so crappy and non-productive I could scream. I think Seinfeld sums it up right now:

"I am so busy doing nothing . . . that the idea of doing anything—which as you know, always leads to something—cuts into the nothing and then forces me to have to drop everything."

You gotta love Jerry Seinfeld. He's not only very funny but usually right.

● ● ● ●

We both knew we wanted to include a chapter touching upon the importance of making time to relax, contemplate, think, recharge, or just be, but after more than a few pow-wows, we still hadn't come up with any solid ideas for an expert. A rabbi or a priest? Someone from another religious community? A therapist? A spiritual healer, a yogi, a health care practitioner? They all made sense yet somehow, none seemed quite right.

So here we were—stuck again. But why?

And then it hit us. So much of our journey and subsequently this book have brought a sense of clarity. Seeking clarity wasn't the point when we started this project, but that's what we came away with. *How* we achieved this, though, came in different ways for each of us. We found clarity on our own, in our own individual ways. No one else could have told us how to achieve clarity. There really isn't any "expert" who can tell *you* how to relax, or contemplate, or find clarity. It is really up to you to find what works.

Professionals, the clergy, and others will all tell you how important it is to look within to find some serenity in your life. They may share tools and ideas to help you be more reflective, more focused, more present. They will show you different ways to slow down, to be still, or to step away. But only you know what will get you there.

And so throughout our 52 Weeks we, as well as our guest bloggers, all found different ways to relax, reflect, and recharge.

Our friend Laurey shared a post with us on our blog about the day she spent with a drumming circle. Quiet introspection and meditation this definitely was not. Research has shown that personal drumming has the ability to release anger, create joy, alter brain rhythms, induce trance, and create empowerment. Laurey said, "As moms, we are juggling everything all the time. I tried yoga and could not calm my thoughts of all the 5,000 things I had to do that day, that week, that month. Drumming allowed me to focus on one thing only: the *downbeat*. I actually *felt* the downbeat, the rhythm, and thought of nothing else. I was transported to a meditative state . . . the kind of state I have never felt before unless I was painting. My eyes were closed, and when I opened them after eight minutes or so and adjusted to the light, I saw that my friends were all in the same zone, doing the same thing."

The sudden death of Karen's father-in law led her to think about spirituality and religion in a new way. She is still searching for some spiritual guidance but she came away with a better understanding of what she wants from religion. Visiting the Kabbalah Center also helped her gain some clarity and insight. She knows she needs a safe harbor, a place where she can feel supported and can go when she needs guidance or a connection to others. On another occasion, laughter ironically led Karen to look within. Feeling pensive after her friend's death, Karen unexpectedly met someone extraordinarily funny (at a manicure salon!). She was in a bad mood, in a sad mood, was annoyed by everyone around her, and then she met a comedian at the salon. His words made her laugh, made her forget, and made her think. This simple, unexpected encounter triggered something for her. She came away happier and realized that complaining was not the answer.

Pam's visit to Ground Zero was not only a time to reflect on the events of the past, but in a crazy roundabout way led her to find closure with moving to a new home and the mixed emotions she was feeling about this major life event. When she needs time to just think and "be" she visits a special quiet spot in Manhattan's Central Park that has personal meaning to her. The nature hike she took was a conscious decision, but it was only because of her 52 list that she made time for what became a reflective outing.

So what does this all mean? It's really about just *being*. If you want to think about nothing, that's fine. If you want to take stock, re-evaluate and make a plan, that's even better.

And our advice? Just plan a 52 list that includes all the things you want to do, in all areas of your life. Sometimes our greatest moments of clarity came to us when we least expected them. Perhaps part of getting unstuck is being open to whatever comes your way. If you create new and different experiences in your life you will be surprised and rewarded by what you learn about yourself.

NEXT STEPS

Make time for reflection

Remember to put this on your list. It's so easy to overlook: meditation, spiritual awareness, a run in the park, a swim in the water, reading, visiting a special place, lying on the hammock, a walk in the woods, or even a long drive alone.

Find a way that feels right for you

Finding a way to reflect that is meaningful is key. Discover a way to quiet your mind through whatever means work for you. Karen likes to take a drive when she needs to be alone or just "be." She also likes to walk through street fairs, flea markets, and art shows. Despite the hustle and bustle around her, she finds it comforting and it allows her to think. For Jennifer Gardner Trulson, a contributor featured in our "Flying Solo" chapter, writing her book was cathartic and therapeutic—a way for her to take stock and regroup.

Find a place that feels right for you

It's important to find that safe haven. Whether it's the beach or your backyard, a museum or a memorial site, find a place that feels comfortable where you can just think, just like Pam's spot in the park. While it is shared by tens of thousands of visitors, it's a special place for her. She shared this story in Chapter Five, "Relationships." It was donated in loving memory of a dear friend of hers who passed away. Interestingly enough, it doesn't make her sad when she visits. Just the opposite. When she needs to think, she goes to sit there. She walks away with a renewed appreciation of her good fortune. She also goes just to recharge. It's her spot.

SOME TAKEAWAY ADVICE AND QUOTES TO GET YOU GOING

➢ "Follow effective action with quiet reflection. From the quiet reflection will come even more effective action."—Peter F. Drucker

➢ "Who in the world am I ? Ah, that's the great puzzle." —Lewis Carroll, *Alice in Wonderland*

➢ Look again. You don't always see what's right in front of you.

➢ Moving on doesn't ever mean forgetting.

➢ Acknowledge the bad memories but preserve the good ones.

➢ Surround yourself with people and places that make you smile.

➢ Look in your own backyard. You don't always need to look far to find something new. It could be right in front (or in this case, in back) of you.

➢ Breathe in the air. Really.

➢ A hike is good for the head as well as the heart.

IDEAS FOR THE READER

Take time to relax, reflect, and recharge. For some suggestions, check out Chapter 11, "Your 52."

- Explore Kabbalah.
- Go on a hike.
- Visit a memorial.
- Remeber to laugh to clear your head.
- Enjoy solitude.
- Do nothing.

Chapter Nine

Changing Course

"Adults are always asking little kids what they want to be when they grow up because they're looking for ideas."

—Paula Poundstone, comedian

Career Tune-Up

I was having a conversation with an acquaintance recently and after mentioning to her that I am looking to go back to work on a full-time basis again, she said to me, "No offense, but you really aren't that marketable." Not marketable? Wow! That stung.

Pam

Later that day, I took my car in for an inspection. My mechanic said that the tires on the car needed to be rotated. I didn't need new ones, but they needed to be switched around, rearranged, and changed for optimum performance. They'd then be up and running and good as new.

Sounds crazy, but I went home and thought about what the acquaintance had said AND about the tires that needed to be rotated. And then it hit me.

I needed a "career tune-up."

I've always heard about career counselors but never thought that was something I would seek out. I mean, what could they tell me that I didn't already know I should be doing? I'm a former teacher, a reading specialist, and I worked in the non-profit sector for several years. I have always thought that the "helping professions" were where I wanted to be, but I felt like something was lacking in my career. So while I often turn my back on these types of coaches or self-help programs, this time I decided to give it a go and at least try to be open-minded. Isn't the 52 Weeks all about doing something that I could benefit from but that may be out of my comfort zone or routine?

Enter Pamela Weinberg of Mind Your Own Business Moms.

MYOBMoms is dedicated to helping moms re-enter the workforce or explore new career opportunities. Faced with a similar professional identity crisis several years ago, Weinberg and her business partner, Barri Waltcher, turned their own situations into a successful and rewarding second act. They took their experiences as a seasoned writer and successful lawyer, respectively, and really thought about how they could repackage the skills they had acquired. They ultimately received degrees in career management, becoming career advisors to other women with similar experiences.

I must admit, as I knocked on Weinberg's door, I had no idea what to expect. But my meeting with her was unexpectedly enlightening. Weinberg listened and, more importantly, heard. Part therapy session, part strategic business meeting, our conversation definitely opened my mind and forced me to look at my goals in a new way. She also made me really think about what I am looking for in a career (or even just "a job") and what I am capable of. I think sometimes women of a certain age lose their self-confidence. Weinberg really addressed that with me—and then some.

The meeting was very productive. We discussed my previous work experience and sifted through what I liked and disliked about my past jobs, really focusing on which skills I liked using the most and when I felt most satisfied. We decided *that I would create a new resume presenting my qualifications in a skills-based format, highlighting skills rather than former jobs—an effective technique often used for career changers and people re-entering the workplace after a "break." I also came away with a few contacts and leads so I could begin the important task of networking and arranging informational interviews to learn more about the fields I was interested in pursuing.*

Weinberg even gave me a homework assignment. Ugh! She guided me through a career values exercise. It sounded hokey to me at first, but it actually helped me sort through what factors were important to me career-wise (i.e. flexibility, earning potential, autonomy). The questionnaire allowed me to see that sometimes the job you think you want may not be the job that fits your values.

Like so many other forty-something women who left the career track behind, switched into a slower lane or pulled over completely (mainly to raise a family), I now am faced with trying to squeeze back into the moving lane. Just as a car may need its tires rotated or a new paint job, this mother needed a little tune-up and repackaging too to help get back up to speed!

From Fashion to Passion

This is a guest post by Marni Heller. Full disclosure: Marni is one of Karen's oldest friends since their college years. She is creative, driven, funny, and fashionable. She is a wife, mother, daughter, sister, and a great friend, and was inspired to write for the52weeks.com when she found herself embracing a new career after many years out of the fast lane and exciting world of fashion.

The 52 Weeks

Design trips to Europe, trade shows, and parties in Las Vegas, frequent trips to Los Angeles—this is how I spent the bulk of my twenties and thirties in the fast-paced world of fashion.

Driven at a young age to be independent, I ventured out on my own and opened a small showroom on 42nd and Broadway representing West Coast designers. Soon, it became clear I would need a business partner or I would not have anything resembling a personal life. Not having to look far (down the hall from my office), I met a fellow overachiever. Together, we plunged head-first into what would be an exhilarating eleven-year ride of hard work, financial struggle, glamour, and, let's face it, a whole lot of fun.

We worked hard, shopped hard, and played hard. All was wonderful until one day, I found myself married with twins, moving to the suburbs, and simultaneously trying to keep up the same pace as I did when I was twenty-four and single. Needless to say, I was exhausted!

The decision to change my lifestyle at the time was one of the hardest that I have ever made. It is amazing how your career can become such a big part of your identity. As much as I loved my life with my husband and beautiful twins, I felt lost. How could I, the same woman so driven for so many years, now be a "stay-at-home mom?" I couldn't bear it. Luckily, I had my hands full with number three on the way and all the joy and exhaustion that came with it. But all along, I knew that, to feel complete, I needed to make a move toward a professional future . . . at some point.

After leaving the garment center, I took some classes in what always was a personal passion: exercise. I took classes at New York University, received a bunch of certifications, and began teaching spin classes and personal training. Quickly realizing that teaching adults was not my forte, I began teaching after-school yoga programs and kickboxing. Okay, so keeping our youth fit, not bad, right? But I knew something was missing.

When my twins turned five, it was time to put them in day camp. I decided to check out a Jewish Day camp across the bridge in Nyack, New York. It was known for its diverse programming, large Israel focus, and spirituality. I met with the director, and in no time at all, I had a job as the kickboxing and yoga instructor at Ramah Day Camp in Nyack. Fast-forward to what became a life-changing experience for my whole family: I quickly became a division head for the camp and moved my whole family there that summer. It became our "summer home" for many years to follow. I was also brought on to recruit campers and staff during the off-season. Granted, I was the only person on staff who immediately changed into my four-inch platform shoes and skinny jeans as soon as the campers were on their way home, and I quickly became the staff "personal shopper" and style consultant. It was almost exactly ten years after I left the fashion world, but my experience at Ramah, initially started as something to help my kids go to the right camp, resulted in, once again, finding a passion that could be a career: the not-for-profit world of Jewish camping. But the fashion world was still gnawing at me. Was that part of my life really over?

Recently, my former business partner from those glamorous years, who also had left the business world to raise her children, re-entered the fashion industry. Honestly, I thought that it was only going to be a hobby and expected it to be very short lived. Much to my surprise, she has now moved into a showroom and is back in business . . . without me. How was this possible?

This is when I found myself stuck. At a crossroads in my career, I began to question my direction. I started daydreaming of being back in the fast-paced, glamorous world of fashion.

I even went as far as staying up all night creating a concept, a label, registering a name and a website. The next morning, when the rest of the world woke up, I was on high speed, telling anyone who would listen that this was going to be MY re-entry into my past life. I must admit, it could have worked. It was good stuff. Still, when the adrenaline rush wore off, I felt torn, once again, stuck. Was this really what I wanted? Was I ready to take the last ten years and pretend that they never happened? Was I like Dorothy waking up after the tornado only to realize that what she thought was reality was only a dream? I knew that I needed to take a step back, have a few glasses of wine, hit the gym (not necessarily in that order), and hopefully in a few days all would be clear.

Then it happened, browsing through a weekly email of job listings that I have been receiving for years, I came across a listing that literally jumped off the page. There it was: clarity. This needed to be my next endeavor: sending high school-age children to Israel. My heart began to race as I read about the Alexander Muss High School in Israel. A secular Israel experience that instills, at a young age, a love for the land and history of Israel as well as a deeper understanding of what it means to be Jewish. Not religious, Jewish.

My parents sacrificed so much to send me to Israel when I was a senior in high school. That experience began what has been a lifetime of evolution that has helped me instill in my family a love for a country as well as a people who defend a place where I may not have my own address but where I always feel at home.

So here I am, forty-six years old, and I finally get who I am: I am a four-inch (sometimes five-inch!) platform-heel, skinny jeans-wearing "fashionista," wife, friend, mother of three, ready to utilize all of the experiences and passion that led me to where I am today and embark on this new path. This journey has taught me to embrace it all: where I've been, where I am today, and most excitingly where I may be tomorrow.

And even though we know better now than to ever "sell" our daughters on the fantasy of Cinderella, I can honestly say that a good pair of shoes CAN change your life. You just have to walk around for a while, preferably in four-inch spikes, to find the career you want.

How a Mensch Got Me
to the Theater . . . Finally

This is a guest post by Robin Gorman Newman. Robin became a midlife mom at age forty-two, and it changed her life in ways she couldn't have imagined. Soon, Motherhood Later . . . Than Sooner (MLTS) was born—an organization for older moms. Robin is Associate Producer of Motherhood Out Loud, *an off-Broadway show in New York now touring. As a love coach and author—*How to Meet a Mensch in New York *and* How to Marry a Mensch *(now adapted for the stage)—she has made appearances in shows including* Dinner with Friends *and* I Love You, You're Perfect, Now Change. *Robin is a featured expert in our "Flying Solo" chapter.*

It's never too late to see your passions come to fruition, even as a mom caught up in parenting. I wanted to share my story with The 52 Weeks *so that others might be inspired.*

I've adored theater my whole life.

My first role in high school was a part in the ensemble of Anything Goes. *While singing is not my strength, I won the role of an Angel—a big deal for me at the time. My family came to cheer me on, and it was an experience I'd not soon forget, and which still makes me smile. When I graduated college, my dream job was to become a professional theater critic. But, when the* New York Times *hired Frank Rich that very year, my bubble was burst. He had scooped up the job I yearned for.*

But I kept going. I kept my finger on the pulse of theater by writing reviews for the Queens Tribune *and other local publications. I took a corporate job because it felt like the "safe" thing to do, but my heart was always with theater.*

Over the years, reality set in, as did the lure of a paycheck, and as I ultimately found my way to a career in public relations, my theater critiquing took a backseat.

Then I became an author. My books, How to Meet a Mensch in New York *and* How to Marry a Mensch, *were published. As a little girl, I dreamed of writing books and seeing someone actually reading or buying them. But in the back of my mind, the thrill of theater always loomed.*

When I was about forty, I decided to explore what it might be like to become a theater producer. I reached out to some producers, and they were kind enough to meet with me. One, who has sadly died way too young, became my cheerleader and would invite me to readings of shows so I could experience that part of the process. Then, one day, out of the blue, he said to me, "Mensch: The Musical," and I said, "What?!" And, he repeated as if it were a no brainer.

Shockingly, he envisioned my books as being performed in the theater. He was interested in the project. I was stunned—thrilled—and scared out of my mind. I didn't have playwriting experience. I took some classes and took a stab at it, but had no confidence in my ability. So, I tabled it . . . but never forgot.

Parenting became my focus, and I launched a worldwide organization and blog, Motherhood Later...Than Sooner, *after being tired of feeling like the oldest mom in the playground. I've worked on it tirelessly for about seven years now. One day, a wise friend said to me that* Motherhood Later *was really my "platform." I knew what that meant but didn't grasp what it was leading to or what specifically she might have been alluding to. Did she see something that I couldn't? It turned out she was right.*

One day, I got wind of a show that had just closed in Los Angeles called In Mother Words. *I reached out to introduce myself and didn't think I'd hear back from anyone. Then, I got a pleasant surprise. The co-creators/producers contacted me via email and suggested we chat. I wasn't sure if they had an agenda or what I even had in mind, but I wanted to know more about the production to see whether Motherhoodlater.com might somehow support it. Clearly, we were curious about each other, and that's a good place to start.*

What emerged from our phone conversation was so much more. The chat was stimulating and, supportive, and I felt a connection to kindred creative spirits. The project was something I wanted to be part of. I was psyched! Little did I know, they were planning to next bring it to New York. The name became Motherhood Out Loud, *and they sent me the script. After a read and further discussion, and a meeting with the New York-based producer, I was sold. Associate producer became my title, and I've embraced it with everything I am! The show had a successful run at Primary Stages in New York City and is poised to tour worldwide. It just completed a run in Tucson, Arizona.*

I'm also now working on Mensch: The Musical. *I've hired an experienced, award-winning playwright to "coach" me, and under his guidance and encouragement, I've completed my first draft. Additionally, I blog about theater on MotherhoodLater.com. I've made theater come to life in my life!*

It's never too late to keep pursuing your life's dream—even "on the side" and in between real life. That much I learned as I look back with fondness on my first theatrical role in Anything Goes. *Now I know why my parents were smiling even though my vocal talent left a bit to be desired. They knew I was doing something I loved from the beginning: following my passion for the stage.*

Becoming a 45-Year-Old Intern

Jodi Garner is the associate director of Development and Institutional Advancement at The City College of New York. She is also an aspiring Broadway producer. She lives in New York City with her twelve-year-old twins. When Jodi heard that one of the chapters in our book was about mid-life career changes, she contacted us and wanted to share her story.

It was a chilly March day in 1992. I was in my twenties and recently engaged. The Dow was just above three-thousand, and I was in my final semester of business school. I had just registered for my dream china with my fiancé. It was the perfect moment to set a wedding date.

My fiancé didn't really care, so I deliberated with myself. I have a December birthday that is often usurped by the holiday season. I wanted my anniversary date to have its own day in the sun—without competition with the gift-giving season.

The marriage didn't last, but what my now ex-husband said on that fateful day did; actually, it was prophetic. Upon hearing how I arrived at our wedding date, he said, "You know, Jodi, not everyone measures the year in terms of gifts."

True, but some people do. Not only are there people who measure the year in terms of gifts, but they also are paid to do so. They are called fundraisers. Their job performance is measured on the number of gifts they receive throughout the year. I know this because after a twenty-year career on Wall Street that ended with a spectacular finale—the fall of the House of Lehman—I became a fundraiser. Midlife reinvention. I had to email the52weeks.com to share my story.

From the start of my career on Wall Street right up until the financial crisis, I rarely thought about what else I could possibly do. As a single parent with nine-year-old twins to support, I thought I had to do what I had always done. Work was work, right? It took a near global financial meltdown for me to change my views.

In 2008, when I was aboard the mighty ship of Lehman Brothers and it started to sink, the venerable investment bank tried saving itself by throwing its employees overboard. Most of us in Leadership Development were among the casualties. Just like that, my career on Wall Street came to an inglorious end.

I tried to look at the bright side: what better time to get laid off but right at the start of summer? It had been eight years since my divorce, raising my twins as a single parent, I was relieved to have a break. Having gotten divorced when my kids were just six months old, I never really had the chance to lose that baby weight. So I hopped on my bike and started circling Central Park. I was in good spirits and good

178

company—thousands of people were laid off in 2008 as a result of the financial crisis, and the park was packed. It was like summer vacation, and when a friend invited me to go hiking with her in Montana, I jumped at the chance.

I returned ready to hit the pavement and look for a job, but the rug was pulled out from under me when Lehman Brothers declared bankruptcy and the entire financial system was on the verge of collapse—everyone was pounding the pavement for jobs that were few and far between.

After months of fruitless interviews, and then no interviews, like any well-trained person with a Master of Business Administration from Columbia Business School, I hung out my consulting shingle. Business was rough. And while things looked like they might pick up in April 2009, including two corporate interviews, the money just kept running out.

I wouldn't say I was despondent, but I was tired, really tired. I had started out as a bond trader; one marriage, two kids, and a divorce later, I was stuck in leadership development. The fact is, it wasn't really a great passion of mine. So I sat down, fired up my laptop, and said, "Well, I need to figure something else out." As if fated, my phone rang: Mary Burton, a top career coach I'd met ten years prior was on the line. And on that sunny morning in 2009, my new beginning arrived.

Mary had reached out to see how I was and tell me about a career transition group forming in a few weeks. Mary is a Harvard University graduate and powerhouse. I jumped at the opportunity to work with her. As I expected, more minds were much better than my one. Like with so many things, it took a village to help me make my midlife career transition.

To be clear, it took work—lots of work. Every day for seven intense weeks, in between dropping the kids off at school, shuttling them to and from their after-school activities, doing the laundry, and making dinner, I committed to doing everything that Mary told me to do to find a new career.

So after more than twenty years on Wall Street and lots of self-reflection, work, and brainstorming with my career-transition group, my career answer

materialized: nonprofit fundraising. I had helped raise money for my kids' schools,
but I never had considered it a career possibility. But why not?

Contacting friends and family and anyone else I happened upon, I conducted
more than thirty informational interviews during the six weeks that followed our
group work: on the phone, over coffee, over drinks. Ten lattes, five salads, and three
glasses of prosecco later, I was convinced that it was a perfect fit and set out to look
for a job.

With each ad I answered, and each letter and email I wrote, I proudly explained
that I was making a career transition from Wall Street to the nonprofit arena and
how excited I was to apply my transferrable private-sector skills to achieving
sustainable funding for your organization (fill in the blank—you name it). When
no responses came back, it finally occurred to me: unlike sex, when it comes to jobs,
nobody wants to be the first: you can't get hired unless you have experience, but
you can't get experience if no one will hire you. We had a name for that in college,
and it was called an internship. So I made myself into a forty-five-year-old intern.
I researched which organizations would give me the best exposure to nonprofit
fundraising and offered to work . . . for free. It wasn't easy, but I got through it and
with a positive outcome.

And the rest, as they say, is history. I got to put that unpaid experience on my
resume and secured a paying fundraising job at a top-tier medical center in less
than six months. Fast-forward to today: three years and three jobs later, I have
been moving up the fundraising corporate ladder. Currently, I'm the associate
director of Development and Institutional Advancement at The City College of
New York.

I've heard that the only thing constant is change, and maybe some people
(read: me) are hard-wired to keep moving, to keep reinventing themselves. So, I have
another idea percolating. My grandparents gave me this record when I was a kid,
and I've recently secured the rights to make it into an Off-Broadway show: How
to Succeed in Childhood Without Really Whining: A Child's Introduction to

Grownups. *I have this crazy plan to get a bunch of celebrities to rotate through the narrator role, but that's another story for another time.*

• • • •

It's no secret that a big part of what was making us itchy to get moving again was a bit of tedium. We were busy, but busy with routines and managing the minutiae of family life. We always seemed to be orchestrating for others. You could say we were the nucleus of it all, but we felt it was now time to start making things happen for ourselves outside of our insular environment.

The last few years had brought some changes for us both. Karen ran her own highly successful public relations company for many years, and Pam was teaching, but both of us officially left the workforce full time when our kids reached elementary school. While we left for different reasons and still were taking on the occasional project to help bring in a paycheck, both of us felt a void in that area. Especially Pam.

For Karen, the private clients she maintained from her public relations consulting business kept her going, but there was always "something missing," and she was, without even realizing it, looking for another, new entrepreneurial challenge. When we launched the blog, we never thought this would turn into a new career path. We just wanted to have fun and get "unstuck." However, when www.urbanbaby.com called us for an interview, it was as if Pam could see a light bulb turn on above Karen's head. All of a sudden, the blog and the possibility of making the52weeks.com a "bigger" thing was Karen's new passion. The publicity inspired her to take it to a whole new level. So much for just playing without purpose! Okay, yes, there were personal and growth goals on the agenda from the beginning; that's why the blog was created. But it was Karen who saw it as more than that. The blog itself was the very thing that got her unstuck! And, of course, some golf lessons, drawing classes, dance lessons and trying to just grow and be better.

Pam kept busy, taking care of her husband and two girls, tutoring students part time, and getting way too involved in her daughters' school board. All were fulfilling to a degree and definitely kept her busy. However, the desire to try something new and get going again was never more acute for Pam than when the topic of "going back to work" full time came up. It weighed on her—from a financial perspective as well as for continued personal growth.

As we spoke to more and more women of a particular age, it became clear that this was an area of concern and discussion for many others as well. Yet, the idea of changing careers or going back to work is something that stops many women dead in their tracks. Many women just don't know now how to jump back in.

For Pam, this was a story she knew all too well. So many bright, educated, formerly driven women lose confidence as the years pass. Leaving the work force for the Mommy Track brings with it a whole new set of emotions and insecurities once your children get a bit older. Many of us didn't think of this in our twenties or thirties when we decided to have kids. We never thought we'd wake up one morning a decade or two later saying, "What's next?" but without the confidence to answer the question.

We had the good fortune of meeting many exceptional women who have made career changes later in life. We've shared stories from Marni, the *fashionista* who realized what she really wanted to do was leave the fashion industry and work in non-profit; Jodi, the single divorced mom who lost her job, became a 45-year-old intern and reinvented herself; and **Robin Gorman Newman**, the theater junkie who held on to her dream and has now written and produced a Broadway play after years of doing just about everything else. We also met quite a few women who returned to graduate school, hoping to begin a new career path or finally fulfill a long sought after goal. Even one of our experts in our "Just for Fun" chapter, comedian **Michele Balan**, reminded us that she was a successful account executive in a computer company, but always wanted to be a comedian. Nearing forty, she left her high-paying job, with a pension and health benefits, to do stand-up. It wasn't always a smooth path and she had to go through some financial challenges, but she's now a successful comedian who makes a living making people laugh!

As we said earlier, writing this book became Karen's new endeavor. The business of the 52 Weeks—learning social media from scratch, writing a book proposal, reaching out to literary agents, and the thrill of securing great experts—put Karen back on track. Pam was right there with her, but sometimes not as enthusiastically! Perhaps it was Karen's comfort zone and she did also fear that she was reverting back to what she knows best. She was used to working. She was good at it. It was a tough realization to accept that maybe, in the end, the business of 52 overtook the original purpose of the blog. Perhaps she will still change course, but it got her back in the game.

As for me, well, I'm still searching. I do know this project helped confirm what I like doing and not doing. For me, writing a book was a lot harder than I ever imagined. It was a challenge—a BIG challenge. While I've never run a marathon (that's a whole other 52 list item maybe I will explore someday), I imagine this is what it might feel like emotionally. It began as something fun but has morphed into meeting and conquering a challenge and seeing it through to the finish line.

I've also realized I don't particularly enjoy being an entrepreneur or working from home. I like being out there with others. It energizes me. What I do want to do is still up for grabs. I know that I want to return to the "helping" field or to public service and really do miss the children I worked with on a regular basis, even more so now that my own girls are growing up.

I'll probably end up back on the teaching track or in the education nonprofit sector in some way within the next year or two; I'm just not sure in what capacity.

Our research for this chapter led us to some incredible experts who offer advice on recharging one's career, making a change, or reentering the workforce at this time in your life. This information should help get you going and thinking about making that "change in course" as you navigate your way to a new or different job.

Pamela Weinberg, a career counselor and the founder of Mind Your Own Business Moms, myobmoms.com, was our first stop. Weinberg had experienced that feeling of stuckness before she embarked on her present career path. She, too, felt an eagerness to "get back out there." She had authored the hugely successful parenting resource guidebook, *City Baby*, ran groups for new mothers in and around New York City, and was a frequent speaker for the expectant and new mom community.

"The career suited me well when I had young children, as it offered me flexibility and allowed me to spend a lot of time with my children when they were young," said Weinberg. This is something many of us are thrilled to have in our twenties and thirties as we navigate the world of new motherhood or recent marriage.

Then, as was also the case with us, Weinberg began to have more time to devote to her career as her children grew. This is the time when many women begin to reassess what their skillset is and how they can return to the workplace after taking time off to raise children. Weinberg began to reassess.

After considering her options, she went back to school and parlayed her talent and expertise into a thriving new career. She and her partner, Barri Waltcher, now run MYOB Moms, a career counseling firm dedicated to helping women get back into the work force.

If you are feeling stuck, a way to get going is to re-evaluate your career. Weinberg suggests brainstorming with a friend or family member. Ask them what he or she thinks you are good at—sometimes others are better at assessing our strengths than we are ourselves. Be open-minded.

When our friend and guest blogger featured in the "Wellness" chapter, Amie Valpone, wrote in to tell us about her long battle with an undiagnosed illness and her subsequent journey to recovery, we never thought that her story would make us think about changing career course. But interestingly enough, her journey led her to not only get better, but it put her on the path to an entirely new career. Her research and new-found knowledge of her illness led her to find her true passion. She's now a nutritionist, best-selling food writer, and cookbook author. Wow, talk about reassessing and finding your true calling.

Sometimes being in the right place at the right time is also a way to get back into the workforce. That's why we at the 52 Weeks feel so strongly that it's important to get out there and try new things. Often one experience leads to another. Connections are often made in the strangest ways. This was never more apparent than with another of our experts, Vivian Steir Rabin.

"Think back to your childhood, and remember what you wanted to be when you grew up. Are you doing what you thought you would? Why or why not? If you could have a dream job, what would that be?"
—*Pamela Weinberg, career coach*

Vivian Steir Rabin is co-founder of iRelaunch. com and best-selling co-author of *Back on the Career Track: A Guide for Stay-at-Home Moms Who Want to Return to Work* with Carol Fishman. They run a successful national organization dedicated to helping women re-enter the workforce and provide valuable information on the topic. Rabin returned to work after a seven-year hiatus that included raising five children, relocating for her husband's career, and, as she said, "going into reproductive hibernation.I let go of all of my professional ties and focused completely on my brood."

But when her youngest child started preschool, it was time to relaunch. Rabin said she lacked confidence and didn't know what she wanted or could do. And then, the beginning of her journey began literally right in her own backyard! One of her neighbors who had his own executive search firm heard about Rabin's background and asked her if she wanted to work with him. Once she began networking, the solution turned up right under her nose. Talking with him about her interests and background led to a job offer and got her back into the workforce. Of course, this was just the beginning of her journey, but she now has a success story. Rabin went from being a stay-at-home mom to a recruiter to a successful author, entrepreneur, and businesswoman. She now helps other women do the same.

"The best way to predict the future is to create it"
—Abraham Lincoln

What are some practical, simple steps one can take to jump-start a career change or re-enter a former career? Both Rabin and Weinberg suggest some.

One of the most important and feared steps is to start talking to people that have careers that interest you to find out more about what those jobs are really like and how your qualifications

"There is nothing wrong with change, if it is in the right direction."
—Winston Churchill

would be viewed by those in the sector. The best way to learn about jobs, industries, and careers is by speaking to people in the field. Whether it's a former colleague, family member, your next-door neighbor, or a fellow PTA member, don't be afraid to let them know you are looking to make a change and would love to speak with them. Informational interviews will help you narrow your options and help you decide whether you need any additional training. Remember, you aren't asking for a job—just some information—which is much easier and way less stress-inducing.

It also is important for people who are unsatisfied in their caeers to do what Rabin refers to as a career self-assessment. "We recommend that people who are considering returning to work after a break, or those who are unhappy in their jobs and are seeking to make a change, do some deep thinking about what they would really like to do professionally," she said.

Rabin said there are many of tools and resources to help people do this—including self-assessment diagnostics (such as the ones included at the end of this book), the Strong Interest Inventory, a few sessions with a career coach, if you can afford it, or some great books that are out there on careers. Even if you discover through this process that your dream career is not a practical choice at this point in your life, you may be able to reorient your job search or goals in a direction that will be fulfilling in a different way. Some people know what they want to do, but most do not. And employers want people who are directed, not people who say "I can do anything."

> **"I was resistant to taking one of these assessment quizzes. I wasn't sure if I was afraid of what I'd find out or just thought they were silly. But after agreeing, I found that it was really helpful and enlightening. It didn't give me an 'a-ha' moment, but it did give me a direction. It got me thinking about choices, and ideas, and what I am suited or not suited to do within the framework of my lifestyle."**
> *—Pam*

Weinberg and Rabin's advice, as well as our own experiences, all lead to the same conclusion. Women who want to reenter the work force often stall or feel paralyzed, so getting out there is of the utmost importance, even in the smallest ways. These baby steps are what will propel you forward. Even if you don't initially follow through, these first steps will get you going.

NEXT STEPS

Self-assessment

Do some soul searching. Rabin calls it a self-assessment, Weinberg calls it re-evaluating. Whatever you want to label it, it's important to take a long, hard look at yourself, contemplate what you want reality to look like, and reassess whether you are looking for a change. Our friend and guest featured in our "Flying Solo" chapter, **Linda Orton**, did just that. At forty-seven, newly divorced and on her own, she started writing a novel and doing stand-up comedy! Talk about looking within and seeing who you really are and what you are really all about. Weinberg pointed out that sometimes our hobbies and old interests resurface when we are re-evaluating, and these reignited passions can often become careers. Another fan of the 52 Weeks, Susan Boyles, wrote to tell us that after years of trying many different things—including a twenty-year stint in the US Army—she realized that her love of cooking and working in the food industry on and off for many years is what made her the happiest. She's now teaching cooking classes, running a culinary store, and blogging about all things epicurean.

Network

This is probably the most important next step you can take. In order to bulk up your resume, you need to get out there and meet others, get ideas, and speak with people about options. Rabin also emphasizes viewing every event as an opportunity to build relationships that could lead to your next role, even your son or daughter's soccer game.

Case in point: when Karen finally decided to explore her long-standing interest in the field of art and antique appraisals, she talked to lots of people. She has always had an interest but never considered it a real option until the 52 Weeks. But then she started to make calls, and met with the head of a continuing education program at a local college, which led her to speak with someone from the New York School of Interior Design. She also took a class in design and collecting. All of this networking put her in touch with more and more people and also opened her eyes to what this endeavor would really encompass. She's not quite ready to jump in head first, but the networking did helped her figure out the direction she can go in if she pursues this career change at some point. Karen also made some great contacts that she keeps in touch with in case she decides to go that course.

Personal branding

Once you have done some evaluating and started to network, you can polish up your resume and LinkedIn profile, which should include a professional photo, strong summary, references, skills, and keywords. Creating an online presence also is key. Comment on industry blogs and become active in relevant social media groups.

SOME TAKEAWAY ADVICE AND QUOTES TO GET YOU GOING

➢ Be confident.

➢ We've said it before, but we'll say it again: it's okay to ask for help. Another point of view often puts it all in perspective.

➢ Repackage yourself.

➢ "It is never too late to be what you might have been." —George Eliot

➢ "Cinderella is proof that a good pair of shoes can change your life." —Anonymous

➢ Take a class in your field to get back up to speed.

➢ Don't just join LinkedIn; use it!

➢ Sit down and finish that resume.

➢ Talk to people, and network. As great as social media is for a job search, few people get jobs by sitting at home in front of their computers.

➢ *Do not* sell yourself short. You are qualified and you are marketable. You just may need a little updating.

IDEAS FOR THE READER

- Take an online course.
- Take a class at your local community college.
- Subscribe to newsletters from organizations that interest you.
- Volunteer.
- Become an intern.
- Check out job listings or other opportunities for advancement at your current place of employment.
- Speak to a career counselor.
- Contact your alma mater. Universities and colleges often have alumni-outreach offices and programs dedicated to helping alumni reenter the workforce, complete with individual counseling.
- Contact your local community college or a university. Many offer executive education and career-retooling weekends, weeks, and seminars.
- Enroll in short-term certificate programs such as massage therapy, financial planning, etc.

Chapter Ten

Flying Solo,
with Jami Kelmenson

"It seemed to me that the desire to get married—which, I regret to say, I believe is basic and primal in women—is followed almost immediately by an equally basic and primal urge—which is to be single again."

—Nora Ephron

Single in the City

Jami Kelmenson, our contributing author for this chapter, was one of our first guest bloggers for the52weeks.com. She is happily single, lives in New York City and is continuously getting "unstuck" doing amazing, interesting things. Jami is a marketing professional and is writing her first novel.

Let's face it: we all know that being single is different than being married. Of course, each has its own unique set of "stuff"—both good and tough, challenging and rewarding. Generally, when you're single, you have more opportunities to try something new, so getting "unstuck" is not always as challenging as it may be for your married friends who often have a kids at home. But even single people may need a little nudge now and then, so here's my "top ten" list for getting yourself unstuck, based on my experiences over the past 52 weeks.

1. **Strike a pose.** *I have avoided Level 2 yoga classes for a long time. Yoga is supposed to be relaxing, not work! But I "enjoy" my gym workouts a bit too much and just haven't gotten to yoga at all. Recently, I was rained out of my normal Thursday morning run, so I decided to go to a yoga class. I expected to feel weak and out of place. I did; but I also realized a few things: I could "bind." I could lift my toes up in "crow pose" for a split second—hey, it counts. And I don't have to climb the wall in handstand if I don't want to. And I don't want to. At least not yet. So now that I've survived Level 2, I can comfortably return to Level 1 where I can relax. After all, it is yoga.*

2. **Turn up the volume.** *I have a stereo system from the last millennium with one working speaker and enough broken, plastic CD cases to fill a bookshelf. My music needs a makeover. I just splurged and spent sixty dollars on a docking station. Now all my favorite songs sound new—I can hear words and notes I'd never noticed. So how does this count as getting unstuck? Well, I finally made over my entire music experience. I will now have every genre of music loaded on my iPod and can listen to the songs as they were intended to be heard: jazz, classical, country (OK, Lady Antebellum might not really be country, but I'll keep working on it). Any suggestions?*

3. **Little house on the Hudson.** *Last summer, I rented a cabin in the woods in beautiful Dutchess County, New York. I rented a car, which is colossal for me, because living in Manhattan, I rarely drive. I grilled on an outdoor barbecue,*

which is also colossal for the same reason. I sipped local wine while sitting in a rocking chair on my porch watching the sun dip behind the tall pines. I entertained friends from the city. But mostly, I just hung out with myself and my thoughts. People asked, was I afraid of being out in the woods alone? Not really, if you take the bears out of the equation. It was the weekend of Chelsea Clinton's wedding in nearby Rhinebeck, NY, and yes, I did consider crashing, but Owen Wilson was nowhere to be found.

4. **Strangers on a Eurail.** *I traveled and hiked the Swiss, Italian, and French Alps with a tall, handsome, almost-stranger. We'd met once in Manhattan at a networking party. I was the media professional. He was the crasher (red flag, anyone?). When he asked me to join him for an "adventure," (he was living in Geneva, and I was traveling to the area) I consulted a few friends, then ignored their advice and met him anyway. I will leave the rest to your imagination given the limited space here, except to say he spoke four languages, looked like Harrison Ford, and built me a campfire on the side of a mountain. Indiana Jones and the Temple of Swoon.*

5. **Haitian by association.** *When I heard Sean Penn speak about how the media attention had died down only months after the Haiti earthquake while the need was only growing bigger, I felt moved to do something. And then I woke up the next morning, went to my job, and forgot about Haiti. Until a friend of mine from said job quit to start Community2Community, a nonprofit with a mission to establish self-sufficiency in Haiti. The next thing I knew, I was among a crowd of Haitians at a jam-packed fundraiser in Brooklyn. When my friend handed me the microphone to share my experience as a volunteer, I spoke about Sean Penn. I spoke about the people of Haiti. I spoke about being Jewish, and I spoke about how we can't stand aside while others suffer. And it was there and then I was proclaimed "Haitian by Association." I am proud of this.*

6. **Match schmatch.** *I signed off of Match.com. That may seem like the opposite of getting unstuck if you want to meet someone. But after many go-nowhere*

dates, I'm taking an even bigger leap of faith—actually steadily dating one of my "Daily 5" (i.e.- the five prospects Match sends to your inbox each day). I look forward to potentially feeling the good kind of "stuck"—with M—assuming he'll have me as his glue. (I didn't just ask someone to go steady in a book, did I? No pressure, honey!)

7. **Guatemala or bust.** *Costa Rica wasn't enough. I had to give my mother an even bigger heart attack by traveling 14 hours by plane, van, and then boat to a remote little town on the edge of Lake Atitlán, Guatemala. I took writing classes while looking out at a spectacular view of three volcanoes. I contributed to the local economy by buying handwoven tote bags and scarves with personalized tags from "Isabel," the woman who labored over her spinning wheel to weave them. I watched local artists capture the scenery in their paintings. I drank margaritas (not frozen!) made with brands of tequila I'd never heard of. And I learned that scorpions in that part of the world are not poisonous when a friend of mine was bitten and lived to tell about it. (Sorry, Mom, but there's a world out there!)*

8. **Listen to Sally Struthers.** *I was so touched by the colorful native dresses and dark soulful eyes of the children in Guatemala that I signed up to sponsor one with Children International. Ana Cecilia stole my heart. Her picture hangs on my refrigerator, with a note saying how much she enjoyed the coloring books and markers I sent her. There is a dearth of shoes for children in Guatemala, but thanks to Children International, Ana now has a pair of black school shoes.*

9. **A novel idea.** *My life may sound interesting, and maybe I enjoy telling stories about my escapades. I know, I should write a book. So I am. I'm halfway through a draft of my first novel about the choices women make in life and love.*

10. **Blogging.** *Trying something new really does get you going again. That's what I did; this is really quite a list. It's exhausting being me. I should take a break and cozy up on the couch for a while. Nah! There's always the next 52 weeks!*

Soaring on Long Island

This is the first guest post that appeared on the52weeks.com. It was written by Rochelle Paris Sanders. Our blog inspired her to go gliding for the first time as she faced the possible dissolution of her twenty-five-year marriage. It doesn't get any braver than this. Rochelle lives in Westchester, New York, and has two college-age sons.

"Soaring on Long Island" was the title of the pamphlet. Sore and reeling, I had been emotionally "soring" on Long Island, in Westchester and Manhattan for months. My husband had moved out. My life had spun out of control. Then it went dark. Literally.

My 16-year-old son and I were trapped in a dark house surrounded by downed power lines and massive snow drifts. He lit candles, gave me a tea and vodka ("Did he learn that in Home Economics?" I thought). As I lay wailing in a heap on the floor of a cold, dark house, he put his hands on my shoulders and looked me in the eyes. He made me repeat these words: "I am strong; I can get through this." I was proud that my son was growing into a wonderful young man. However, I will always feel badly that he was with me at that dark moment. You never want your kids to see you so distraught.

It became a year of firsts: shoveling snow, surviving power outages that lasted for weeks. The spring brought an infestation of ants, school functions attended separately as mom and dad, and even a holiday without my children since we tried to be equitable about where they spent their time. I developed an uneasy relationship with a power drill as I hung a Horst photograph I admired but hadn't dared to display when I lived with "Him." I hung it next to my new gunmetal-colored chaise lounge ("is it pleather?" The Ex had asked). The summer brought the annual beach vacation without the rituals of going to the farm stand and beach together. The warmth of summer was replaced by rain, and then more rain.

"I am strong; I am courageous; I can get through this" was my mantra. With each new challenge, I became stronger. The old therapy adage one step forward, two steps backward was the rhythm of my new life. The unwavering support of my friends and family smoothed out the edges and indignations along the way.

In the midst of adjusting to my "new normal," I saw the pamphlet hanging on a bulletin board in a tiny bakery in town. "Sky Sailors-Soring on LI-Glider Rides" (it truly was misspelled—how ironic). "Our experienced pilot will take you high above the earth in our sleek silent glider."

On the first August day when the sun finally emerged, before I could reconsider, the tow-plane was taxiing down the runway past the solid airworthy Gulf Streams and Citations, dragging the glider behind it with me attached. Panicked, random thoughts ran through my head, such as wondering if my boys would survive without me for a few hours or at the very least remember to check themselves for ticks when they left the beach.

Then I remembered to breathe deeply and chant my mantra: "I am strong; I am courageous; I can get through this." My stomach lurched as we ascended over the Pine Barrens, the quarry pit now used to train police officers for high-speed chases, the local shopping outlets, and a shooting range. At about 5,000 feet up, the pilot shouted something; I felt a terrifying start and a jolt. The tow plane had released the glider. For the first time in months, I found myself in complete silence, and my anxiety and sadness began to dissipate.

Gliding over the east end of Long Island, I looked down at the twin forks and the small smidgens of land between them (Shelter Island, and that mysterious "research" facility, Plum Island) stretched out before me. Connecticut and The Berkshires beckoned to the north. We turned toward the west and soared silently over Dune Road with the Atlantic Ocean just beyond. A hazy Manhattan skyline poked *through the horizon. As promised in the pamphlet, the ride was "smooth, quiet, peaceful, and spectacular." "Time to head back to the airport," screamed the pilot, and I was jolted out of the peaceful moment, and we sharply banked, seemingly 180 degrees, and then took a nosedive of 500 feet (it was probably only 25 degrees and 50 feet but I couldn't tell in my panic). "I can do this," I told myself. Several bumps later, we were back on terra firma. Big sigh of relief.*

According to the Soaring Society of America, a glider stays aloft without an engine because of the pull of gravity and sources of "lift." The glider stays in flight if the air mass in which it is flying is rising at a faster rate than the sailplane is gliding downward. The earth, when heated by the sun, warms the air next to it, causing it to expand and rise just like steam coming from a boiling kettle. Rising warm air forms into columns called thermals. Barring unanticipated changes, the glider smoothly navigates these predictable natural forces. However, an unexpected change of direction may disrupt the tranquil experience of gliding. "The pilot must accept and adapt to these changes," according to the Soaring Society's website. I remind myself of this as I try to navigate through new territory. We all should as we face unexpected currents and bumps in life.

Finding Funny at Forty-Seven

This is a guest post by Linda Orton. Linda is a mommy, an optimist, a storyteller, a comedian, and a serial entrepreneur. Owner of Intelligent Video Solutions, she works across the United States helping major corporations tell their stories. We love Linda's honesty about her many "firsts," and we're happy she wanted to share her story with 52. The fact that she is doing stand-up for the first time in her forties is great. She lives in Westchester, New York, with her two children.

I have always been defined by my intelligence. It was what mattered most to my mother; it was what influenced my choices in work, in friends, in a husband, and in my parenting. My focus on being smart and seeking smart got in the way of so many other more important things, such as compassion and fun. But then, life happened, and an amazing shift occurred: being smart gave way to being funny and emotional.

The past few years have turned my safe bastion of cerebral focus into one wild ride full of emotions, instinct, and creativity. I didn't realize outside factors — seemingly so disconnected from one another—would have such an effect on me. Perhaps I was simply ready: tragedy and hardship had paved the path for humor and optimism.

My marriage of twenty years officially ended on November 28, 2012. It had unofficially ended at least five years earlier, but my ex-husband moved out on Memorial Day 2010. Two weeks later, he said he had something important to tell me and I should sit down. I said, "I don't need to sit down. I know exactly what you are going to tell me. She's Asian, she's a black belt, and she's in her twenties." He looked at me and said, "You think you're so bloody smart. . ." long pause; "She's thirty-two." I was right about the other two things, though, and so the harsh reality that our marriage was not only over, but also that he had moved on quickly set in.

The 52 Weeks

On Memorial Day 2011, my mother died. She and I had shared a tumultuous relationship for most of my life. I met her death with a sense of peace and gratitude and her funeral service was my first attempt at stand-up comedy—as strange as that sounds. She had led a sad and unfulfilled life—driven by alcohol and sarcasm; we rarely shared the mother-daughter bond that many have. She met my children only four times before she died. One time a year—starting when they were three and six— we got together. I carefully recorded and preserved these times for my kids to look back on one day, if they choose.

Once my mother died and my ex-husband moved out, I had an epiphany that gave me great joy. I was funny. In fact, I was hysterical, not just to myself, but also to others. It was instantly clear: I simply had the wrong audience most of my life. This small fact, but major realization, was more liberating than anything that had come before.

When I realized that I could use my brain for humor as well as for deep discussion, an entire world opened up. It's not that I was dry and boring before . . . more that I just didn't allow myself to experience or create humor even though I enjoyed it immensely. It was about finding the funny inside of me and letting it out. Around the same time I also discovered sex toys.

I never had discussed this subject with anyone and was much too dependent on third parties to make myself feel good. For someone so smart in certain ways, I was incredibly limited in others. Discovering humor and vibrators around the same time could have made for a challenging situation; I could have been liked the caged monkeys in the experiment and never left my bedroom, but alas, I had my children to care for and two companies to run. Everything in moderation became my mantra.

I also was given a guardian angel in the form of a Verizon salesman. Unlike everyone I grew up feeling attracted to, he was street-smart, cocky and a nonstop talker. He was tough and shy, and in a bizarre twist of fate, we became friends, really good friends, within the confines of his Verizon store in my suburb of Westchester, New York. We talked about photography and religion, my divorce, and my son with special needs; we talked about his failed relationship, and about life and death. I fell in love with him, and we communicated through email even after the owners closed the store and he moved on to a new job, in a new town.

He was there for it all and supported me through all my creative pursuits, my divorce, my mother's death, my work, and my challenges with my kids. He always seemed to contact me when I needed him the most. After almost a year, he finally agreed to have dinner with me. We covered every possible topic in one night at my house. We talked about my taste in art, and he was the first one to shed light on why trees were always prominently featured in the art in every room of my home. He said they provided me with the roots I longed for. I listened to him and tried to provide the forgiveness he sought for actions he had taken in his youth. We talked about things I had never spoken about with anyone.

When he left my home, the gates at my complex wouldn't open for some reason. He texted me and said it was a sign I was trying to lock him in. I said I'd come to let him out, and I saw his bright blue eyes behind his helmet stare deep into me. Later in the summer, he was killed in an accident. We had never talked again after that night. I believe he came to say hello and goodbye to me in one six-hour conversation. I served him tomato sauce from a jar and he wrote, "Yea, that really killed me." Oy, words can often prove prophetic.

I learned I could love again. I mourned the death of someone I was never physically involved with more deeply than I mourned the death of my mother. I learned you never know what gifts will be dropped into your life and then be taken away with no clear reason. I learned that life is so very fragile and I was so very grateful.

I was so angry that my intelligence did not help me identify and fix the problems in my marriage and with my mother. That it did not save my dear friend from dying. I could not think my way out of any of it and so I was left to feel. To feel deeply and profoundly and to move the grey matter so far out of the picture that only nerves were left in my body and my brain.

Once the anger subsided, sometime last year, I realized that the emotions I had were healthy and that my brain was still there; they just were learning to coexist with the other parts of my being. No longer vying for top seat, intellect and emotion were collaborators, guiding my being to my future funny self. One filled with joy, with happy and sad memories of the past, and with incredible hope for the future.

• • • •

For many, the journey is not one made with a partner, but one made "flying solo," whether by choice or circumstance. These are women who are making the journey solo—never married, divorced, widowed, or otherwise unattached. So we decided to explore not only why we—two women in our forties with husbands and children—were stuck, but also why single women are stuck, and more importantly, what they can do to get unstuck. Of course, whether single or married, you can be stuck in a million ways. However, if finding a relationship is what you need to get going again, then this chapter will point you in the right direction.

Because it's been a while since we've been unattached, we decided to seek the help of writer and blogger Jami Kelmenson, who in her own words has been "single, mostly by choice, for almost three decades." That's a lot of direct experience, but Kelmenson also sought experts of her own—including **Dr. Helen Fisher**, renowned biological anthropologist and author of *Why Him? Why Her*, and **Robin Gorman Newman**, author of *How to Marry a Mensch*—to help us understand the stickiness of singledom. Here's what Kelmenson has to say.

When Karen and Pam reached out to me for this chapter, I jumped at the chance to put it together. Travel, adventure, yoga, volunteer work, the pursuit of passions, and, of course, men—they were all part of my amazing experiences as a single woman in Manhattan. But as I told Karen and Pam when I first heard about The 52 Weeks, single people get stuck too! All that opportunity and a blank slate can really overwhelm a person, even to the point of inaction. So much to do, so *much* time!

Whenever I get to know someone new, it inevitably comes up: the subject of my singleness. "I can't believe you're not married!" is usually the response, from both men and women, often accompanied by a look of disbelief. Of course, there are two ways to interpret this reaction. "You're not married," as in: *I can't believe some lucky man hasn't scooped you up by now!* Or, as in: *What's wrong with you?*

On a recent trip to Haiti (two ways I get unstuck are traveling and volunteering), one of the workers at my hotel asked me about my family. I started talking about my sisters, and he shook his head. "No, I mean *your* family," he said in broken English. "I don't have one," I responded sheepishly. He looked shocked. I had never experienced this level of reaction to my single status. He couldn't believe the concept of not marrying and forming a family by a certain age.

I wanted to cry. You see, despite my usually sunny disposition, there are most certainly drawbacks to being single. For me, some of these are: not having plans on your actual birthday as well as major holidays, attending weddings or social functions where everyone else is part of a couple, dealing with the death of a parent on your own, and—believe it or not—inclement weather. While the rest of New York City was seemingly holed up—and coupled up—in their apartments during Hurricane Sandy, I was "snuggled up" with meteorologist Jim Cantore of The Weather Channel.

That's why I've been so relieved by the trends highlighted in Eric Klinenberg's 2012 book *Going Solo*, which gives us "still-singles" reason to celebrate. According to Klinenberg, more than 50% of American adults are single, about 17 million women are contemporary solo dwellers, and the percentage of Americans living by themselves has doubled since 1960. Simply put, Klinenberg observes that "for the first time in centuries, the majority of all American adults are single" and "the typical American will spend more of his or her adult life unmarried than married." And, interestingly, most of them prefer it that way and are "crafting new ways of living in the process."

I have just one word to say to Mr. Klinenberg: hallelujah! At last, redemption! Or should I say permission, to be, well . . . me.

Somewhere along the way, I was "supposed to" get married, move into a house (or at least a one-bedroom apartment), maybe have a kid or two, possibly even a dog and/or an SUV. I haven't accomplished any of these things, not even the dog adoption, and it hasn't been for lack of trying. Marriage just didn't happen. But now, thanks to Klinenberg, I can breathe a sigh of relief knowing what I have always felt to be true: I am not an outcast, old maid, spinster, loser, neurotic (okay maybe a little), commitment-phobic, or any one of other such terms used to describe the nagging question of *what is wrong with me?* There's only so much therapy a girl can take, after all. Maybe the incredulous looks will start to subside.

So what does this have to do with The 52 Weeks, you may be wondering? It's very simple: single people—whether by choice or circumstance—get stuck too. How you arrived at being single varies, of course. While being single wasn't my intention, I just haven't found the right one. Others perhaps, have sadly lost someone they loved or ended a bad relationship .

Why we, as single women, lost momentum can often be attributed to different reasons than people who are attached. Even our way of coping with being stuck is unique. I've asked some of these women to weigh in, along with the experts, to find out what they think of the trends in singledom and how the notion of getting stuck—and unstuck—applies to those who are, or know someone who is, flying solo.

I talked with **Dr. Helen Fisher** about the art and science of romantic love. It's important for me to say again that many women flying solo aren't focused on finding romantic love, and it isn't even on their list—even a 52 list; but for those who are single and want to change their status, Fisher was overflowing with advice to get them going again. Fisher, a biological anthropologist and author of *Why Him? Why Her?*, echoes my sentiment about the incredulous looks, saying people tend to make assumptions about her and other solo people that are not correct. Assumptions like, we can't get men. "That's not true," she said. "We are choosing to fly solo until the right one comes along. We're not desperate.

"Sometimes you have to stand alone to prove that you can still stand."
—Anonymous

We're happy; we have huge networks of friends and relatives; and our lives are no longer defined by whether or not we are in a romantic relationship."

Culturally, we are wired toward romantic love, Fisher says. Her research has identified three different brains systems: sex drive, intense romantic love, and attachment, which all bring calm and security. It's natural to want to look for a romantic partner, she says. "But in this day and age, anyone can have an exceedingly full life without someone. It's a tremendous moment in human evolution, and our modern world supports and accommodates women who fly solo."

Still, she purports, we are built to form bonds. I asked Dr. Fisher why some women tend to shut out this normal biological inclination toward pairing even if they want to find someone.

"Some women are working too hard," Fisher said. "Dating takes time. They need to go out regularly and follow through. Maybe they are not happy with themselves. They need to be competent in dating. They need to set goals and proceed on schedule."

Single women can be stuck in many ways, she says. "They can be stuck in a bad relationship, stuck in routines, stuck at home, even stuck in friendships that are no longer working." Fisher talks more about the friend phenomenon in the chapter on relationships. Despite the advances of women in the workforce, Fisher believes they also can be stuck economically or in a job they don't enjoy. This can impact their attachment needs and, in turn, their relationships.

Contrary to what Klinenberg's research might indicate, Fisher refers to demographic studies that suggest between 85 and 90 percent of Americans will marry by middle age. However, they are staying single longer and getting out of bad marriages and therefore becoming single again for longer periods of time, perhaps waiting to remarry. So while it may look like all these single people are living by themselves, the fact is both men and women go in and out of relationships, what she refers to as "serial monogamy. It's no longer until death do us part," she said.

But don't make dating all work, she cautioned. It's important to play! 52 Weeks talks more about this in the "Just for Fun" chapter. Any kind of "play" drives up dopamine levels in the brain, which increases feelings of energy, optimism, creativity, mental flexibility, curiosity and focused attention. "Novelty can spur the mind. We're built to play," she stresses. "Laughing is good for you." Fisher herself is flying solo now for the first time in thirty years. "I am really enjoying it," she said. "I get to read my science magazines at night, get up when I want, exercise, do what I want, and I'm catching up with girlfriends, meeting men, and having a ball." Life is a pile of opportunities, she believes; it's just that we don't get them all at the same time.

While she loves the freedom she is currently enjoying, Fisher admits she sometimes misses having someone to sleep next to. This quandary, she believes, is the key issue facing twenty-first-century women—striking the right balance between autonomy and attachment. Women need to decide what kind of attachment they want to build so that they still have enough autonomy and independence within that attachment. The trick is finding someone who feels the same way you do.

It may not be easy, but it's worth trying to design our lives the way we want so that our innate need for independence is reconciled with our innate need for attachment in constructive ways. This way, everyone is comfortable and can feel enlivened and expanded by both drives.

Until then, it's okay for women to be flying solo until the right person comes along—and they're doing it because they can, because social trends have enabled, even encouraged, it.

For more insight about the art of finding "the one," I reached out to **Robin Gorman Newman**, author of *How to Meet a Mensch in New York* and *How to Marry a Mensch*. She couldn't agree more with the concept of finding romantic love, as the titles of her books would suggest. And like Dr. Fisher, she believes not everyone has to be married; it's a personal choice. But if after significant reflection and self-understanding, the inclination is *Yes, I want a life partner*, Gorman Newman has some steps to show you how to get exactly what you deserve.

She believes that all women essentially want and deserve the same thing—to be treated well, to find someone who stands the test of time, who will really be there and put them first, love them through thick and thin, and make them feel supported. And, of course, there's got to be chemistry on top of all that. In short, we want a *mensch*.

In her experience as a love coach, Gorman Newman finds that the women she coaches have reached a point in their lives where they've accomplished a lot—but if they're stuck, they need to pause to ask themselves a crucial question: *How did I get to this point?* Maybe they thought things would be different. "Understanding yourself," she said, "is step one of finding a mensch of your own." In her love coaching practice, Gorman Newman asks her clients to take stock of their emotional inventory—what they have to offer, what their dating history is, their challenges. "You have to love yourself and be in a positive place," she said. In a sense, you have to be a mensch to get a mensch.

Gorman Newman offers the example of women who say they want to meet someone but don't do anything about it. A popular complaint is, *I go to bars, but nothing happens*. Gorman Newman asks them, "Did you even talk to someone? Did you give them your number? Very often they say they're ready, but, when probed, they're not prepared. It's not enough to just show up."

"Marriage is not a panacea," she said. It takes work to share your life with someone. Not everyone is that prepared to share. But if you believe in your gut that you are ready, it helps to try new things, break old patterns, live fully, think out of the box, and feel good about yourself.

Gorman Newman agrees with Dr. Fisher that women having careers has changed the playing field considerably. Whereas Fisher sees the balancing act as one of autonomy vs. attachment, Gorman Newman sees another dimension, that of stability vs. the unknown. Too often women stay in marriages or relationships because they're afraid of the alternative. One of the reasons *Eat Pray Love* resonated so, she believes, is that Elizabeth Gilbert's story "spoke volumes to women who weren't happy by showing them a recognizable character who had the strength to trust her own gut when it comes to making a change."

For divorced women who still may be wary because they see their marriages as failures and don't want to repeat their mistakes, Gorman Newman advises them to consider what worked during the marriage. It could be a bigger failure, she suggests, to stay in a bad relationship. "If they're divorced, we need to look at why they're divorced. What went wrong in the marriage? Women have a fear that this can happen again, so we need to determine what they've learned from it so they don't repeat their mistakes," said Gorman Newman.

It can be much more complicated in many ways for women who have lost a spouse. "Many in our age group are more familiar with one of our parents losing a spouse at this point in our lives," say Karen and Pam. "As painful and difficult as that is, it's really a completely different thing when a peer loses a partner." So the 52 Weeks spent some time talking with women who unfortunately have experienced this type of painful loss. While losing a life partner at a young age offers unique challenges, we found that the road forward was similar for them. **Jennifer Gardner Trulson**, who lost her husband on 9/11, shared a bit of her story.

Trulson was a 35-year-old happily married mother of two children, ages two and four, living the cliché of "having it all." She had a successful law career, a great marriage, two beautiful kids, and two beautiful homes. Then, 9/11 struck, and her husband, Doug, was killed. Trulson movingly and painfully speaks about the days, weeks, and months after the devastating moment that changed everything in her book, *Where You Left Me*.

As a young widow reeling from the aftermath of 9/11, Trulson had to navigate her way back not just for herself, but also for her children. The advice and the steps she took to move forward resonated with us. She talked about how in the days and months after her husband's death, she took great comfort in the support of friends. "You cannot do it alone," she said. "It is crucial to have a network of people to help you through." She also said that the small moments of each day gave her pause for distraction and helped her to move forward. We like to refer to them as baby steps at the 52 Weeks—but even these seemingly inconsequential moments helped her get through each day. Checking off one little item on her to-do list—going to the market, getting a manicure, meeting someone for coffee—first was an escape but soon became her new reality.

While she slowly repaired her world and moved forward with her family, she was convinced and content that she would remain single, and she felt that was good enough for her. I know many single women, including myself, who reach a point (usually when the biological clock has ticked out) at which finding romantic love isn't a goal anymore. We are so busy living life, working, enjoying friends, and giving back that the idea of another person coming in to upset the balance sounds less than ideal. This was how Trulson felt, too, but for different reasons. She had her children, her friends, and the memories of her husband. She was as fulfilled as she needed to be at that time. As Trulson said, "I was not looking for a new husband; I was resolute and content to be single forever. Then it happened." Had she not been cajoled to go out with her friends one night, she wouldn't have met *him*. She was clear that she does not, and never has subscribed, to the idea that everything happens for a reason—because it will never be okay that her husband was murdered and taken from her children—she does believe that the healing is in the connections we have with each other.

"The best lesson we can learn from any traumatic loss is that while we may be helpless to stop bad things from happening, perhaps there are signs and road maps to help us recover and reconnect, provided we know where to look." The loving support of her friends gave her the impetus to grab hold of the lifelines that appeared before her. It did take some time until she felt she was truly ready, but she believes this is what led her to the possibility of a way back, and ultimately to Derek, her husband of seven years.

Understandably, Trulson doesn't have any quick answers on how to get through this kind of loss. "If it is fresh, I probably wouldn't offer much advice at all. I would most likely wrap someone who has just lost a spouse in a warm hug and offer her a sympathetic ear. In the early stages, a devastated widow needs a patient and kind listener. I might also encourage her friends and family to keep in close contact for an extended period. Grieving isn't a linear process—one can have a good day followed by three awful ones."

"If a woman has lost a spouse, the key difference is that it is often very difficult for her to believe a new start is even out there," said Robin Gorman Newman. "And to do that, I help her understand her past and determine if she is indeed ready to move forward."

Whether never married, divorced or widowed, Gorman Newman's essential premises still stand: know when you're ready, and then really be out there; don't just act like you're out there.

You may be reading this and still not feel like you're ready to move on. We can hear you saying, "I just wanted to get moving again; it's not about finding someone right now." That's why there is only one chapter about finding love and companionship, or moving on from a divorce or devastating loss. When you're stuck, you're stuck. It may be the perfect time for "Trying Something New" (Chapter 1), "Giving Back" (Chapter 7), or doing something "Just for Fun" (Chapter 3) all while flying solo! As we like to say, "the possibilities are endless."

NEXT STEPS

Like yourself

If you don't, no one else will. If you can't stand to spend the night alone, why would someone else want to spend his or her time with you? Really. Make your own fun; feel good about yourself so others can feel good about you.

Figure out what you like to do . . .

Don't worry about what your potential partner might like to do. We've all heard stories of women who take up golf because it's a great way to meet guys. I don't love skiing, but if I meet a guy who skis, suddenly I'm willing to invest in a pretty, new pink parka with fur on the hood. Not the best strategy. I've met more guys hiking (which is what I love to do) than I ever will on a ski slope.

Don't obsess over the marriage question or the biological clock

It was a huge relief for me once I was technically past the biological-clock mark in life (although never say never). It opened my options, not just to guys who don't want kids, but also to a life that doesn't include marriage. Now, wanting kids is a perfectly legitimate goal, and you should go for it if you want to be a parent, but if you obsess over the need to get married and have kids, you might be putting out vibes that are counterproductive to your ultimate goal. Relax; it will happen if it's meant to.

Don't be too picky

If you know for sure you would like to find a partner, don't judge too quickly. Dr. Fisher offers this advice: after you've met nine men, pick one to get to know better. The more you get to know someone, the more you can find things to like about him or her, and the more you can see how you are alike or different.

Remember to have fun

No one likes a wallflower. Plus, having fun makes you smile. If you're not sure how to have fun, try a few different things, just for laughs. For me, it was karaoke (I know, terrifying!), but there are some cute guys out there singing their hearts out—badly.

Take your time

If you are grieving the loss of a partner or spouse, go easy on yourself. Understand recovering will be a marathon—not a sprint—to recover. Surround yourself with family and friends who are there with hugs and support for the long haul.

Try something new

It's fun, and it stimulates dopamine, which may bring new people into your life, not to mention new ideas and a new perspective. Do novel things to drive up dopamine, which is linked to feelings of curiosity and romantic love.

Give back

Get out of your head. You might find your own situation isn't as bad as you think it is. And when you can spend just a few hours of your time in a way that affects someone else for a lifetime, it lifts your spirits, which can make you more attractive. There were so many people who rose to the occasion in the northeast after Hurricane Sandy that giving back actually became "cool." For more about the importance of volunteering, see Chapter 7, "Giving Back."

Don't give up on the future you see for yourself

It's never too late to find love. And life can still be fulfilling until then. But it's also important to remain open to changing your own life view as you grow older. You just might find a new future for yourself that is equally, if not more, fulfilling.

Take time for yourself

Never underestimate the power of a little pampering from time to time. Or of some "me" time doing whatever you love to do—without guilt. This goes back to liking yourself. Treat yourself well. You're worth it. More importantly, *enjoy* yourself, too.

IDEAS FOR THE READER

Here are a few things I've done (or thought about) to get myself unstuck while flying solo that you can try as well.

- Travel solo for pleasure. (Try Abercrombie & Kent, Friendly Planet Travel, REI, or www.cruisemates.com.)
- Travel solo with a purpose. (Make a difference with Habitat for Humanity, www.habitat.org; World Wide Opportunities on Organic Farms, www.wwoofinternational.org; International Volunteer Programs Association, www.volunteerinternational.org; or VolunTourism.org, www.voluntourism.org.)
- Try online dating. It works for some people; why not you?
- Be a PANK (Professional Aunt, No Kids) to other people's children (Visit savvyauntie.com for more info).
- Adopt a rescue pet (Petfinder.com, ASPCA.com, or Stray From the Heart in NY).
- Clean out your closets, then freshen your habitat with everything that is uniquely you.
- Meditate on where you see yourself in the future, and don't underestimate the power of verbal or written affirmation.
- Cook a gourmet meal for yourself (then repeat it for someone else if it works!).
- Go out alone, and survive it!
- Find your passion (this applies to people who are in relationships as well!).

SOME TAKEAWAY ADVICE AND QUOTES TO GET YOU GOING

- ➢ Make a plan, stick to it, and go no matter what your mood.
- ➢ Get out of your comfort zone, and take a risk.
- ➢ "I feel very adventurous. There are so many doors to be opened, and I'm not afraid to look behind them." —Elizabeth Taylor
- ➢ Acknowledge the bad memories but preserve the good ones.
- ➢ Repackage yourself. Times change, trends change, you change. Embrace change, and use it to your advantage.
- ➢ "My knight in shining armor turned out to be a loser in aluminum foil." —Anonymous
- ➢ "Being single is getting over the illusion that there is somebody out there to complete you and taking charge of your own life." —Omkar Phatak, writer

Chapter Eleven

Your 52

"You have brains in your head. You have feet in your shoes. You can steer yourself any direction you choose."

—Dr. Seuss

Now it's your turn!

This chapter is devoted to your next steps.

"Your 52" includes many of the things we tried and many things we just never got around to. There are also many great ideas that weren't on our original 52 list but may be right for you. The suggestions in this chapter were culled from our informal research, experts, our blog followers, friends, family, and trendsetters.

Did you know that Facebook co-founder Mark Zuckerberg sets one new personal challenge every year? We didn't! His first annual personal challenge was vowing to wear a tie to work every day in 2009. Then Zuckerberg pushed himself to learn Mandarin the next year. One year, he insisted on personally killing any animal he ate (causing him to become almost a complete vegetarian). And then more recently he pledged to return to his roots and spend time programming each day like he did when he started the company. Now, we didn't include Zuckerberg's personal to-do's in this chapter but we thought it was pretty great the CEO of the successful social network also carved out personal time to do new things and challenge himself.

One thing we know for sure: The ideas in this chapter will inspire you to get going again, explore, and move forward in many areas of your life. Some may not interest you at all; others may spark another idea; and some will certainly end up on your own 52 lists.

We've included lists covering each chapter topic to help get you going. Start at the beginning of each list or mix it up like we did.

 If you want to use our template, you will find a **Create Your Own 52** on page 247. Have fun, volunteer, learn to tango, take drum lessons, love a little more, forgive, bake a cake, or plan a day to relax and do nothing. Allow yourself a simple little pleasure, or go for broke! And as we've been saying for a while now, no matter where you are in life, be inspired to get better, get moving, or get over it!

Trying Something New

Sometimes you have to shake it up to get "unstuck." Break out of your comfort zone, and try new things. It's good for your health and your brain.

1. Go on a horseback ride.
2. Take up Saori weaving.
3. Go tandem skydiving.
4. Buy a lottery ticket.
5. Go skinny dipping.
6. Découpage a piece of furniture.
7. Eat a food you've never tried before.
8. Read a classic novel.
9. Swim with dolphins.
10. Learn a language.
11. Travel across the country.
12. Make out with a stranger.
13. Take a yoga class.
14. Enjoy a candlelit dinner.
15. Go paragliding.
16. Mentor someone.
17. Make a red velvet cake.
18. Take a drawing class.
19. Go out to eat by yourself.
20. Get your caricature done by a street artist.
21. Become a pen pal to an overseas soldier.
22. Have a photographer take some hot photos of you.
23. See one of the seven wonders of the world.

24. Watch a meteor shower.

25. Ride a mechanical bull.

26. Play strip poker.

27. Throw a surprise party.

28. Enroll in an improv or storytelling class.

29. Take a dance lesson.

30. Patent an invention.

31. Write your memoir.

32. Schedule time with parents or grandparents and record the conversations.

33. Plant a garden.

34. Take a flying lesson.

35. Complete a random act of kindness.

36. Learn how to drive a "stick-shift" car.

37. Eat at a five-star restaurant.

38. Go whale-watching.

39. Fill and bury a time capsule.

40. Go to a nudist beach.

41. Compliment someone you don't like.

42. Fall in love.

43. Write a book.

44. Have a picnic near a pond or lake.

45. Paint a room.

46. Take a cruise.

47. Try scuba diving.

48. Get banned from somewhere.

49. Build a bonfire in your backyard and roast marshmallows.

50. Go on a "Polar Bear" plunge.

51. Eat kimchi.

52. Learn to play Texas Hold 'Em.

Wellness

Wellness really is about making small lifestyle changes. Toss the white bread, eat an apple, laugh, move, and don't forget your vegetables. Mom was right.

1. Take the stairs instead of the elevator.
2. Freeze blueberries as an easy way to add antioxidants to your diet.
3. Use a treadmill or walk for 15 minutes every day.
4. Get a therapeutic massage.
5. Learn effective breathing techniques to reduce stress.
6. Take up gardening. It's relaxing and provides Vitamin D.
7. Go to the beach, and watch the waves.
8. Try a new class at the gym.
9. If you sit at your desk all day, get up every hour and stretch or take a walk.
10. Watch a funny movie. Laughter releases endorphins.
11. Use smaller plates to help control portion size.
12. Break the bedtime TV habit: turn everything off.
13. Don't watch or read anything upsetting before bed.
14. Learn a short exercise routine you can do anytime, anywhere.
15. If you have the chance to grab a 20 minute nap, take it (but keep it at 20 minutes!).
16. Have an extra glass of water every day for a week.
17. Take a calcium supplement if needed.
18. Try going vegetarian one day a week.
19. Cut back on coffee and soda.
20. Eat whole-grain bread instead of white bread.
21. Eat an extra serving of fruits and vegetables every day.
22. Grab a jump rope for some old-fashioned fun and fitness.

23. Stroll through a flower show and literally smell the roses.
24. Try acupuncture.
25. Go bird-watching.
26. Enjoy dark chocolate and wine at dinner.
27. Visit the ASPCA and pet the puppies and kittens for an instant mood lift.
28. If you're going to snack while watching TV, have some popcorn or kale chips.
29. Watch the sunset with friends.
30. Listen to classical music or any music that works for you.
31. Try oils on your pulse points to de-stress.
32. Do 10 minutes of meditation a day.
33. Add chia seeds to your cereal.
34. Try healthy food swaps.
35. Limit your sugar intake.
36. Make the switch to environmentally friendly cleaning supplies.
37. Forgive people.
38. Nurture your relationships.
39. Make a smoothie with fruits and vegetables if you're having trouble getting them into your diet.
40. Quit smoking.
41. Exercise.
42. Download a fitness app to your smartphone.
43. Train for a 5K.
44. Try hypnosis to kick a bad habit.
45. Give up something you eat too much of for a week.
46. Enlist a friend or hire a personal trainer to kick-start a strength-training program.
47. Spend a week trying heart-healthy recipes.
48. Go out and help someone. It's good for you.

49. Take a walk.

50. Try an eco-friendly dry cleaner.

51. Go to bed an hour earlier than you typically do.

52. Take up knitting.

Just for Fun

Make time to play. Do something for no reason. Take a few minutes, an hour, or an entire day and just have fun!

1. Make snow angels.
2. Eat whatever you want for a weekend.
3. Play in the backyard with your kids.
4. Go sledding.
5. Rendezvous with your significant other.
6. Get dressed up for a dinner at home.
7. Line dance.
8. Paint your toenails different colors.
9. Put bright red streaks in your hair.
10. Go commando.
11. Climb a tree.
12. Attend a Renaissance fair.
13. Go on a hayride.
14. Visit a psychic for a tarot card reading.
15. Join a flash mob.
16. Make it into the *Guinness Book of World Records*.
17. Have a water balloon fight.
18. Play Quarters at your next book club meeting.
19. Attend a baseball game on opening day.
20. Have a movie night with friends.
21. Learn to make sushi.
22. Use a Hula-Hoop; see how many times you can spin.
23. Have a "Make Your Own Pizza" night.
24. Read a book.

25. Cannonball into a pool.
26. Join a dodge-ball league.
27. Get a tattoo.
28. Visit your Alma Mater.
29. Crash a wedding reception.
30. Send a message in a bottle.
31. Take a continuing-education class.
32. Get a makeover.
33. Go for a walk and discover a new street or neighborhood.
34. Have a tequila tasting party.
35. Participate in a competitive eating contest.
36. Stop to listen to a street or subway musician.
37. Get a lap dance.
38. Give a lap dance.
39. Camp in the backyard.
40. Have a day with nothing on your schedule.
41. Plan a Spy Day.
42. Celebrate the Chinese New Year at a traditional banquet.
43. Go on a trip to a city you've never visited.
44. Spend time with pets at a humane society.
45. Order in and catch up on the DVR.
46. Get a celebrity's autograph.
47. Eat popcorn for dinner.
48. Spend a weekend at a vineyard.
49. Take a helicopter ride.
50. Sample oysters.
51. Try indoor rock climbing.
52. Test-drive a ridiculously expensive sports car.

Arts and Culture

Dance, paint, explore, listen, create! Fill your senses and you will feel better. We promise.

1. Learn glass blowing.
2. Attend a pottery class.
3. Go art gallery-hopping.
4. Visit Montreal, Canada and get some French attitude.
5. Look for graffiti in unexpected places.
6. See experimental theatre.
7. Help paint a mural.
8. Make a recipe that has been in your family for generations.
9. Read the entire works of William Shakespeare.
10. Watch an opera in its original language.
11. See theater al fresco.
12. Put on a puppet show for kids.
13. Sit under the stars at the Acropolis.
14. Go to the ballet.
15. Visit a new museum every week for a month.
16. See the touring company production of a Broadway show.
17. Listen to Handel's *Messiah* in a beautiful setting.
18. Learn to play a musical instrument.
19. Read *War and Peace* by Leo Tolstoy.
20. Take a photography class.
21. Visit Chinatown and have dim sum.
22. Go to a Buddhist temple and meditate.
23. Attend a concert by a living legend.

24. Watch Ken Burns' *The Civil War*.
25. Take the stage at a MOTH storytelling event and share your tale with an audience.
26. Go to a luau.
27. Visit Graceland.
28. Have an Éric Rohmer film-watching marathon.
29. Shoot your own documentary.
30. Check out the Henry Ford Museum.
31. Attend a murder mystery dinner.
32. Re-read F. Scott Fitzgerald's *The Great Gatsby* and throw a Roaring Twenties soirée.
33. Try to be an extra in a TV show or movie.
34. Attend a music festival.
35. Dress up for a screening of *The Rocky Horror Picture Show*.
36. Experience Mardi Gras.
37. Participate in an authentic Japanese tea ceremony.
38. Compose a song.
39. Take a continuing education class.
40. Become an oenophile.
41. Travel to a remote locale where English isn't spoken.
42. Learn origami.
43. Participate in a war re-enactment.
44. Start a correspondence with an artist.
45. Peruse albums at an old-school record shop.
46. Perform a song or read a poem at an open-mic night.
47. Walk the streets of Philadelphia where George Washington, Thomas Jefferson, and Benjamin Franklin once walked.
48. Go to the symphony.

49. Stroll through a botanical garden.

50. Explore beautiful landmarks.

51. Take a music appreciation class.

52. Rent a François Truffaut movie and learn a bit about French cinema.

Relationships

Friends and family are what life is all about. Take time to make sure you nurture your relationships. Forgive, forget, and make an effort.

1. Call a family member just because.
2. Make a photo album for your extended family.
3. Don't cancel your monthly girls' night out.
4. Have a picnic with someone special.
5. Start a new family tradition.
6. Kiss your partner in the morning.
7. Go for mani-pedis with the friend you never get to see.
8. Create a family tree and give your family members copies.
9. Use a long weekend to visit a friend who lives in another city.
10. Go sailing with your significant other.
11. Have high tea with the older generation of women in your family.
12. Try something new with friends.
13. Give one compliment, or a thank you, to your partner every day.
14. Start a book club.
15. Do a favor for someone and don't mention it.
16. Recreate your first date with your significant other.
17. Plan a cousins reunion.
18. Accompany a friend visiting someone in the hospital.
19. Make chicken soup for someone who is sick.
20. Try something new with your partner.
21. Go to the beach with your kids and collect rocks and shells.
22. Go to a sex toy shop with your significant other.

23. Smile more often.

24. Spend an afternoon decorating cookies with your children.

25. Take a nightly walk with your partner and use it as an opportunity to communicate and get fit.

26. Offer to babysit for a friend in need of a break.

27. Have a block party.

28. Shop for and make dinner together as a family.

29. Record a marathon of a friend's favorite shows and invite him over.

30. Forgive and move on.

31. Join a sports team with your partner.

32. Roll a joint, listen to some classic rock, and have a relaxing night with friends.

33. Watch an adult movie with your spouse.

34. Have a tech-free night spent playing cards or board games.

35. Leave a note in your partner's briefcase or your kid's backpack.

36. Train for a marathon with family and friends.

37. Play hooky with your child one day and do something fun together.

38. Host a potluck meal and invite everyone over.

39. Take your kids to the zoo or aquarium and then adopt an endangered animal.

40. Start a craft club with friends.

41. Have a family day at an amusement park or county fair.

42. Don't forget to ask "How was your day?"

43. Take your favorite uncle to lunch.

44. Have a wilderness weekend and go camping.

45. Take a shower with your partner.

46. Give a massage to someone.

47. Plan a weekend away with your sister.

48. Rent a boat or canoe for two.

49. Teach your kids how to roller skate.

50. Go to a bar with your spouse and pretend to pick each other up.

51. Go on an old-fashioned sleigh ride with your family.

52. Buy beautiful stationery, then send letters to family and friends.

Facing Fears

Take a deep breath and start facing your fears.

1. Go on a rollercoaster.
2. Go skinny dipping.
3. If you don't like heights, go rock climbing.
4. If you are nervous about public speaking, try karaoke to get things going.
5. Accept a dare.
6. Read. It calms the soul.
7. Say *no* for a change. Try it for one week.
8. Go without makeup for a day.
9. If you always weigh yourself, hide your scale for a week.
10. Buy a set of "worry beads."
11. Go to sleep earlier for seven days. Sleep reduces anxiety.
12. Start a journal.
13. See a cognitive behavioral therapist to work on your stuff.
14. Invest in a media or public speaking coach.
15. Ask your employer for a raise or review.
16. Research and try energy tapping for anxiety control.
17. For one week, wear red instead of black. Be bold.
18. Take a risk and plan an adventure that's outside of your comfort zone.
19. Listen to soothing sounds or music.
20. Make a list of your accomplishments.
21. Slightly change your daily routines for a week.
22. For one week, learn to be still for a few moments each day.
23. Volunteer. Helping others can decrease anxiety.
24. Learn as much as you can about your fear. Knowledge is power.
25. If you are scared to drive through tunnels, bring a friend for support.

26. Learn the art of persuasive speaking: take a class, read a how-to book, or work with someone.
27. Fill that prescription if you need it.
28. Ditch the coffee. Check out high tea at a fancy hotel.
29. Learn how to breathe properly. Shallow breathing causes anxiety.
30. Dive into the pool.
31. If you are afraid to travel alone, plan a solo trip to pursue a passion.
32. Spend a week acknowledging your fears and owning them. That's the first step.
33. Try something new. Fear fades when you are learning new things.
34. Find the right therapist.
35. If you think you've lost your mojo to middle age, prove to yourself that you've still got it. Go flirt with someone!
36. Take a course to learn to calm your flying jitters.
37. Trust your instincts—they've gotten you this far.
38. Strive to know when to say yes and when to walk away.
39. End a bad relationship and move on.
40. Don't rely on others for approval.
41. If you fear commitment, try to date someone for at least one month.
42. Find a career, job, or calling that makes you feel good about yourself.
43. Go to a comedy club, or make plans with your funniest friend. Laughter reduces anxiety.
44. If you can, face a fear full-on for the week. Book a flight if you don't like to fly; hop on the express train if you are afraid of the subway. Just try.
45. For one week, tackle a fear little by little.
46. Take a baby step. Make just one call for information about the thing you're afraid of.
47. Do something that scares you.

48. Expose yourself to something you're afraid of.

49. Think about what makes you happy.

50. Spend a week taking care of yourself. It will decrease anxiety.

51. Spend a week trying to think only positive thoughts.

52. Face a person or situation head-on.

Giving Back

Whether it takes ten minutes, ten hours, ten days, ten months, or even ten years, find a way to help others. It will help you feel better too.

1. If you love to bike ride, ride for charity.
2. Help out with Toys for Tots.
3. Plan a Mission trip (building houses for victims of disaster).
4. Teach English as a Second Language.
5. Help out at an animal shelter.
6. Volunteer at a soup kitchen.
7. Offer to tutor your neighbor's child.
8. Make sandwiches for the hungry.
9. Be a library volunteer.
10. Be a docent at a museum, zoo, or art gallery.
11. Volunteer to coach a neighborhood team.
12. Donate a suit to Dress for Success.
13. Be a blood or bone marrow donor.
14. Work with people with disabilities.
15. Help a new neighbor move in.
16. Bake someone a cake for no reason.
17. Cook someone a meal who is stuck at home sick or homebound.
18. Help an elderly neighbor with his or her errands.
19. Offer to help carry someone's bags.
20. Get a haircut and make a donation to Locks of Love.
21. Buy a stranger a meal.
22. Send a letter of encouragement to a friend.
23. Donate clothing to a homeless shelter.

24. Plant a tree.

25. Pick up trash around your neighborhood.

26. Bring flowers to someone to cheer them up.

27. Send a thank-you note to someone who has helped you.

28. Have a bake sale for a charitable event.

29. Cash in loose change and donate it to charity.

30. Volunteer to clean up a local park.

31. Mentor a child.

32. Give a compliment.

33. Start a blog or website dedicated to a cause you are passionate about.

34. Send phone cards to the troops overseas.

35. Vote.

36. Shovel snow or rake leaves for a neighbor.

37. Make a gift or card for someone.

38. Adopt a pet.

39. Make someone laugh.

40. Take action against ocean pollution.

41. Use environmentally friendly cleaning supplies.

42. Babysit for a single parent.

43. Make snack packs for those staying at the Ronald McDonald House.

44. Help without being asked.

45. Donate supplies to a school in need.

46. Write a letter to a serviceman or servicewoman.

47. Pay the toll for the car behind you.

48. Get your friends together and dedicate a year to a specific cause.

49. Explore how you can get involved in Habitat for Humanity.

50. Volunteer at a summer camp for kids—even for a day.

51. Give a blanket to a homeless person.

52. Let a distressed shopper cut in line at the grocery store.

Reflection

 Almost anything you do can be an opportunity to reflect and look within. What works for one person may not work for another. Take time to think and clear your mind. You may find answers you didn't even know you were looking for.

1. Practice yoga.
2. Read and write a poem.
3. Learn to paint.
4. Bake a cake.
5. Explore a new part of your hometown.
6. Travel.
7. Spend a weekend alone.
8. Take a train ride.
9. Challenge your beliefs.
10. Forgive someone.
11. Tap into your faith.
12. Accept and reflect on your mistakes.
13. Make a list of your dreams, hopes, and aspirations.
14. Spend time in nature.
15. Read.
16. Take a warm bath.
17. Enjoy a spa day.
18. Learn to play an instrument.
19. Be patient.
20. Talk with friends.
21. Write in a journal.

22. Avoid greed, anger, and ignorance.

23. Respect others.

24. Smile.

25. Be the change you wish to see in the world.

26. Be positive.

27. Look at old photographs.

28. Try not to worry.

29. Make a plan.

30. Be a leader, set an example.

31. Begin again with a clean slate.

32. Listen to classical guitar music.

33. Learn to rely on yourself.

34. Purposely eat alone.

35. Immerse yourself in solitude.

36. Don't confuse a job with purpose.

37. Go fishing.

38. Take a random road trip with no destination in mind.

39. Learn chess.

40. Pick up a new hobby.

41. Stop rushing.

42. Have a technology-free day.

43. Take a hot air balloon ride.

44. Clear clutter.

45. Finish what you start.

46. Explore Kabbalah.

47. Take a walk in the woods.

48. Visit the 9/11 Memorial.

49. Visit any memorial—think about our history.

50. Go back to your religious roots.

51. Read old love letters.

52. Just be still.

Changing Course

Take just one step forward toward making a career change or comeback. It will get you going and spark ideas. Don't sell yourself short. You are ready.

1. Be an apprentice.
2. Join an Employment Meet Up.
3. Go to a networking cocktail hour.
4. Buy a new interview outfit.
5. Set up a LinkedIn account.
6. Take a skills-assessment test.
7. Dye your hair.
8. Put away money for a rainy day.
9. Relocate.
10. If your dream job involves travel, take a language class.
11. Go on an informational interview.
12. Apply for an internship.
13. Invest in a new computer.
14. Create inexpensive business cards.
15. Make a vision board.
16. Find a mentor.
17. Get certified in an area that interests you.
18. Don't buy into ageism.
19. See a career coach.
20. Visit your school's alumni office.
21. Start a side business on eBay or Etsy.
22. Write a guest article or blog post.

23. Shadow someone in an industry you want to learn more about.

24. Learn a new skill.

25. Update your resume.

26. Treat yourself to a personal shopper and create a new look.

27. Know when to move on from a dead-end job.

28. Volunteer; doing so could lead to paid opportunities.

29. Don't become obsolete. Make sure your skill set is relevant.

30. Make a list of interesting activities worth trying.

31. Sell your paintings or jewelry designs at weekend flea markets.

32. Identify your dream job and email, write, and call the CEO until you make something happen!

33. Take the **MYOB Moms Inventory** in this book.

34. Help someone out: do a favor and that person will do a favor back.

35. Go to graduate school informational sessions.

36. Join a gym or athletic league and make new contacts while releasing beneficial endorphins.

37. Ignore the naysayers and listen to what your heart is telling you.

38. Become a consultant in your area of expertise.

39. Make a family recipe then sell it at a farmers market.

40. Complete the **Career Values Worksheet** in this book.

41. Dedicate a week for the library: read about your dream job.

42. Make a list of things you loved as a child.

43. Join a group like Toastmasters.

44. Be a freshman again.

45. Start a blog.

46. Take the **Relaunch Readiness Quiz** in this book.

47. Resist the urge to complain.

48. Give tennis lessons to kids.

49. Peruse the classified listings.

50. Write your autobiography: it might reveal things you forgot about yourself.

51. Audit a college class.

52. Start conquering your fears; they may be preventing change.

Flying Solo

 Be sure to check out the other lists too, but if you're flying solo by choice or circumstance then this list is for you.

1. Go solo on an adventure vacation.
2. If you never do, go to a movie by yourself.
3. Take a walk, alone, through the park.
4. Set personal goals. You have a better chance of succeeding if you write them down!
5. Go on a wellness retreat.
6. Buy thoughtful gifts for relatives or friends.
7. If you don't like what you do, explore a new career.
8. Start a blog.
9. Change your look.
10. Buy yourself flowers.
11. Learn a foreign language so you can breeze through Europe alone.
12. If you eat on the run, cook a gourmet meal.
13. Focus on your friendships.
14. Spoil yourself rotten.
15. Spend a day at a spa.
16. Redecorate your bedroom.
17. Make an online dating profile.
18. Be passionate about a cause, volunteer overseas, make a difference.
19. Adopt a pet.
20. Take a continuing education class in a subject you always wished you had studied.
21. Learn to dance.

22. Go dancing.

23. Go to a concert.

24. Start a DIY project. Isn't it time to organize those photos?

25. Appreciate the small things.

26. Start a book club, movie club, online dating club, or any club.

27. Sing karaoke with friends.

28. Spend a day being lazy.

29. Visit a museum.

30. Smile.

31. Flirt.

32. Join a bowling league, softball league, or any league.

33. Go to a comedy show.

34. Throw a divorce party.

35. Plan a potluck dinner with old friends.

36. Join a gym.

37. Make a budget, finally.

38. Go soaring alone in a glider plane.

39. Fill your home with plants and flowers.

40. Learn about art and start your collection.

41. Renovate your kitchen or bathroom.

42. Reorganize your files, and toss the ten-year-old receipts.

43. Join a meditation group.

44. Seek out spiritual enlightenment.

45. Explore a new book genre.

46. Go to a networking event.

47. Visit your parents spontaneously.

48. Drive with no destination in mind.

49. Take surfing lessons, or any lessons.

50. Throw a dinner party.

51. Start your own nonprofit organization.

52. Don't always fly solo; if you are tackling something big in your life, join a support group.

CREATE YOUR OWN 52

MY 52

1. _____
2. _____
3. _____
4. _____
5. _____
6. _____
7. _____
8. _____
9. _____
10. _____
11. _____
12. _____
13. _____
14. _____
15. _____
16. _____
17. _____
18. _____
19. _____
20. _____
21. _____
22. _____
23. _____
24. _____

25. _____
26. _____
27. _____
28. _____
29. _____
30. _____
31. _____
32. _____
33. _____
34. _____
35. _____
36. _____
37. _____
38. _____
39. _____
40. _____
41. _____
42. _____
43. _____
44. _____
45. _____
46. _____
47. _____
48. _____
49. _____
50. _____
51. _____
52. _____

Afterword

A Note from Karen

The night we conceived the52weeks.com, Pam and I were on the same page. We both felt the same way: stuck.

I love being with Pam. I value our friendship. She's sharp, witty, and "gets" me. She has years of experience as an educator, and while she may no longer be in the classroom, she is always a teacher. A few months into our project, I began to see the52weeks.com as a bigger idea. I began to see it as a way to inspire and help a lot of women who felt like us, and it was around that time that Pam must have noticed the entrepreneurial sparkle in my eye. She probably thought to herself, "What did I get myself into? I just want to have fun and do things." I think I stressed her out a bit, planning future workshops, arranging for us to appear at the 92nd Street Y with other bloggers, visualizing our book, reaching out to agents—these weren't really part of Pam's original plans; in fact, it was not in either of our minds when we hatched the52weeks.com. But we continued moving forward. We continued checking things off our respective 52 to-do lists, sometimes together, mostly on our own. We supported and pushed each other when we needed to, but ultimately the blog became something different for each of us and we didn't know it until it was all over.

For me I came to realize that in a way the "business" of 52 Weeks was another way to stay in a comfort zone. Or maybe Pam first pointed that out to me.

I already knew how to be an entrepreneur. That was, for some reason, a comfortable place for me. That's where I was effective. That's where I was confident.

*Did I create another business from the52weeks.com, in part, to avoid many of the personal hurdles I needed to conquer? Was I hiding behind another business to avoid really tackling the personal "stuff" on my 52 list? My first reaction was to get upset at this possibility. Then I stopped listening to my persistent inner critic. The blog was a success. It succeeded because I **did** try new things and crossed off many of my 52 to-do's off my list. The blog became the very thing that got me going again. It gave me a new passion and purpose.*

And the personal stuff? Well, I tried new things, had fun, succeeded, and failed. The blog was an effective way to monitor it all. Without the blog, all of those "things" would be floating around the universe, around my brain, unfettered and without a home. The book process forced us to look back and look forward. It forced me to look at what it was all for, what things on the list to pursue now and in the future; what to throw away and what I never should have tried to begin with! It made me realize that what is really most important is to find pleasure and happiness in life's everyday moments, and don't take it all too seriously because there is another 52 around the corner. Things come up, things change and, as they say, no matter how much you plan, "God laughs." I learned the real purpose of the blog by accident. It was my big "oh, that's it!" moment.

I also walked away with some great memories and a sense of pride in planning something with my good friend and following through; for starting something and finishing it; for making progress on the tough things and learning to accept where I need help. Most of all, I came away with a greater sense of calm because I finally got it: a 52 project will work to get you going again and it's fun. But first and foremost you need to accept who you are, own who you are, and be ready for some surprises.

"Some of the biggest game-changing inventions and discoveries of our time were not the product of calculated genius, but accidents that happened to work out," said a 2010 Newsweek article. "These lucky mishaps have given the world everything from the awesome Slinky toy to the lifesaving antibiotic penicillin." The 52 Weeks

was, in many ways, my medicine. Now it's really time to get going. Or, maybe its just time to really do nothing and not worry so much about it!

A Note from Pam

I never intended to write a book—but somehow here I am. What began as a genuine and fun experiment to "try something new, something different, or something I was afraid to do," turned out to be that and much more. Getting here has been a long and arduous journey for Karen and me, filled with a rollercoaster of emotions. It has brought us closer, it has pushed us apart at times; it has been trying for our families, it has been a source of pride for them.

When we came up with our plan, there wasn't a bigger agenda other than a desire to try something a little different and follow through on a commitment, to myself and someone else. But I knew I had to embrace the idea of being accountable: it was the only way we'd succeed. And so a blog was born. But, in fact, sharing my personal exploits with others proved rather difficult. I'm an extremely private person, and so this reluctant writer took on my first challenge— overcoming my hesitancy to share my personal triumphs and tribulations. I am happy to say I succeeded.

Before I knew it, Karen and I were thrust into all things "blog," and got carried away with bringing it to life. Working through my "52 to-dos," talking to others online, people liking what we were doing . . . it didn't stop. So many new things. Soon, an idea for a book began to take shape. Taking those baby steps, as we often say, led the way to a much bigger adventure.

Of course, I could not and would not have succeeded without Karen. Anyone who knows her as well as I do knows that it is nearly impossible not to get sucked into the "Karen vortex." She is a whirling dervish of frenetic energy and can make anything happen that she sets her mind to. She has a heart of gold and is always there for her friends. We are a rather unlikely team, but somehow her yin works to my yang and we accomplished what we set out to do. While we were each the taskmaster at different times, it was Karen's incessant pushing, cheerleading, and vision that enabled me to complete "my end" of the project. She was focused and excited about getting 52 out there. I, on the other hand, often felt ambivalence and trepidation. During the book's development process, we spent countless hours stuck behind our computers. We argued. We wrote. We argued some more. What we did agree on, however, was the irony of the whole situation; we started our blog to "get out there" and the book brought us back to our apartments! We often had to stay put to write the book and meet deadlines. Had we moved away from our original intent? How could we talk about getting out there and doing new things if we were glued to our laptops? We laughed at the irony.

But then, after what seemed like 52,000 weeks, I realized that the original intent for launching The 52 Weeks didn't get away from me. I did, in fact, accomplish what I had intended to do. There was reason for the blog, beyond just our own personal goals and friendship pact.

The 52 Weeks isn't about checking off each individual item on your "52 list." What I came to realize, and hope our readers do too, was that the biggest 52 was never even on my list. My success was the project as a whole and where it led me. I challenged myself and I sure as hell tried new things (write a book, anyone?). I am still a reluctant writer. We are all still a work-in-progress. Perhaps my ideas and experiences will inspire others to go for it, whatever it may be. The message? Do things, anything. You never know where it will take you.

Meet the Experts

Michele Balan

Michele Balan was one of the finalists on NBC's *Last Comic Standing*. She has appeared on *The Joy Behar Show*, *Comics Unleashed With Byron Allen*, and *The Outlaugh Festival* on Wisecrack for MTV's LOGO network, and was voted one of the "Top 10 Comics" by *Backstage Magazine*. Balan headlines all over the country at comedy clubs, corporate events, on cruises, and more. Along with her stand-up, Balan writes for many other well-known comedians, and is a contributor to a variety of magazines. Often told she was naturally funny, the Brooklyn native left a high-paying position at a computer company to pursue comedy, and has been performing ever since.

Andrea Blanch

Andrea Blanch is a New York-based award-winning fashion, fine art and conceptual photographer who began her career working with Richard Avedon. Referred to as "the woman who knows how to capture a woman," her work has appeared in *Vogue*, *Elle*, *Details*, *GQ*, *Rolling Stone*, *New York Times Magazine*, and *Harper's Bazaar*. Her photographs are owned by collectors worldwide. She is the founder and editor-in-chief of *Musée Magazine*, a magazine dedicated to emerging photographers. Blanch teaches at the International Center for Photography and is a member of American Photographic Artists.

Marie-Yolaine Eusebe, CEO, Community2Community (C2C)

Haitian-born, humanitarian, speaker, facilitator, entrepreneur and actor, Marie-Yolaine Eusebe is the definition of moving from spectator to participant. After the devastating earthquake in Haïti on January 12, 2010, Eusebe was compelled to take action. In May of that year, she resigned from her position at American Express to launch Community2Community (C2C), a nonprofit service organization dedicated to creating self-sufficient communities by working with the people of Haiti. Currently, C2C is focusing on business development, education, health and rebuilding infrastructure.

Helen Fisher, Ph.D.

Helen E. Fisher, Ph.D., a biological anthropologist, is a research professor and a member of the Center for Human Evolutionary Studies in the Department of Anthropology at Rutgers University. She is also the chief scientific advisor to the Internet dating site Chemistry.com, a division of Match.com. Fisher is a journalist and has conducted extensive research and written five books on the evolution and future of human sex, love, marriage, and gender differences in the brain, and how personality types shapes who you are and who you love.

Joi Gordon

Joi Gordon is CEO of Dress for Success Worldwide. Since assuming the role of executive director of the New York program in 1999 and then overall leadership of Dress for Success Worldwide in 2002, Gordon has been devoted to establishing Dress for Success as a recognized leader in the economic and social development of disadvantaged women.

With global responsibility for the organization which is composed of more than 110 affiliates in twelve countries, Joi's day-to-day duties include strategic organizational planning, new program development and implementation, board cultivation, resource development, brand fortification, and the maintenance of a welcoming place where disadvantaged women are empowered towards financial independence and self-defined success.

Under Joi's direction, Dress for Success's signature suiting program has grown tremendously while the organization has expanded its services to offer career counseling, interview preparation, financial literacy, and other programs and tools to assist women in their efforts to grow professionally.

Now serving more than 50,000 women globally each year, Dress for Success, through the vision and leadership of Joi Gordon and the support of the staff, affiliates, donors, volunteers, partners, and Board of Directors, has touched the lives of more than 600,000 women around the world and is still Going Places. Going Strong!

Lauren Kantor Gorman, M.D.

Lauren Kantor Gorman, M.D., is in the private practice of psychiatry in New York City. She specializes in psychotherapy and psychopharmacology of adults with a range of psychiatric issues and works with many patients, specifically to help them cope with fears and anxieties. She is a member of the faculty of the Icahn School of Medicine at Mount Sinai in New York City, where she teaches and supervises psychiatry residents. Dr. Gorman received her Bachelor of Arts degree from the University of Pennsylvania and her Doctor of Medicine from the College of Physicians and Surgeons–Columbia University. She did her psychiatric residency at The Mount Sinai Hospital in New York and was an attending at Montefiore Medical Center before opening her private practice in Manhattan. She is a recipient of the Greta Herman Award for excellence in teaching from Mount Sinai, is listed as a top doctor in the nation by Castle Connolly Medical Ltd, and is co-author of several important publications in psychiatric journals.

Barbara Hannah Grufferman

Barbara Hannah Grufferman, nationally recognized expert on positive aging, is the author of *The Best of Everything After 50: The Experts' Guide to Style, Sex, Health, Money and More,* a best-selling resource book addressing the concerns of women over fifty with the wisdom of top experts in different fields, including Diane von Furstenberg, Frederic Fekkai, Dr. Patricia Wexler, and many others. She writes a weekly column for the *Huffington Post,* is the positive living expert for AARP, hosts a weekly AARP YouTube video series, and serves as positive living editor for *Glow Beauty Magazine.* Grufferman is currently at work on her second book.

In 2013, the National Osteoporosis Foundation named Grufferman its first ambassador for bone health in recognition of her support of women over fifty, and advocacy of positive and healthy aging. The NOF also honored her with its Generations of Strength Award.

Grufferman has been a guest on the *TODAY Show, The Early Show,* and *Good Morning America.* She is a regular guest on numerous radio and internet programs, including *NPR, Dr. Oz,* and *Sirius Radio* on the Oprah Channel, as well as *Sirius Doctor Radio.* She travels around the country, speaking about health, nutrition, career, fitness, sex, and other topics related to positive and healthy aging.

Grufferman lives in New York City with her husband, two teenage daughters, and Gunther the Wonder Dog, who was rescued through the National Brittany Rescue Network.

Enda Junkins, LCSW

Enda Junkins, licensed clinical social worker, is a motivational speaker who brings a sense of fun to everything. She has an important philosophy about the power of laughter being applicable to all areas of life. As a professional speaker, she has a unique ability to draw people in and make them anxious to participate. In addition to making her audiences laugh, she provides people with practical, unique tools that invite and create laughter in everyday life. She is a practicing psychotherapist, encouraging people to use their laughter to heal serious issues. Junkins is funny and informative, sharing her useful approach to the power of laughter with a warm connection. She leaves her audiences with the potential for lower stress levels, tools for clearer communication, and a stronger connection to one another. Junkins developed her laughter expertise over years of working with serious issues where resolution involved coping, surviving and healing through the positive energy of laughter.

Jami Kelmenson, Contributing Author, "Flying Solo"

Jami Kelmenson is a freelance writer and blogger who lives in New York City. Her work has been published by Match.com's *Happen Magazine*, *The 52 Weeks* blog, and most recently www.shelfpleasure.com, the destination spot for women who love reading. She is seeking representation for her first novel, *Crossing Paths*. Read her ongoing tales of travel, life, love, and the pursuit of getting published in New York City at her blog, jamikellywriter.tumblr.com.

Ellen Leikind

Ellen Leikind, the creator and founder of POKERprimaDIVAS™, established her organization to help women win through poker. According to Leikind, poker will help in every aspect of life, including improving business skills, getting a new hobby, finding a date, challenging the mind, or improving one's social life. She believes that by mastering poker skills women will be better negotiators, more confident in their decisions, and learn to take risks.

Leikind is an accomplished corporate executive who has been involved in poker for many years. When she took a hiatus from the Fortune 500 world and rediscovered poker, a game she had learned as a teenager, she saw the similarities between the card game and the larger "game" of business and personal fulfillment. Inspired, she wrote her first book, *PokerWoman—How to Win at Love, Life, and Business using the Principles of Poker*. Ms. Leikind has worked in major marketing positions at large consumer packaged-goods companies, including Pfizer and L'Oreal. She spent seven years in the infomercial business and now is president of EDL Marketing Group in New York. She has an Master of Business Administration in marketing from Fordham University and is a native New Yorker and avid animal lover.

Alex Lickerman, M.D.

Alex Lickerman is a physician, former assistant professor of medicine and director of primary care, and current assistant vice president for Student Health and Counseling Services at the University of Chicago. He also has been a practicing Buddhist since 1989. Dr. Lickerman has been quoted in *Crain's Chicago Business*, *Playboy*, *The Chicago Tribune*, *Men's Health*, and *Time Magazine*, and has had articles appear in *Psychology Today* and *Medicine on the Midway*. He also has written a television pilot called *Sessions* that was optioned by DreamWorks Television, as well as several movie screenplays, including an adaptation of John Milton's *Paradise Lost*. Lickerman's first book, *The Undefeated Mind: On the Science of Constructing an Indestructible Self*, was published in 2012.

Lisa Lillien, The Hungry Girl

Hungry Girl is not a nutritionist. She's just hungry. Lisa Lillien, a.k.a. Hungry Girl, is a *New York Times* best-selling author and creator of the Hungry Girl brand. She is founder of www.hungry-girl.com, the free daily email service that entertains and informs hungry people everywhere. Lillien is a typical woman battling the same food issues most struggle with every day. She considers herself a "foodologist," not because she has some kind of fancy degree, but because she is obsessed with food — how wonderful it is, and how much of it she can eat and still fit into her pants.

More than 1,000,000 fans eagerly wait for Hungry Girl's recipes, food finds, and tips & tricks each weekday. What started as a daily email to friends and family has turned into a nationwide, multimedia phenomenon! In addition to the million-plus die-hard subscribers to her daily emails, Lillien also writes a weekly column on WeightWatchers.com, regularly contributes to *Redbook*, and makes recurring appearances on television shows such as the *Dr. Oz Show*.

Lillien is author of seven best-selling books — five of which debuted at number one on the *New York Times* best-sellers List. Her most recent book, *Hungry Girl to the Max! The Ultimate Guilt-Free Cookbook*, launched in the number-one spot.

Her television show, *Hungry Girl*, airs on the Food Network and Cooking Channel. A self-proclaimed "mad scientist" in the kitchen, Lillien dishes out guilt-free recipes, tips & tricks, supermarket finds, and survival guides for real-world eating situations.

Debbie Magids, Ph.D.

Debbie Magids, Ph.D., is a counseling psychologist with a thriving private practice in New York City. Always client-focused, Dr. Debbie's groundbreaking methodology and results-oriented process consistently help her clients flourish so they can live their best life. Dr. Debbie is author of *All The Good Ones Aren't Taken: Change the Way You Date and Find Lasting Love*. She regularly contributes her advice to *Cosmopolitan*, and has been quoted in *Glamour, Self, and Time Out New York* magazines, as well as on MSN. com. A popular television guest, Dr. Debbie has appeared on *The Anderson Cooper Show, NBC's Today* and *The Nate Berkus Show, HLN's The Joy Behar Show, FOX's The Morning Show with Mike and Juliet, CNN Headline News, The Jane Velez-*

Mitchell Show, *Your World with Neil Cavuto*, *The Tyra Show*, *The Montel Williams Show*, and on primetime's *Pregnant in Heels*. Dr. Debbie's commentary also has been featured on *The Howard Stern Show*, where she's offered her expertise on the mental health of Howard and the gang. Dr. Debbie holds a Master of Arts in organizational psychology and a Master of Education in psychological counseling from Columbia University's Teachers College. She earned her Ph.D. in counseling psychology from Fordham University. Dr. Debbie has been a member of the American Psychological Association since 1989.

Jennifer Mieres, M.D.

Dr. Jennifer H. Mieres is one of the leading experts and patient advocates in the fields of nuclear cardiology and cardiovascular disease in women. In her role as leader of the North Shore-LIJ health system's Office of Community and Public Health, Dr. Mieres, has oversight of the Katz Institute for Women's Health, all of North Shore-LIJ's health and wellness, community education and healthcare access programs, as well as corporate social responsibility. She is also the health system's Chief Diversity and Inclusion Officer, and Medical Director of the Center for Learning and Innovation, North Shore-LIJ's corporate university.

A graduate of Bennington College and Boston University School of Medicine, she is a Fellow of the American Heart Association (AHA), the American College of Cardiology (ACC), and the American Society of Nuclear Cardiology (ASNC) and in 2009, she served as the first female President of the ASNC and is board certified in cardiovascular diseases and nuclear cardiology.

Dr. Mieres is an active volunteer for the AHA, serving on the national board of directors from 2004 to 2006 and is a current member of the Founder's Board of the AHA. She is very involved in community service and is a national spokesperson for the AHA's Go Red For Women movement, and past chair of the AHA's national Professional Education Committee. In acknowledgement of her work as a cardiologist, researcher, patient, and community advocate, she was the recipient of the 2011 AHA Louis B. Russell, Jr. Memorial Award, presented annually to an AHA volunteer for outstanding service in addressing healthcare disparities and/or service to minority and underserved communities. In 2012, she received the AHA Founder's Affiliate health care service award at Yankee Stadium. She is also a recipient of a 2008 Woman's Day Red Dress Award for her contributions to Women's Heart Health. In 2005, she received the Long Island AHA Award for Outstanding Service as President and was the recipient of the AHA's William Groom Award for Volunteer of the Year. She was also awarded a 2002 New York State Governor's award for excellence in health care.

Dr. Mieres is routinely called upon by the media to comment on heart health, appearing in national and local media outlets on such programs as 20/20, the Today Show, Good Morning America, CNN, and The Martha Stewart Show. As a producer of the PBS documentary *A Woman's Heart* (2003) she was nominated for an Emmy for Best Documentary in the Health Science category at the 46th Annual New York Emmy Awards. In November 2008 she was featured in *SHAPE Magazine* as one of the Women Who Shape the World. In 2009 and 2010, Dr. Mieres was featured in *New York Magazine* as one of New York's leading doctors in cardiovascular disease. In 2008 her book, *Heart Smart for Black Women and Latinas: A Five Week Program for Living a Heart-Healthy Lifestyle* was published by St Martin's Press. She was recently featured in *The Best of Everything After 50: The Experts' Guide to Style, Sex, Health, Money, and More*.

Robin Gorman Newman

Robin Gorman Newman is founder of Motherhood Later . . . Than Sooner, an international organization for mothers who are thirty-five or older. Robin publishes the monthly eZine *Baby Bloomer* and blogs on her site and for *The Huffington Post* about parenting and entertainment. A work-at-home mother, Robin is associate producer of *Motherhood Out Loud*, a touring play that had a successful off-Broadway run. As a Love Coach (LoveCoach.com) and author of *How to Meet a Mensch in NY* and *How to Marry a Mensch* (being adapted for the stage), she has made appearances at off-Broadway shows including *Dinner with Friends* and *I Love You, You're Perfect, Now Change*. She's been seen on CNN and *The Today Show*. She is a member of The American Society of Journalists and Authors and has more than twenty years of experience in public relations and a master's degree in marketing. She lives in Great Neck, New York, with her mensch husband, son, and pet cockatiel.

Vivian Steir Rabin

Vivian Steir Rabin is co-author of the acclaimed career-reentry strategy book *Back on the Career Track: A Guide for Stay-at-Home Moms Who Want to Return to Work*, and co-founder of the career-reentry programming website www.irelaunch.com.

Rabin and her co-author and business partner, Carol Fishman Cohen, are Harvard Business School graduates and relaunchers—between them, they have nine kids, and they each returned to work after multi-year career breaks before writing *Back on the Career Track* and starting iRelaunch. They have presented their return-to-work strategies to more than 10,000 people at 150 events since 2006. They are regularly quoted in the national press, including *TIME*, the *Wall Street Journal*, National Public Radio, the *New York Times*, the *Boston Globe*, *Money*, *Entrepreneur*, *Fast Company*, *Family Circle*, and MSNBC.

Daniella Ohad Smith, Ph.D.

Daniella Ohad Smith received her Ph.D. degree from the Bard Graduate Center for Studies in the Decorative Arts, Design History, and Material Culture.

For the past two decades, she has been committed to education in design history, theory, and the decorative arts. She has been a faculty member at the Department of Architecture, Interior Design, and Lighting of Parsons the New School for Design since 2000, and has taught at Pratt Institute, Bard College, and Bezalel Academy of Art and Design in Jerusalem. Smith has been teaching, conducting, and curating public lectures, as well as speaking in conferences and publishing in scientific journals and magazines for years. As an art advisor, she has assembled distinctive private collections of twentieth-century furniture and decorative arts. Smith takes part in the museums arena as a member of several acquisition committees of major museums in New York City.

Nadia Stieglitz

Born in France and raised in the Alps, Stieglitz lived in Paris and London before settling in New York with her husband and three daughters. Stieglitz worked as creative director in publishing for ten years, after which she became a consultant with an innovation firm. Over the course of her career, she has become attuned to the unique needs of women. In 1998, after the birth of her third daughter, Stieglitz began organizing girls' activities with her friends to shake up an existence that she feared had become too serious and timid. Yearning to reconnect with her love of playfulness, she challenged herself to learn new skills and discover more about herself. She invited her girlfriends to join her. With activities such as trapeze, a Roaring 20's dress-up photo shoot in Harlem, a Mixology Contest, and Burlesque, the group has explored many new playgrounds together. They've had many thrills and laughs while pushing their boundaries. Whenever she would gather with friends, she kept thinking about the saying "When the cat is away, the mice will play!" so she named her group Mice at Play.

Jennifer Gardner Trulson

Jennifer Gardner Trulson is the author of the memoir *Where You Left Me*, which was named Best Non-Fiction of October 2011 by the readers of *Elle*. She has been featured on the *TODAY Show* and *20/20* and has had an essay published in *Harper's Bazaar*. Trulson founded the Douglas B. Gardner Foundation, a nonprofit organization dedicated to helping at-risk children in New York. She graduated from Tufts University and received a Juris Doctor from Harvard Law School. She lives with her husband and children in Manhattan.

Pamela Weinberg

Pamela Weinberg is an author, career coach, and founder of MYOBMoms (Mind Your Own Business Moms). MYOBMoms was co-founded by Weinberg to help women discover their personal passions and use them as a guide as they consider re-entering the workforce. MYOBMoms is dedicated to helping women who have been out of the workforce, perhaps raising families, stay connected to the professional world or explore new career possibilities. The options seemingly are endless: return to a former career, start a new one, go back to school, become an entrepreneur, and work full time or part time. MYOBMoms was founded to help women create exciting new opportunities for themselves, and to help support women through that process. Weinberg also is co-author of *City Baby*, a best-selling parenting guidebook. It is in its third edition and has been called "the Bible for New York City parents." In addition to her writing, Weinberg speaks frequently on child-related issues and careers at luncheons and seminars in Manhattan. Weinberg has been interviewed on *NY1 News* and *Saturday Today in New York*; she also has been featured in the *New York Post*, the *New York Daily News*, *Martha Stewart Living*, and other publications.

Julie Weiss, Marathon Goddess

After the death of her father following a battle with pancreatic cancer, Julie Weiss was determined to make a difference. She decided to turn her passion for running into a purpose, and embarked on a journey to run 52 marathons in 52 weeks to raise money and awareness for pancreatic cancer. To date, she has raised $180,000 for the Pancreatic Cancer Action Network through her website marathongoddess.com. By day, Weiss works as a real estate accountant. She has two children, ages twenty and twenty-four. She also volunteers as a pace leader for the Los Angeles Marathon owned LA Roadrunners. Weiss is honored to help so many people, and hopes that others will notice and take action to help make a difference too.

CHANGING COURSE WORKSHEETS

Relaunch Readiness Quiz

By Carol Fishman Cohen and Vivian Steir Rabin

Co-authors, *Back on the Career Track: A Guide for Stay-at-Home-Moms Who Want to Return to Work*

Co-founders, iRelaunch, www.irelaunch.com.

Reprinted with permission.

Part I. Appetite for work

1. I miss working.

Not At All   Somewhat   A Lot

| 1 | 2 | 3 | 4 | 5 | 6 | 7 | 8 | 9 | 10 |

2. For the time being, I am happy being a stay-at-home mother.

Agree Strongly   Agree Somewhat   Disagree Strongly

| 1 | 2 | 3 | 4 | 5 | 6 | 7 | 8 | 9 | 10 |

3. I have a hobby or volunteer work that engages me.

Agree Strongly   Agree Somewhat   Disagree Strongly

| 1 | 2 | 3 | 4 | 5 | 6 | 7 | 8 | 9 | 10 |

4. I could see myself going back to work in _____ years.

10	9	8	7	6	5	4	3	2	1
1	2	3	4	5	6	7	8	9	10

(Choose your answer in the top row, then circle the number in the second row below it.)

5. The average number of hours per week that I am willing and able to spend working is:

0	5	10	15	20	25	30	35	40	40+
1	2	3	4	5	6	7	8	9	10

(Choose your answer in the top row, then circle the number in the second row below it.)

6. Our family could benefit from me earning money.

Agree Strongly				Agree Somewhat				Disagree Strongly	
1	2	3	4	5	6	7	8	9	10

Add up the numbers you circled. This is your score for Part I:_____

Interpretation of scoring for Part I

If you score 50 or above, you have a strong desire to relaunch. Even if your scores for Parts II and III are low, you may wish to explore child care options to enable you to go back to work.

If your score falls between 30 and 50, you have a moderate appetite for work. Combined with a high score in Parts II and III, you may decide to give it a go.

If you score less than 30, you're not very motivated to return to work at this time. Consider investing more time in volunteer work and hobbies, particularly ones that might open up career options for you later.

Part II. Child care and elder care responsibilities

1. Number of children not yet in school:

    3+   3   2   1   0

    1   2   3   4   10

    (Choose your answer in the top row, then circle the number in the second row below it.)

2. Number of children in preschool:

    3+   3   2   1   0

    2   3   4   5   10

    (Choose your answer in the top row, then circle the number in the second row below it.)

3. Number of children in elementary school:

    3+   3   2   1   0

    3   4   5   6   10

    (Choose your answer in the top row, then circle the number in the second row below it.)

4. Number of children in high school:

    3+   3   2   1   0

    4   5   6   7   10

    (Choose your answer in the top row, then circle the number in the second row below it.)

5. Average number of hours per week I spend between 8:00 AM and 6:00 PM on weekdays taking care of my children and/or an elderly or ill relative:

50	45	40	35	30	25	20	15	10	5	or less
1	2	3	4	5	6	7	8	9	10	

(Choose your answer in the top row, then circle the number in the second row below it.)

Add up the numbers you circled. This is your score for Part II:_____

Interpretation of scoring for Part II

If you score 40 or above, you have time to explore relaunching your career. Couple this with a high score in Part I, and you're raring to go.

If you score between 30 and 40, you have reasonably demanding family obligations. If you score high in Part I and III, however, you have the motivation and support for a successful relaunch. A high score in Part I and a low score in Part III will make it more difficult, but nothing is impossible.

If you score below 30, you have a lot going on in your household. If you score high on Part I and III, however, don't be discouraged. If you are willing to explore child care options for part of the week, you still can relaunch. This most likely will be necessary if you score low on Part III.

Part III. Spousal and/or other family support

1. My spouse has some flexibility in his schedule.

Very Little				Some					A Lot
1	2	3	4	5	6	7	8	9	10

2. My spouse is/would be supportive of my going back to work.

Disagree Strongly				Agree Somewhat					Agree Strongly
1	2	3	4	5	6	7	8	9	10

3. My spouse or another adult family member is/would be available to help me an average of ___ hours per week between 8 a.m. and 6 p.m. during the week with child care- or elder care-related tasks.

    1   2   3   4   5   6   7   8   9   10

Add up the numbers you circled. This is your score for Part III:_____

Interpretation of scoring for Part III

If you score 20 or above, you have strong spousal or other family support for a relaunch. Couple this with a high score in Part I, and you're off to a strong start, regardless of your score in Part II.

If you score between 15 and 20, you have a reasonable amount of support for a relaunch. Coupled with a high score in Part I and II, your challenge is manageable. If you have a low score in Part II, you may need to engage outside child care resources in order to relaunch.

If you score less than 15, you're not getting much spousal or other family support for a transition back to work. However, if you scored high in Part I and II, you may not need that much support to pull it off. If you scored low in Part II, you almost certainly will need to engage outside resources to help you with your child care responsibilities. You should continue to revisit the relaunch issue with your spouse or other close family members to see whether you can garner more support.

Pamela Weinberg and Barri Waltcher's MYOBMoms Inventory

Self-exploration Questions

- What do you do well? What do your friends and family members ask you to help them with?

- What would you do if you couldn't fail and money was no object?

- What did you want to do/be as a child?

- What do you most enjoy doing? Thinking about? Reading about? Studying? What are your hobbies? What section of a bookstore do you gravitate toward?

- What do you love to do? What activities or hobbies do you like to do in your spare time?

- What are the most interesting jobs you can think of?

- Think about a time when you felt satisfied (at work or in your personal life). What was satisfying?

- What have you liked about past jobs? What have you disliked? What's been missing for you?

- What ideas have you had for jobs, careers, or business?

- Do you have any (career) regrets?

- Where do you see yourself in five years? Ten? Twenty?

Career Values Worksheet

Modified from Career Paths Online, 1996,
Reprinted with permission.

Values are the things that are most important to us in our lives and careers. Our values are formed in a variety of ways through our life experiences, our feelings, and our families. In the context of career planning, values generally refer to things we value in a career. For example, some people value job security, money, structure, and a regular schedule. Others value flexibility, excitement, independence, and variety.

Values are things we feel very strongly about. For example, most of us will say having enough money to live comfortably is important, but many are willing to work for less because what they value most is not money, but something else, such as working for a cause, helping people, or having free time. Being aware of what we value in our lives is important, because a career choice that is in line with our core beliefs and values is more likely to be lasting and positive. To gain awareness of your work values, complete the following checklist.

Directions

In the following checklist, consider each work value carefully and indicate whether it is Very Important (1), Somewhat Important (2), or Not Important (3) to you.

It's important to me to:	Value	Importance
Experience change and enjoy a variety of tasks.	Variety	1 ○ 2 ○ 3 ○

Have little chance of job loss or loss of income.	Security	1 ○ 2 ○ 3 ○
Have defined responsibilities and a hierarchy in the workplace.	Structure	1 ○ 2 ○ 3 ○
Have a high income.	Money	1 ○ 2 ○ 3 ○
Keep a routine without too many surprises.	Stability	1 ○ 2 ○ 3 ○
Be given opportunities to travel and see new places.	Travel	1 ○ 2 ○ 3 ○
Work with a diverse group of people and share ideas.	Teamwork	1 ○ 2 ○ 3 ○
Make my own hours and have little direct supervision.	Independence	1 ○ 2 ○ 3 ○
Take part in higher education and ongoing training and upgrading.	Education	1 ○ 2 ○ 3 ○
Experience adventure, changes and challenges.	Excitement	1 ○ 2 ○ 3 ○
Take on responsibility and help a group reach collective goals.	Leadership	1 ○ 2 ○ 3 ○
Have time and energy to spend with family and close friends.	Family	1 ○ 2 ○ 3 ○

Spend time on hobbies and interests outside of work.	Leisure Time	1○ 2○ 3○
Work in an occupation that fits with my religious beliefs.	Religious Beliefs	1○ 2○ 3○
Be recognized and respected for the work I do.	Prestige	1○ 2○ 3○
Work outside, close to nature.	Working Outside	1○ 2○ 3○
Work in comfortable surroundings, inside.	Working Indoors	1○ 2○ 3○
Have my own tools and working space.	Personal Space	1○ 2○ 3○
Meet a variety of people and work with and/or for others.	People	1○ 2○ 3○
Work with facts and abstract concepts.	Information	1○ 2○ 3○
Work with concrete items.	Things	1○ 2○ 3○
Make a difference in people's lives.	Helping Others	1○ 2○ 3○
Make the world a better place on a grand scale.	Community Impact	1○ 2○ 3○

Have little chance of on-the-job injury or danger.	Safety	1 ○ 2 ○ 3 ○
Have positive and friendly relationships with colleagues.	Relationships	1 ○ 2 ○ 3 ○
Learn and develop a variety of skills in my work.	Skills	1 ○ 2 ○ 3 ○
Use my artistic talents in the work I do.	Creativity	1 ○ 2 ○ 3 ○
Be in charge.	Authority	1 ○ 2 ○ 3 ○
Work in a casual and relaxed atmosphere.	Informality	1 ○ 2 ○ 3 ○
Become completely wrapped up in the work I'm doing.	Passion	1 ○ 2 ○ 3 ○

Fill in the values that are most important to you (every number 1 that you selected above) and then fill in below:

My Work Values

1.		2.		3.	
4.		5.		6.	
7.		8.		9.	